"Mike Nappa's research definitely reveals more about us than it does our teenagers. We can't expect youth to believe what they have not been taught at home or in the churches they attend. This book will challenge parents and youth leaders alike to pass their faith to students with accuracy and authenticity."

—**Wayne Rice**, co-founder, Youth Specialties; author, *Reinventing Youth Ministry (Again)*

"Every parent, youth worker, pastor, and Christian educator should read *The Jesus Survey*. Passing on the true faith to the next generation is one of the most critical needs of our day and this book will help us in that challenge. Mike Nappa gives us insight into not only what our kids do and do not believe, but why they are failing to embrace the core beliefs of the faith. Read and study this book; you will be glad you did."

—**Josh McDowell,** bestselling author and noted youth speaker

"If you're a youth worker or a parent of a teenager, you're committing malpractice if you don't read this book. The questions about basic Christian doctrine Mike Nappa asks teenagers, and their responses, will give you both a roadmap for where you need to head in your discipling journey with kids and the fuel to help you get there. Buried in the middle of this book is a question that represents our core challenge: 'So, at what point does the supposed faith of our teenagers actually become a false religion that's more idolatry than genuine relationship with God?' That's a question we're all compelled to answer."

—**Rick Lawrence,** executive editor, *Group Magazine*

"This book is full of interesting and informative data for parents, youth workers, and everyone else who cares about young people. Nappa gives us a rare glimpse into the spiritual lives of the next generation—and we walk away with a sense of hope and fresh challenge."

—**Amy Simpson**, small groups editor, *Christianity Today*;
author, *Into the Word: How to Get the Most from Your Bible*

"Lace up your biblical boot straps; we are in a spiritual battle with and for our teens. *The Jesus Survey* offers a sobering insight. You hold in your hands valuable reflections into the thoughts and beliefs of the next generation."

—**Mike Jones,** co-founder and executive director, Reach Workcamps

THE JESUS SURVEY

THE JESUS SURVEY

What Christian Teens Really Believe and Why

MIKE NAPPA

a division of Baker Publishing Group
Grand Rapids, Michigan

Published by Baker Books
a division of Baker Publishing Group
P.O. Box 6287, Grand Rapids, MI 49516-6287
www.bakerbooks.com

Printed in the United States of America

Library of Congress Cataloging-in-Publication Data

Nappa, Mike, 1963–
The Jesus survey : what Christian teens really believe and why / Mike Nappa.
p. cm.
Includes bibliographical references (p.).
ISBN 978-0-8010-1444-4 (pbk.)
1. Jesus Christ—Person and offices. 2. Teenagers—Religious life. I. Title.
BT203.N37 2012
232—dc23 2011045089

To protect the privacy of those who have shared their stories with the author, some details and names have been changed.

The internet addresses, email addresses, and phone numbers in this book are accurate at the time of publication. They are provided only as a resource; Baker Publishing Group does not endorse them or vouch for their content or permanence.

This book is published in association with Nappaland Literary Agency, an independent agency dedicated to publishing works that are: Authentic. Relevant. Eternal. Visit us on the web at: NappalandLiterary.com

12 13 14 15 16 17 18 7 6 5 4 3 2 1

In keeping with biblical principles of creation stewardship, Baker Publishing Group advocates the responsible use of our natural resources. As a member of the Green Press Initiative, our company uses recycled paper when possible. The text paper of this book is composed in part of post-consumer waste.

For Amy!
who makes it easier to believe

"Every generation blames the one before."

—Mike & The Mechanics

CONTENTS

Part Two What Difference Does Jesus Make?

FOREWORD

Dr. Steven W. Smith

The reason this book is important is simple: *Jesus is everything.*

Christ is not just first, not simply best; he is everything.

Like the sun in our sky, he's the fixed essence of the universe around which all things exist. They—we—exist at his behest. Yet unlike the sun, he's not fading, he doesn't dim, and he has no other competing solar systems. He is everything, and he will not compete with what I think I can't live without. Money is not everything, family is not everything, church is not everything. Jesus is everything.

Colossians 1:15–18 reveals that God put everything under Christ's control, that Christ is the reason all things were created and that Christ is the means by which they were created. Christ completes God's plan. And, perhaps most importantly for this discussion, Christ is the exclusive means by which God is accessible; he's the "image of the invisible God" (v. 15). Therefore, if students don't know Christ, they don't know God.

It's against this biblical backdrop that those of us who work with students took notice a few years ago when sociologist Christian Smith concluded, in his provocative study *Soul Searching*, that the religious faith of teens could best be described as "moralistic therapeutic deism." What's more alarming is what students call moralistic therapeutic deism: *Christianity*. If there's any hope for the future, it will be in getting teens to God *through Christ*. This is the only way.

Building on the research of Smith and others, my friend Mike Nappa recently set out to find out not what just "teenagers" believe, but to discover what our own youth-group bred "Christian teenagers" actually think about the Christ they call their Savior. The results were astonishing—in both good and not-so-good ways.

Through a national survey of more than eight hundred Christian teenagers, Mike measured how youth in our churches understand—and believe or disbelieve—four key doctrines of Christianity: (1) The Bible is trustworthy in what it says about Jesus; (2) Jesus is God; (3) Jesus died and rose again; and (4) Jesus is the only way to heaven.

If you're curious about what Mike found, you might want to stop reading this foreword and skip to the intermission. (It will make you want to read the rest.) Or go ahead and start in chapter 1 and work your way through to the end. The results may not shock you, but they did me.

I've known Mike Nappa since we were both teenagers ourselves, growing up together in the church where my father was the pastor. Even then I could see the passion in Mike's eyes. He loved Jesus as a teenager. He wanted us all to love Jesus. He even started a midweek students-only service for us. During lunchtime at school, he taught the Bible to anyone who'd come hear it. He loved God's Word. And he lived it. Some thirty years later, Mike still exudes that fire, that passion for Christ and for teens, that absolute certainty that Jesus is indeed *everything* . . . and therefore our teenagers deserve to know about him.

When I reflect on my own journey, I think that at times I simply added Jesus to my already well-appointed life. To my shame, ministry was everything, and Jesus was just something. Reputation was everything, and Jesus was something. Money was everything, Jesus was something. Just like the ancient Colossians, we must decide if Jesus is just something, or if he is everything. I'm not saying this as a prophet, but as a penitent. My own nature is to ask Christ to rotate around the vortex of my ambition. But Jesus is not a God who can be patronized by my willingness to put him in my stratosphere. He is not in my world; I am in his. I am not anything; Jesus is everything.

It's not all that ironic that today I'm writing this foreword for Mike's insight on student belief. Perhaps it's even predictable. I'm still getting the benefit of his passion. I hope you will too.

So I encourage you now: take *The Jesus Survey* for your own. Dig deeply into the results of this nationwide study, wrestle with it, rejoice in it, mourn when you must. But mostly, let Mike Nappa's example and expertise be the spark that ignites within you a new, world-changing passion for Christ and for his teenagers.

Because . . . Jesus is everything.

Steven W. Smith, PhD
Dean, The College at Southwestern
James T. Draper Chair of Pastoral Ministry,
Southwestern Baptist Theological Seminary

INTRODUCTION

This Little Light of Mine . . .

Let's try an experiment.

First, we enter a darkened room. No light peeks through the curtains; nothing illumines the crack beneath the door.

Now, the match.

With a practiced flourish, you strike a flame and transfer it easily to a candle set up in the middle of our darkened room. (Nice job, by the way. I can tell you've done this before.) Immediately the tiny fire dances in our vision. Sure, this is a big room, so the candle's flame doesn't flood our surroundings with light, but it does fill our retinas and cast new shadows in every corner.

In fact, no matter where we stand, our backs to the flame or facing the candle, there's no place in this room where we can't see evidence of this little candlelight. Even if we close our eyes, behind our eyelids we still see ghosts of the flickering glow that burns in the room.

Ah, now let's take this experiment a step further. Suppose that I, ornery guy that I am, don't like that pinpoint of brightness you've created with your candle and its flame. Suppose I want nothing more than to douse that light and make it practically invisible to anyone else who might come into this room.

Well, obviously, I could pour water over the candle, or blow out the flame, or even smash the wick between my thumb and forefinger to extinguish that light. But what if your candle, once lit, couldn't be put out? What if gale force winds, an ocean of water, or anything else I could muster was incapable of un-lighting that tiny flame in our darkened room?

What would I do then?

Hmm.

The answer is not too difficult, really. First, I would set a flashlight beside your candle and turn it on. Next, I'd click on the lamp in the corner. Maybe I'd even install an overhead fixture and let that brightness flood the room as well. In fact,

I'd find any artificial light I could muster and set it up in our previously darkened room until—and this is the sneaky part—that pure light from your candle's flame was so surrounded by lesser lights that it became practically invisible to anyone who came into our room.

This little trick of light-masking is not new. In fact, if you live in a city of any reasonable size, it happens to you every single night. Those in the know call it "light pollution," that is, "the glow from street and domestic lighting that obscures the night sky."[1]

Think about it. There are, literally, millions of stars in the sky right now . . . so why can't you see them? It's because all the artificial lights that surround you—street lamps, building lights, billboard lights, automobile headlights, porch lights, and so on—shine just enough to obscure the brilliant night-lights in the sky and make them seem (mostly) invisible.

Now, back to our little experiment. (You see where I'm going with this, don't you?)

Picture the single, powerful candle that lit up our darkened room. In a symbolic sense, Jesus himself is that unquenchable flame: the true, pure light that no man, woman, or other being can ever completely extinguish. Scripture tells us that when Jesus Christ began his earthly ministry, it was a fulfillment of this prophetic declaration of Isaiah: "People living in darkness have seen a great light."[2] Well, what if you are someone who doesn't like that flickering light of truth? What if you want, with great passion, to obscure the light of Christ? What will you do?

You'll do all you can to distract from the real light of truth by placing any and all artificial lights of falsehood in people's realms of vision. You'll surround the truth of Jesus Christ with plausible (or even fantastical) lies. You'll hope to obscure Christ by means of almost-Christs, with part-true theories and speculations.

Jesus was a good man, a righteous teacher, and a noble person—but he was not God.

Or . . .

Jesus's "death" on a cross was actually some kind of hoax that was later covered up by his followers and the Catholic Church.

Or . . .

Other highly regarded religious books, such as the Qur'an or the Book of Mormon, are just as important as the Bible in teaching people about who Jesus really was.

Or . . .

Jesus actually escaped death on the cross, married Mary Magdalene, and started a political dynasty.

Or . . . well, you get the idea.

Light pollution, really. Attempts to dim the true light of heaven with the brightness of imitations from somewhere below. And for many, such imitation is enough to substitute for the real, eternal light.

Now, before you think me a prophet of doom and despair, I want to make it clear that this kind of spiritual light pollution around the person of Christ is nothing new. It's been around for centuries—millennia even. And in spite of it, the light of Jesus shines just as brightly today as it did some two thousand years ago.

But I am a curious man by nature, and a former youth pastor by profession. Over the last decade I've seen a resurgence in zeal among those in our society who would prefer to eliminate the light of Christ—especially among teenagers for whom these kinds of anti-Christian conspiracies are new and (potentially) exciting. And it made me wonder . . .

What do Christian teenagers today believe about Jesus Christ?

What difference does that belief make in their lives?

That's how this book began.

ABOUT *THE JESUS SURVEY*

Over the course of three months during the summer of 2010 (June–August), my friend Mike Jones did me a favor I can never repay. He gave me access to over eight hundred churchgoing teens and let me ask them any and all the questions I wanted.

Yeah, Mike's a stud. And he's someone who actually cares about teenagers and their spiritual experience in the twenty-first century. That's why, since 1992, Mike has served faithfully as the executive director of Reach Workcamps (www.reachwc.org).

Every year, thousands of students from church youth groups all over the nation join Reach in weeklong missions of Christlike service to low-income communities. With the aim of helping teenagers live the life of service that Jesus exemplified, Reach organizes and coordinates the completion of basic home repair projects for elderly, disabled, and low-income families. The construction aim of a workcamp is to provide "neighbors" (see Mark 12:31) with warmer, dryer, and safer homes. These workcamps also help restore lost pride and hope to the neighbors' lives. In many cases, the repair work also helps to reduce utility costs. Still, the primary goal of a Reach workcamp is to meet the emotional and spiritual needs of the neighbors, while helping with their physical needs.

At the same time, the teenagers get to experience a large-scale youth group program/church meeting every single night of a workcamp: singing praises to God, digging into Bible studies and devotional experiences, joining with others in small groups where they can encourage each other toward authentic, active Christianity—both now and after the workcamp is over. Fun stuff.

Back in 1997, Mike Jones allowed me to survey his campers with questions about their expectations and experiences in youth groups all over the nation. The results of that study later became the groundbreaking book *What I Wish My Youth Leader Knew about Youth Ministry*. The impact of that study on youth ministry during the late 1990s and early 2000s was very rewarding, but—as you can see if you know anything about math—by 2010 not a single person who participated in that survey was still a teenager. In fact, the entire population of teens is completely remade every seven to nine years (depending on whether or not you count junior highers in the teen population).

So, in the spring of 2010, I contacted Mike Jones again. "Hey," I said, "how would you feel about letting me survey your students this summer?" To his credit, Mike not only enthusiastically agreed to let me do that, but he and Reach Workcamps generously bore the brunt of the costs for printing and facilitating that survey. (Like I said, Mike rocks.)

Suddenly my dream of satisfying my curiosity about teen perceptions of Jesus was going to become a reality.

First, a Little Background Music

Now, before we go any further, I think it's time I introduced myself to you. After all, if we're going to be companions on this journey of discovery, you ought to know a little bit about me—and my unrelenting research biases and personality quirks, right?

If you've read my bio, you know the official lines about me. Yes, I'm a former youth pastor. Yes, I worked for several years in youth ministry at two megachurches in Southern California before joining a Christian publisher to work in curriculum and ministry resource development for youth, children, and adults. Yes, I've authored over forty books on biblical topics and edited hundreds more, winning awards and even placing a few titles on bestseller lists. Yes, I hold a degree in Christian education, with a minor in Bible theology. All well and good, but, in the big picture, that stuff's not really important.

What *is* important is that when I was sixteen years old I forced myself to answer two questions:

1. Does God exist?
2. If God exists, who is he (or she)?

I'm going to be honest: the first question wasn't that difficult for me. Sure, I know some atheists and agnostics, and even some Christians, who struggle mightily with doubts about the existence of an all-powerful, all-knowing God. For me, though, the simple realization that this complex universe existed with such orderly consistency was enough to get me to a point of confidence about the existence of God.

The testimony of history—recognizing that every human culture, both primitive and advanced, isolated and interconnected, over all the millennia since history has been recorded has always identified some sort of "god" (or gods) as part of human life—also carried significant weight for me. In fact, if the evolutionists are correct about the idea of "survival of the fittest" (and there are questions about that), then the belief in an all-powerful god of some sort is actually a necessary part of human survival that's lasted with undeniable persistence since humans first appeared on this tiny little planet.

So does God exist? For me, a positive answer to that question was easy to deliver.

Ah, but question 2: Who is God? That was a little harder.

If you glanced at my picture on the back of this book, you probably noticed I'm not an average white guy. In fact, I'm not white at all. I was born in America, but I'm also a full-blooded Arab, thanks to the fact that both sets of my grandparents emigrated to this great nation from Lebanon.

As Arab-Americans, my grandparents loosely followed the Islamic religion. My mother, on the other hand, was the first Christian in our family, and in accordance with her Christianity she raised me in a home where church, Sunday school, and the Bible were normal parts of life. I also had friends who were Jewish, and I was curious about Eastern religions like Buddhism and Hinduism. So once I decided that God existed, the question for me became, "Who is God?"

I spent months wrestling with that question, reading about world religions, asking for advice from friends and family. Finally I realized that, for me, the question "Who is God?" boiled down to one issue: "Who is Jesus?"

You see, from what I could tell, every major religion recognized Jesus as being somehow associated with God—a prophet, a godly teacher, a good man, an example of a godly lifestyle, and so on. But they all stopped short of saying that Jesus was *more* than a man. Only Christians declared he was divine.

So I started reading the New Testament to see if I could find out what Jesus said about himself. Here's what I found:

> "The high priest said to him, 'I demand in the name of the living God that you tell us whether you are the Messiah, the Son of God.' Jesus replied, 'Yes, it is as you say.'" (Matt. 26:63–64)
>
> "Jesus told her, 'I am the Messiah!'" (John 4:26)
>
> "Jesus replied, 'I am the bread of life. No one who comes to me will ever be hungry again. Those who believe in me will never thirst.'" (John 6:35)
>
> "Jesus said to the people, 'I am the light of the world. If you follow me, you won't be stumbling through the darkness, because you will have the light that leads to life.'" (John 8:12)
>
> "Then he [Jesus] said to them, 'You are from below; I am from above. You are of this world; I am not.'" (John 8:23)
>
> "I and the Father are one." (John 10:30 NIV)
>
> "Jesus told her, 'I am the resurrection and the life. Those who believe in me, even though they die like everyone else, will live again.'" (John 11:25)
>
> "Jesus told him, 'I am the way, the truth, and the life. No one can come to the Father except through me.'" (John 14:6)

> "[Jesus said], 'Anyone who has seen me has seen the Father!'" (John 14:9)
>
> "[Jesus said], 'I am the living one who died. Look, I am alive forever and ever! And I hold the keys of death and the grave.'" (Rev. 1:18)
>
> "[Jesus said], 'I am the Alpha and the Omega, the First and the Last, the Beginning and the End.'" (Rev. 22:13)

Wow. That pretty much settled it for me.

Every major religion said that Jesus was a man of God, someone to be trusted in matters of eternity. No one dared to call him a liar. Yet Jesus himself said he was more than just a man—claiming he was the Messiah, the literal Son of God, the only way to the Father, that he and the Father were "one." That couldn't be more clear, at least from my point of view.

If God exists (and I believe he does), and if Jesus has any credibility as a representative of God (and every major world religion says he does), then according to Jesus's own testimony (in some miraculous, triune way), *Jesus is God.*

Why do I tell you this here, now?

Because I want to be honest and up front with you before we get too deeply into this book. My perspective as a researcher and a writer is colored and governed by this simple truth: that Jesus is God. If this offends you, or makes you view me with disappointment or disdain, well, you wouldn't be the first to tell me that. And, of course, that's certainly your prerogative, so I offer you my utmost respect even though we disagree.

Still, I want you to know that I'll try to be fair and generally unbiased as I dig into the results from my survey. But you should also be aware that, as you read this book, my opinions and interpretations of the data will be overwhelmingly influenced by my personal belief about who Jesus is. There's just no escaping that intrinsic element of my personality, so do with that as you will.

Now, about The Jesus Survey *Itself*

The Jesus Survey was administered during the summer of 2010 at Reach Workcamps mission sites in Colorado, Indiana, Maine, New York, Ohio, Texas, Virginia, and West Virginia. (You can see a full copy of the actual survey used in appendix A, on pages 177–80 of this book.)

For the purposes of this study, I defined "teenager" as any student in grades 7–12. I realize that means I included a number of twelve-year-olds in the data, and you might argue that twelve-year-olds are not technically teens. You're right. But I included them anyway, because in our modern society we tend to think of both junior high and high school students as "youth" and integral parts of any "youth ministry." So, even though a twelve-year-old is not technically a teen, from a practical, youth-leadership standpoint, that 7th grader is as much a part of teen culture in our churches as any fourteen-, sixteen-, or eighteen-year-old. For this reason, I felt it was important to include 7th graders in this study.

The students who participated in *The Jesus Survey* came from church youth groups in twenty-four states (plus Alberta, Canada). Among those students, there were 877 teens who returned valid surveys. However, I was interested primarily in discovering what *Christian teens who attend church* believe about Jesus, so the first content question I asked was a clarifying one: Do you agree or disagree with the statement, "I am a Christian"? Of the 877 teens who turned in valid surveys, 96% declared themselves "Christian." As a result, I limited the research data to include only those students who considered themselves to be Christian, and eliminated the thirty-plus surveys from kids who indicated they were *not* Christian.

That left me a representative sample size of 845 kids who (a) were involved in a church youth group and (b) identified themselves as Christian. The general demographics for these churchgoing, Christian teenagers were as follows:

- 451 students (53%) were female
- 394 students (47%) were male
- 33 students (about 4%) were in 7th grade
- 56 students (about 7%) were in 8th grade
- 141 students (about 17%) were in 9th grade
- 206 students (about 24%) were in 10th grade
- 168 students (about 20%) were in 11th grade
- 241 students (about 29%) were in 12th grade

A majority of students (517) indicated that their homes were in or near the geographic East Coast (roughly from Pennsylvania eastward, and up and down the coast), and the rest (328) said their homes were somewhere west of Pennsylvania and throughout the rest of the country. In all, twenty-four states (plus one province in Canada) were represented in the survey:

- Alabama
- Alaska
- Alberta (Canada)
- California
- Colorado
- Delaware
- Florida
- Illinois
- Iowa
- Kentucky
- Louisiana
- Maryland
- Massachusetts
- Michigan
- Minnesota
- New Hampshire
- New Jersey
- New York
- North Carolina
- Ohio
- Pennsylvania
- South Carolina
- Texas
- Virginia
- West Virginia

Additionally, in varying numbers, students reported affiliation with the following church associations/denominations:

- Baptist (a general term kids used that includes any and all of the traditional "Baptist" denominations)
- Brethren in Christ Church of North America
- Catholic Church
- Episcopal Church
- Lutheran (both Missouri Synod and Evangelical Lutheran)
- Non-denominational
- Presbyterian Church (USA)
- Undeclared affiliation
- United Church of Christ
- United Methodist Church
- Other denominations:
  Anglican Church; Christian Church (Disciples of Christ); Church of God; Christian and Missionary Alliance (The Alliance); Evangelical Congregational Church; Mennonite Church USA.[1]

Bear in mind that this study examines the viewpoints of *Christian teenagers*—kids who think of themselves as Christians and who are involved in a church youth group. As such, it would be a major stretch to suggest this book represents *all* teen beliefs about Jesus.

Still, this data is clearly a reliable representative sample for extrapolating assumptions about the kinds of beliefs that self-proclaimed *Christian teenagers* have about Christ. And that's the focus here: to get a glimpse of what young people *inside* our churches think about Jesus. (I think it's pretty obvious what kids outside the church think.)

With that in mind, statistically speaking, *The Jesus Survey* is delimited according to population. Though there are no reliably exact numbers regarding America's teen population, recent US Census Bureau estimates (as of 2008) indicate there are just under 22 million fifteen- to nineteen-year-olds in America, and an additional 20 million kids between the ages of ten and fourteen.[2] Based on those numbers, a reasonable (though rough) estimate of the number of teens in grades 7–12 would be around 29 million (or about 70% of the population of ten- to nineteen-year-old Americans). Additionally, according to the Barna Research Group, about 33% of American teenagers regularly attend a church youth group, which suggests our estimated population of churchgoing, Christian teens in America at present is just under 10 million.[3] Thus, with our survey sample of 845 teenagers, *The Jesus Survey* data delivers a 99% confidence level and a margin of error (confidence interval) of plus or minus 4.44%.[4]

Additionally, as you probably already realize, due to rounding figures the total percentages in a particular chart, graph, or summary used in this book may not always equal exactly 100%. Also, non-response items (when a student skipped a question on his or her survey) were excluded from percentage totals for that specific question.

I also wanted a useful comparative tool, so I went ahead and gave *The Jesus Survey* to 252 adult leaders at the Reach Workcamps mission sites, and asked them to answer the questions by "Choosing the responses you think most teens will choose." I wanted to see if our youth leaders are generally in tune with the opinions and perceptions of their students. Their responses were often insightful, so I've included some of the data from youth workers throughout the book as well.

After all the written surveys were tabulated, I also contacted a random sampling of the student and adult participants with follow-up questions on topics related to the data. Their comments are sprinkled throughout the book.

So, What's Next?

Now comes the good stuff. From here on out we'll be digging into the data, jumping to conclusions, trying to make sense of what we find, and hoping to discover how parents and ministry leaders can take any insights and apply them toward creating thriving, life-changing experiences for churchgoing teenagers.

One word of caution, though. In this book I'll be sharing both the data *and* my opinions. I hope that's OK with you. When I wrote *What I Wish My Youth Leader Knew about Youth Ministry*, I did the same thing, and I remember one book critic damned me with faint praise because of it. He wanted just the data, and not so much my opinions about it. For him, my thoughts ruined the book.

Ah, well.

One of the privileges of writing a book like this is being able to share your own opinions—and you can bet I'll be doing that throughout. Still, if you're like that guy who wants only the data, feel free to skip over my comments and tear out the pages of appendix B (pages 181–236) instead. That's where I've included an overview of the main data collected through this survey.

If you're someone like me, though, who wants to interact with the numbers, explore more deeply what the data might mean, and brainstorm ideas for how to apply the data to real life, then I invite you to join me chapter by chapter as we dig into *The Jesus Survey*.

So who do Christian teenagers think Jesus is? And how do their beliefs about Jesus influence the way they live?

I guess now is as good a time as any to find out.

Part One

WHO IS JESUS?

Who do you say I am?

—Jesus Christ, to Peter[1]

1

CAN I TRUST WHAT THE BIBLE SAYS ABOUT JESUS?

All Scripture is breathed out by God.
2 Timothy 3:16 ESV

"Read the words in red. Those are the best parts."

Randy Haynes fingered the Bible in his hands. It was an unfamiliar experience, causing a tingle in his soul. Not long ago a friend had shared this advice with him: "If you ever decide to start reading a Bible, read the words in red. Those are the best parts."

And so, holding a red-letter edition of the Scriptures (that is, a Bible that has the words of Christ printed in red ink), Randy opened the book—and his heart—to read the messages of God for him. That experience was a catalyst that changed his life, now and forever. Randy Haynes has, literally, never been the same.

I'm thinking about my old friend Randy today, as I begin writing this chapter. That's because I too own a "red-letter" edition of the Scriptures, and I'm wondering . . .

What if the Bible were taken from me? What if the message it shares of Jesus's incarnation, life, sacrifice, death, resurrection, and redemption were no longer mine to access?

Or perhaps worse: What if my Bible were available to me at all times—brimming with truth and power that springs from eternity itself—and I dismissed it as unreliable fiction, no different from any other storybook of dubious distinction in history? What would that mean for me? Or for anyone?

Whether we like it or not, the Bible is overwhelmingly the source of faith in Jesus Christ. Without the Gospels and the subsequent theologies explained in the New Testament, humanity's knowledge of Jesus is sketchy at best and practically nonexistent at worst.

Basically, if you could (hypothetically) erase the pages of Scripture from history, you could, in a very real way, erase the religion of Jesus from the world—and from the lives of Christian teenagers.[1]

It's no surprise, then, that the first and most virulent attacks on the Christian faith are always aimed at discrediting the reliability and veracity of what we call God's Word. Charles Colson, an internationally known columnist and apologist, calls this "The Recurring Battle." "Separated by 18 centuries," he says,

> The stories of Scillitan martyrs and of the Chinese house church movement during the Cultural Revolution involve the same dynamics—Christians defending the Word of God, enemies doing their best to destroy it and persecuting Christians for cherishing it. These identical dynamics . . . illuminate the struggle that began with the early Church and continues to this day, always with the same battle lines over God's Word.[2]

Although attempts to undermine the trustworthiness of Scripture are nothing new, the sheer onslaught of attacks in recent years (coming to a peak after Christian voting blocs tipped the scales behind the 2004 reelection of George W. Bush to the presidency of the United States) is impressive, if only for its volume and breadth in modern media.

Hit TV comedies such as *The Big Bang Theory* and *How I Met Your Mother* regularly present people who believe in the Bible (usually relatives, such as Sheldon's mother or Ted's sister) as nutty, ignorant, and bigoted.[3] Reality TV often does the same (check out pretty much any MTV show). Hollywood films and TV procedural dramas are so prone to casting a Scripture-quoting, gun-toting psychopath as the villain that it's actually become a hackneyed stereotype. And anti-Bible (often atheist) propaganda in books like Richard Dawkins's *The God Delusion*, Bart Ehrman's *Misquoting Jesus*, Christopher Hitchens's *God Is Not Great*, and others have sold millions of copies by taking aim straight at the Bible.

The anti-Scripture message is repeated with regular ferocity in all kinds of media, echoing Dawkins's declaration of unwavering confidence: "Ever since the 19th century, scholarly theologians have made an overwhelming case that the gospels are not reliable accounts of what happened in the history of the real world."[4]

As if reviewing a script with nutty characters from a popular sitcom, he also adds this disdainful generalization, "But there are many unsophisticated Christians out there who . . . take the Bible very seriously indeed as a literal and accurate record of history and hence as evidence supporting their religious beliefs."[5]

Ah, well. Richard Dawkins thinks I'm unsophisticated. Guess I'll have to live with that.

At any rate, in the past these kinds of attacks most often raged in the ivory towers of intellectual debate, and as such were generally outside the realistic realm of influence of the typical American teen. In today's society, though, teens are the most voracious and obvious consumers of mass-media products. Thus, this kind of bias against Scripture is on display—and reinforced—nearly everywhere.

So the question must be asked: Since Christian teens in our churches can't help but be part of our pop culture–obsessed society, have they been influenced by our media's recent resurgence of anti-Bible sentiment?

The only way I knew to find out was to ask them.

Is the Bible Trustworthy in What It Says about Jesus?

In the beginning of the content section of *The Jesus Survey*, I presented teens with two questions regarding their beliefs about the reliability of the Bible's teaching, specifically its teachings about Christ. For all questions, I listed a one-sentence statement as though it were a fact, and then asked kids to indicate whether they agreed or disagreed with the statement.

First, in question 6, I asked kids to react to this statement:

> The Bible is 100% accurate—historically, factually, and theologically—and therefore completely trustworthy in what it says about Jesus.

Next—because, decades ago, my statistics professor in college told me it was a good practice—for question 7 I asked the same basic question ("Is the Bible trustworthy?") from the opposite perspective:

> The Bible, though generally accurate, contains some widely acknowledged errors and can't be completely trusted in everything it says about Jesus.

That meant, to be consistent, a student who answered "agree" or "strongly agree" on question 6 should also answer "disagree" or "strongly disagree" on question 7. Likewise, a "disagree" or "strongly disagree" response on question 6 should also be paired with "agree" or "strongly agree" on question 7. At least that's what I thought.

I'm not sure exactly what I expected I'd find in response to those questions—but what I got was nothing like what I could have predicted.

Question 6: "The Bible Is Completely Trustworthy."

The good news is that when asked straight up whether or not they believe the Bible to be trustworthy in what it says about Jesus, nearly 9 out of 10 (a full 86%) teens in our youth groups said that it was.

Some felt more confident about saying this than others. Just under half of our teens (45%) indicated that they strongly agreed with that statement (see fig. 1.1). Certainly it would have been nice to see a higher percentage—more than half, perhaps—answer this way. But it's still rewarding to see that the first inclination of the largest portion of Christian teenagers is to "strongly agree" that the Bible is trustworthy.

There were a good number of teens who, while not as confident as others, still appeared ready to give the Bible the benefit of the doubt on this question. Although 2 out of 5 (41%) Christian teens couldn't "strongly agree" that Scripture was completely trustworthy, they did feel they could "somewhat agree" to that idea. Yes, the modifier "somewhat" indicates that this sizable group of teenagers has some measurable reservations—or uncertainty—about the Bible. Still, at this point at least they don't appear willing to completely abandon the Bible stories we taught them in Sunday school.

Surprisingly, though, there is a small but significant minority of Christian teens for whom the Bible is unacceptable as an authority on matters relating to Jesus Christ. If the responses in *The Jesus Survey* are truly representative of the churchgoing, Christian teen population in America today (and I believe they are), then roughly 1 out of every 7 kids (14%) in your youth group has serious doubts about the trustworthiness of Scripture, choosing "somewhat disagree" or "strongly disagree" in response to that first question on this topic. This is in spite of your teaching, Bible studies, youth group sermons, youth mission trips, national conferences, summer camps, and so on.

Hmm.

It also turns out that, despite what the other 86% initially said, those 14% who said up front that they don't trust the Bible aren't actually alone.

Figure 1.1

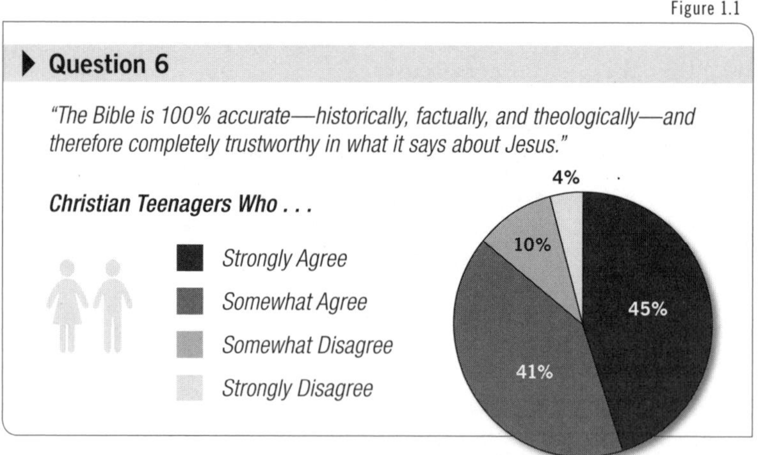

Question 7: "The Bible Can't Be Completely Trusted."

When I turned my attention to the next question on this topic, I got my first real surprise in the data.

Based on the way 86% of our kids responded to question 6, the overwhelming majority should have responded with "strongly disagree" or "somewhat disagree" to question 7. After all, it's basically the same question ("Is the Bible trustworthy?"), but inverted so as to require a "no" response to remain consistent with a "yes" response to question 6.

However, as you can see from figure 1.2, that's just not the way kids saw it.

Figure 1.2*

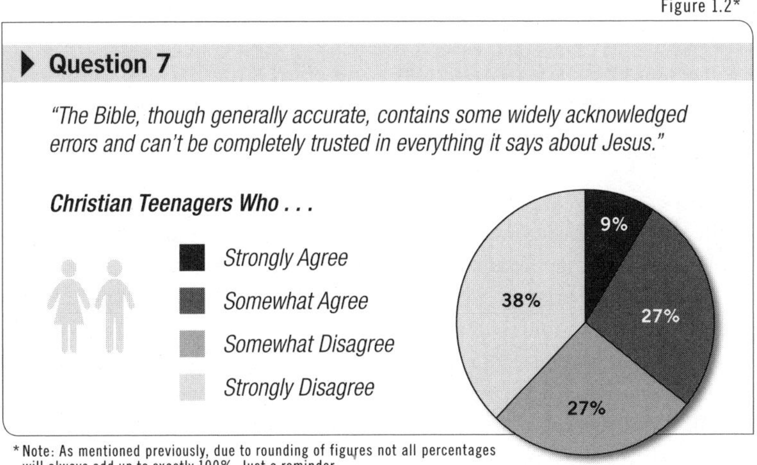

*Note: As mentioned previously, due to rounding of figures not all percentages will always add up to exactly 100%. Just a reminder.

It's important to note that a solid majority of Christian teens (65%) still indicated that they believed the Bible to be generally trustworthy. But it's also important to note that 1 in 5 students (22%) actually *switched* viewpoints when asked this question from the negative perspective.

Back in question 6, 14% of our teens (about 1 in 7) expressed some doubts about the Bible; here in question 7, that number jumped to 36% (more than 1 in 3 of our kids). In fact, 9% "strongly agree" that Scripture *can't* be trusted when talking about Christ, along with 27% who "somewhat agree" to that—despite that many of them had just affirmed the opposite in the previous question.

Even more telling, in question 6, only 4% (roughly 1 out of 20) of Christian teens expressed strong disbelief in the reliability of the Bible. When asked the same question from the opposite perspective in question 7, that number more than doubled to roughly 1 out of 10 kids in our youth groups.

So what's going on? Did our teenagers experience an atheistic epiphany between the time when they answered question 6 and question 7? Were they aware of their apparent hypocrisy? Were they just careless? Or were they simply uncertain of what they truly believe about the Bible?

Well, I have no definitive answers on that, but I can share some speculation.

First, it's important to remember that I write from my generational biases. I'm a member of the leading edge of Generation X, and like many in my generation I value authenticity and consistency. Tell me who you are, and if you act the same way

I will respect you—regardless of whether or not I agree with you. That's something that's become part of the DNA of my generation.

Needless to say, teenagers today continue to value authenticity, but unlike my generation they also appear to be comfortable with personal ambiguity. I discussed this with my good friend Dr. Timothy Paul Jones, and he shed more light on this phenomenon for me.

Dr. Jones is a professor of leadership and church ministry at Southern Baptist Seminary, and a startling intellect in matters of theology, ministry, and pop culture. When I showed him preliminary data on these two questions, he quickly cut through the generational fog.

"This fits perfectly with Christian Smith's research in *Soul Searching* and *Souls in Transition*," he said. "A significant number of teenagers, for fear of seeming intolerant, are perfectly willing to embrace contradictory beliefs about God."[6]

So I checked, and Christian Smith's research does indeed back up Dr. Jones's assessment. "The bottom line," Smith says, "is when it comes to their religious belief about God, U.S. teens reflect a great deal of variance on the matter, and perhaps in some cases more than a little conceptual confusion."[7] David Kinnaman, president of the Barna Group and coauthor of *unChristian*, further documents this unusual characteristic of the current teen generation. Based on his studies of religious attitudes among today's youth, Kinnaman says, "[Young people] view life in a nonlinear, chaotic way, which means they don't mind contradiction and ambiguity."[8]

Well, that's all well and good, and I actually agree with the assessment of these three scholars. Still, I don't like it. Something inside me wants to believe that these teenagers actually do believe *something* consistent about Scripture.

So I decided to dig a little beneath the surface and see if I could find any clues to lead to a more accurate (i.e., less ambiguous!) understanding of what these Christian teenagers are, and aren't, saying.

Unshakeable, Uncertain, Unsettled, and Unbelieving

As I started looking at the data, I realized that if I cross-correlated the tables for answers to questions 6 (the Bible is trustworthy) and 7 (the Bible can't be completely trusted) in terms of consistent beliefs, I could actually see quite clearly four primary Bible belief paradigms among the survey respondents. I won't bore you with the math and combinations, but here's a quick summary of the paradigms of Christian teens that I uncovered.

Unshakeable

These are the kids who appear to have full, unshakeable confidence in the Bible as an authoritative source of truth about Jesus Christ. As an indication of that, they said that they "strongly agree" with question 6 (the Bible is trustworthy) and "strongly disagree" with question 7 (the Bible can't be completely trusted).

Uncertain

These teens initially lean toward the idea that the Bible is trustworthy, but are unwilling to fully commit to that notion like their Unshakeable peers do. It's almost as if they want to give the Bible the benefit of the doubt—for now, or until something happens that pushes them into a fuller commitment one way or the other. They responded to question 6 by saying they only "somewhat agree" that the Bible is trustworthy, and at the same time they only "somewhat disagree" with the assertion of question 7 that the Bible *can't* be trusted.

Unsettled

Like their Uncertain friends, kids in this category are unwilling to fully commit to the idea that the Bible is completely trustworthy. The difference, however, is that these teens are much more conflicted about that uncertainty. Kids in this group responded to questions 6 and 7 in ways that completely contradicted each other. For instance, saying they "strongly disagree" with the idea that the Bible is completely trustworthy, but at the same time saying they also "strongly disagree" or "somewhat disagree" that the Bible *can't* be trusted.

Unbelieving

Like the Unshakeables in their youth groups, these Christian teens have made a clear choice about God's Word—and their decision is that it *can't* be trusted. These kids demonstrated a consistent distrust in the Bible by disagreeing with question 6 and subsequently agreeing with question 7.

Figure 1.3

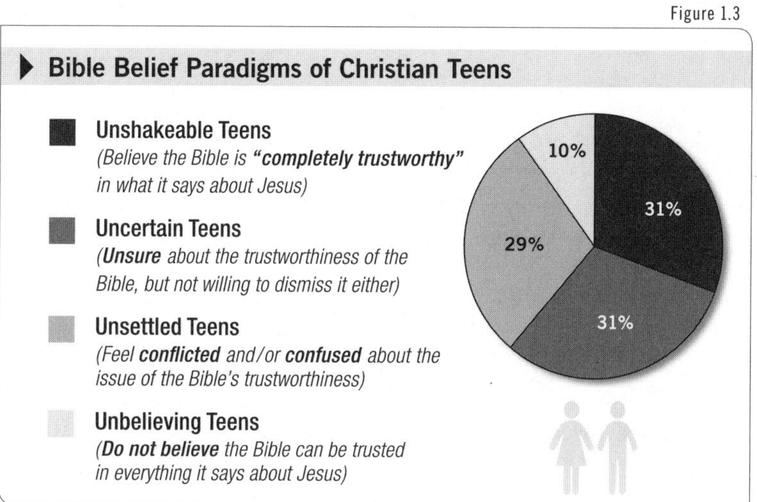

When I finally laid out the cross-correlated data according to teen paradigms, I was dumbfounded by the numbers. I honestly felt a bit shell-shocked, and I'll tell you why.

First, remember, the respondents in this survey meet two core criteria:

1. They are involved in a church youth group.
2. They describe themselves as Christian.

Additionally, these kids (and their parents) paid several hundred dollars to spend a week sleeping on a floor at night and then spending all day doing basic home construction for poor and disabled folks. Of all the kids in our youth groups, these are the ones who are actually trying to live out the lifestyle of service that Jesus teaches us in the Bible.

The former-youth-pastor part of my mind can't help but think that these teens are the cream of the crop in our churches. They are the "good kids" who actually seem to be taking to heart the messages we deliver each week in our churches and who seem to be responding to the discipling influence of our youth ministry. In short, these are *our* kids—the ones for whom we invest our lives in youth ministry. The ones God has given into our care and whom we often feel rewarded to serve.

Now, with that in mind, look again at the numbers in figure 1.3. Do you see what I see?

Among these "cream of the crop" Christian kids in our youth ministries, a full 10% have decided that the biblical accounts about Jesus simply can't be trusted. And the clear majority of the rest (60%) are either uncertain or unsettled and confused about whether or not the Bible can be trusted. As spiritual descendants of the "people of the Book" who spend our days, weeks, and years teaching the Book to teenagers, the news that our finest and most faithful kids simply don't have confidence in God's Word is shocking—and devastating.

Look at it this way.

Let's say that tonight you're leading a group of ten teenagers in a Bible study at your home. When you read the account of Jesus feeding 5,000 people in Mark 6:30–44 to these Christian kids, only three of your kids accept that what you are saying actually happened. The other seven students (quietly, mostly) range from uncertainty about that historical event to outright disbelief in it.

Now, let me reiterate something I said earlier: *If the Bible can't be trusted as an authoritative source of truth—especially in what it says about Jesus—then our faith is both meaningless and unfounded.*

It would be like relying on an electrical manual that you knew was only accurate 90% of the time. You could never be totally sure which instructions fell into that falsified 10% until you tried them—and felt a few thousand volts coursing through your brain. Can you imagine any electrician actually using that manual to, say, reference a diagram on installing a light fixture or laying out the wiring for a new garage door opener? That would be absurd—and dangerous. We'd all toss that manual in the garbage and go looking for one that was trustworthy 100% of the time. Too much is at stake to do otherwise.

Similarly, the harsh truth is if your teenagers don't feel they can trust God's Word to be accurate and legitimate in their lives, they won't listen to it (or you) for long. In fact, other researchers have shown that this outcome is already happening. Kinnaman reports:

> Most young people who were involved in a church as a teenager disengage from church life and often from Christianity at some point during early adulthood. . . . Our tracking research suggests that today young people are less likely to return to church later, even when they become parents.[9]

So where does that leave us? Well, the good news is that on the surface 86% of our Christian teenagers in our youth groups do say the Bible is at least somewhat trustworthy. The bad news is that, in spite of their initial endorsement, the overwhelming majority of our kids (70%) express persistent, measurable doubts—and even outright disbelief in many cases—that what the Bible has to say about Jesus is true. "The Bible was written so long ago," one young woman explained to me in a follow-up interview. She attends a Presbyterian church in New Jersey, and actually supports the idea that the Bible is trustworthy. Still, she says, "All of its eyewitnesses are dead, so it's difficult to trust everything it says. Just as high school textbooks don't always tell the whole story, I sometimes wonder if this is also the case with the Bible."

Houston, we have a problem.

The Leader Factor

OK, deep breath.

In looking at the data, we can take some solace in the fact that although only about 1 in 3 of our Christian kids actually trusts the Bible, another 60% seem at least *willing to consider* the possibility that it's true. The teenagers I've labeled as Uncertain or Unsettled seem to be putting off making a decision on that question, at least for the time being.

For Christian parents and youth leaders, this is not necessarily exclusively bad news.

It does give us a unique opportunity to speak to a generally open-minded audience about the Scripture's claims of truth. That's a good thing. But we must remember that the time we have to seize this opportunity is short—and shrinking daily. We must understand this one principle of faith development:

No decision eventually becomes a "no" decision.

That is, the longer a person puts off making a "yes" decision about an issue, the more likely that person is to settle into a default "no" decision. For instance, imagine that you ask your best girl (or best guy) to marry you. If that sweetheart of yours says, "Give me time to think about it," you and I both know that the longer Honeylips puts off delivering an answer to your invitation of lifelong marital bliss, the more likely it is that Honeylips will eventually decline that invitation. It's just human nature.

Lisa Pearce and Melinda Denton's research in the National Study of Youth and Religion (NSYR) seems to bear this concept out tangibly. As part of their study, Pearce and Denton identified one specific subgroup of teens who (a) express belief in God, (b) occasionally pray, and (c) occasionally attend a religious service. "We call this group Avoiders," say Pearce and Denton, "because it seems as if they are avoiding being either religious or irreligious. They are not Atheists nor dismissive of religion . . . but they are uninterested in having religion be a part of their life."[10] Three scant years after first being identified as Avoiders, these kids were surveyed again by the NSYR. In that short amount of time, fully 11% of these students had already reclassified as Atheists. "Becoming Atheist over these three years involves a clear set of changes," Pearce and Denton say. "These Avoiders decide there is no God, drop private expressions of religion such as praying, and lose any sense of being close to God."[11]

So what does this mean for youth leaders and for Christian parents? Well, for starters we need to get a better, more accurate perception of the teens in our care—and what they believe about the Bible.

As you know, when I surveyed the 845 students represented in this study, I also gave the exact same survey to 252 of the adult leaders from the home churches of those kids. These adult leaders were instructed to answer each question by "choosing the response that you think most teens would choose." Basically, I was asking these adult leaders to demonstrate how well they knew the kids in their ministries by trying to predict—as accurately as possible—the attitudes and beliefs of those kids.

When it came to the question of biblical trustworthiness, these well-meaning adults were woefully out of touch.

As a comparative tool, I sorted the data according to denomination (so that leader predictions were being compared to the results from kids actually in their youth groups or in the youth groups of a similar denomination). Next I measured how many leaders predicted that their kids would fall into the Unshakeable category of believers. As you can see in figure 1.4, leaders were all over the map on that assessment—and frequently wrong.

First, kudos to the Episcopalian leaders and to the youth workers in the six smaller denominations I've classified as "Other." They were able to stay within single digit percentages with their predictions. Everyone else missed the mark widely—by double digits.

Several denominations greatly overestimated the faith their teenagers had in God's Word. Baptist leaders were most out of touch in this regard, predicting that nearly 2 out of 3 (63%) of their kids had confidence in Scripture when, in fact, significantly less than half (40%) actually did. Lutheran, Methodist, and Church of Christ leaders were also guilty of similar stained-glass misconceptions.

At the other end of the spectrum, a majority of denominational youth leaders were actually too pessimistic about the faith their teens had, drastically underestimating the number of Unshakeable teens in their own youth groups. Unaffiliated congregations (non-denominational and undeclared) were most egregious in this negative misperception. Others to join them, in varying degrees, included Brethren in Christ, Presbyterians, and Catholics (more on them in a moment).

Figure 1.4

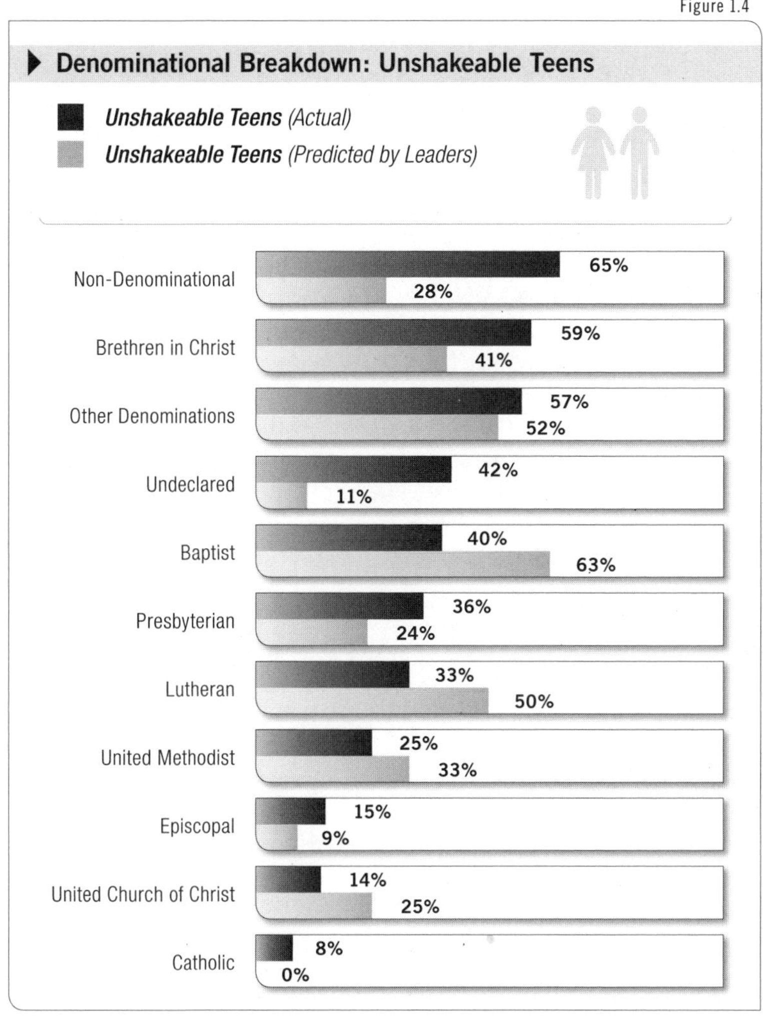

The point here is not that some leaders underestimated their kids' faith in the Bible, or that other leaders overestimated that faith. What's striking—and extremely disappointing—is that so many leaders were wildly off-base in their attempt to accurately assess what their own kids believed.

This reveals a clear disconnect between youth group leaders and their own kids, and would seem to spell disaster for any effort to help teenagers grow their faith in the Scriptures. Now, of course, no prediction in this circumstance could be entirely accurate. There are just too many variables. But the huge margins of error can't be glossed over either.

And it shouldn't surprise anyone that the denominational affiliations performing best here are also among the ones with smaller group sizes and favorable leader-to-student ratios. For instance, according to the survey tabulations, there was at least one adult Episcopalian leader accompanying every two students at a Reach workcamp. That leader-to-student dedication speaks to the value of mentor relationships with teens and shows up in the results here.

If we want to connect our kids to truth, we must also be willing to connect with them ourselves, through friendships and involvement in their lives that foster discussion and action. We need to know our kids personally, to talk with them about what they think and believe. Apparently, when it comes to discussing the Bible and why it can be trusted, we haven't succeeded in doing that. Yet.

Now, I can't simply ignore the Catholic responses in this section. First, please be assured that I hold the Catholic Church in high regard. I spent several years of my own childhood in a Catholic Church, and my best friend of the past thirty years is also Catholic. But the results here are clear: the Catholic Church is not building a generation of Unshakeable teenagers—kids who believe God's Word with full faith and confidence. What's worse: their youth leaders know it.

Of all denominations, Catholic students are least invested in the trustworthiness of Scripture. In fact, only about 1 in 12 dares to believe that the Bible delivers accurate information about Jesus Christ. And that's more than their leaders expected of them! Not a single Catholic leader in this survey predicted their kids would hold an Unshakeable view of the Bible.

That, to my mind, is tragic. For millennia, the Catholic Church has been the single organization to safeguard the Scriptures and the message of Jesus for the world. The stories of our greatest heroes of faith, of our martyrs and missionaries—they are all a part of our shared Catholic history and tradition. Because of that, all of the outrageous claims of conspiracies and hoaxes about Scripture always target the Catholic Church and its leaders as the primary villains in perpetrating those crimes. In fact, many Catholic students and adults who took this survey were angry when, later, I included a question that asked whether or not the Catholic Church was guilty of hoaxing about Scripture (more on that in a future chapter!).

In spite of that glorious history and current protectiveness toward the Catholic name, astoundingly few Catholics in this study seemed to value the Bible that they themselves have preserved. Are, perhaps, mainstream anti-Catholic attacks bearing fruit in our own youth groups? Or have we simply been lazy in helping our Catholic teens experience the life-changing power and authority of God's Word? I have no answers, but sooner or later we must confront that serious problem. (And I pray that it's sooner.)

Question 8: "Other Highly Regarded Religious Books Are Just as Important as the Bible."

The last area of discovery on this topic has to do with the Bible's place among the pantheon of other "holy" books such as the Qur'an (or more commonly, the "Koran"), the Book of Mormon, the Hindu Vedas, the Talmud, and so on.

Because we live in a society that preaches inclusivity often to the point of exclusion, for question 8 I decided to see if our Christian teenagers viewed the Bible as distinctive in its authority or simply "one of many" sources of truth about Jesus. I asked whether teens agreed or disagreed with this statement:

> Other highly regarded religious books, such as the Koran or the Book of Mormon, are just as important as the Bible in teaching people about who Jesus really was.

More than half (56%) of Christian teenagers disagreed with that statement, and just under 1 in 3 (30%) strongly disagreed.

Those results are heartening, because they seem to indicate that a majority of our kids understand that not all religions are the same and that not all teachings about Jesus can be blindly accepted as true. Among this majority, it appears it's almost intuitive to understand that believing what the Bible says about Jesus inherently requires disbelieving what many other accepted "holy" books say about him.

The fact is, religious books like the Qur'an actually contradict—and claim to correct errors of—the Bible. For instance, Sura 19:35 of the Qur'an teaches very specifically that Jesus was *not* God's Son but simply another created being: "It is not for God to take a son unto Him. Glory be to Him! When He decrees a thing, He but says to it, 'Be,' and it is."

Thus, for one who believes the Qur'an, the Bible's promise of John 3:16, "God so loved the world that he gave his only Son," is a lie.

In spite of that—and perhaps due to the contradictory nature of today's teens that we discussed earlier—there are still a substantial number of Christian kids in our churches who equate the Qur'an and other highly regarded religious books with the source of their own faith knowledge, the Bible itself. Nearly half (44%) of our Christian kids readily accept the mistaken assumption that the Bible is just one of many authoritative voices about Jesus Christ.

Among Uncertain teens that number rises to 50%, and I'm sorry to say that it only gets worse from there. For Unsettled youth group members, 3 out of every 5 (59%) believe the Bible is no different from the Qur'an when talking about Jesus. And among our Unbelieving Christian teens, those who think the Bible is uniquely true are outnumbered by more than a 2 to 1 margin (69% to 31%).

I suspect that a lot of this stems from the way our society both demands and enforces relative morality as an approved, inclusive way of life. For most kids, the idea of social tolerance is so ingrained that the mere idea of suggesting someone else is wrong about a religious book is anathema. For many, it would almost be considered bigotry. In fact, in a follow-up interview about this specific question, one teen (a foster daughter of a volunteer leader) commented, "I can't tell someone at my school they're 'wrong' about something without getting punched in the face!" A Presbyterian youth worker added, "This is a result of the moral relativism that exists in teen culture today. In their world, you're supposed to have strong opinions, but you're not supposed to counter anyone else's beliefs."

Christian Smith's research lends credence to that suspicion. He says, "According to emerging adults, the absolute authority for every person's beliefs or actions is his or her own sovereign self." Smith and his research team interviewed young people for clarification on this point, asking what makes anything right or wrong. One study participant summed up the general perspective of his peers by saying, "I think it's your own personal belief system . . . it's just what you think, it's dependent on each person and their own beliefs." Another said, "You know, the Muslim religion is not right for me, but it doesn't make it wrong for them. I just think it's all subjective to each person." "It is individualism," Smith says, "raised on heavy doses of multiculturalism."[12]

That belief seems to hold true for Christian teens in their answers to the question about other sacred books. Among our Uncertain, Unsettled, and Unbelieving kids, Smith's perception appears to be fairly common. In fact, even among Christian teens who say they believe the Bible is completely trustworthy, 2 out of 5 (40%) say they also believe that other highly regarded religious books are just as important as the Bible.

Figure 1.5

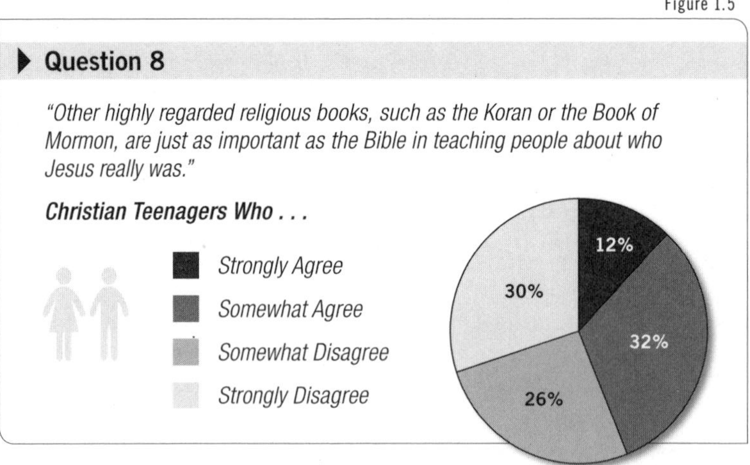

Unsurprisingly, it's the Unshakeables in our youth groups who are most likely to hold out against that trend. For 84% of this group, an all-inclusive, everybody's-OK attitude toward Scripture just doesn't cut it. They alone seem to keep to the traditional belief that the Bible is a uniquely authoritative book on the topic of Jesus. They also appear to be comfortable in the truth that one can disagree with another's religion without having to be hostile toward it. However, it is significant that even among this dedicated cadre of Bible-believing "Unshakeable" Christian teens, roughly 1 in 7 (about 15%) is still willing to assume that a book like the Qur'an or the Book of Mormon delivers legitimate truth about Jesus.

Summary

This has been a lot of information to digest, I know, and believe me when I tell you I feel like I've only begun to scratch the surface here! But this chapter can't last forever, so let me wrap up with a few summary thoughts before we move on to the next chapter.

- *When asked once, the first inclination for Christian teens is to say they believe the Bible is trustworthy in what it says about Jesus.* Fully 86% gave this response—something that's very encouraging for parents and leaders of Christian youth. However, that initial response does mask a few less positive indicators that hide just below the surface. For starters, less than half (45%) of Christian teens feel strongly that their Scriptures can be trusted on the topic of Jesus. And nearly 1 out of 7 (14%) actually disagrees with the idea that the Bible gives accurate information about Jesus Christ. For kids who claim to be Christian and who are involved in church youth groups, this is troubling news.
- *When asked twice about the trustworthiness of Scripture, a significant number of Christian teens appear to lose their nerve.* In fact, about 1 in 5 students (22%) actually switch their view the second time around. The result is an expression of strongly contradictory opinions from the same generic student, with many who first affirm the Bible then say they either have doubts, or simply disbelieve, that the Bible is accurate in its teachings about Jesus. Most researchers acknowledge this to be simply another hallmark of our younger generation. As Dr. Timothy Paul Jones says, "A significant number of teenagers, for fear of seeming intolerant, are perfectly willing to embrace contradictory beliefs about God."
- *Cross-correlating students' conflicting responses to the questions of scriptural trustworthiness reveals a more accurate and consistent picture of what students mean when they say they both trust and distrust the Bible.* In fact, four clear groupings of kids show up when their answers to both questions are taken in conjunction with each other. *Unshakeable* teens appear to have confidence in the Bible's authority to speak truth about Jesus Christ. *Uncertain* teens lean toward the idea that the Bible is trustworthy, but are unwilling to fully commit to that notion. *Unsettled* teens are not only uncertain of the reliability of Scripture, they are also deeply conflicted

and possibly confused by the question of whether or not it can be trusted. *Unbelieving* teens, despite the fact that they think of themselves as Christian, have made a clear choice about God's Word—and their decision is that it can't be trusted.

- *What all this means is that the overwhelming majority of Christian teens in our church youth groups either have measurable doubts about the trustworthiness of Scripture or simply disbelieve it entirely.* Fully 70% of survey respondents fit into this category. What makes this even more surprising is that they doubt the Bible's trustworthiness *on the topic of Jesus Christ.* Honestly, this is shocking, dismaying news. If the Bible can't be trusted as an authoritative source of truth—especially in what it says about Jesus—then our faith (and that of our teens) is both meaningless and unfounded.
- *It's possible, and even likely, that some Christian teens may just be postponing this decision about the Bible for a future time.* Perhaps a good number of our kids simply haven't given a lot of thought to the trustworthiness of Scripture—and they're giving parents and youth leaders more opportunities to weigh in on that decision. That can actually be a good thing. We must remember, though, that the longer this decision is avoided, the more likely it is to turn toward the negative. Over time, "no decision" almost always becomes a "no" decision.
- *Of all denominations, Catholic teens are least likely to affirm the trustworthiness of the Bible.* In fact, only about 1 in 12 dares to believe that the Bible delivers accurate information about Jesus Christ.
- *A majority of Christian teens (56%) disagree with the idea that the Bible, the Qur'an, and other religious books are equally true when talking of Jesus Christ.* At the same time, close to half (44%) of the students in our youth groups feel the opposite, and don't question the socially inclusive mindset that declares all "holy" books are the same.
- *The charge for parents and youth leaders is clear: we must talk to our teens—early, often, and openly—about the trustworthiness of the Bible.* If we neglect to do that, then it's not our kids who have failed to keep the faith—it is us.

Bonus Survey Results

Due to time and space constraints, I obviously can't ramble on about every little permutation of data from *The Jesus Survey*, so here's what I've decided to do: at the end of each chapter, if there are additional data sets I looked at but wasn't able to talk about, I'll include them in table-only form for you. That way you can at least see everything I saw, and then decide for yourself if there are any important insights to be gained from the numbers. I hope that's helpful!

Figure 1.6

Unshakeable Christian Teens (by Grade)

Year in School	***Percentage of Christian Teens Who Are "Unshakeable"*** *(View the Bible as trustworthy when it speaks of Jesus)*
7th Grade	**21%**
8th Grade	**38%**
9th Grade	**33%**
10th Grade	**32%**
11th Grade	**21%**
12th Grade	**34%**

Figure 1.7

Unbelieving Christian Teens (by Grade)

Year in School	***Percentage of Christian Teens Who Are "Unbelieving"*** *(Disbelieve that the Bible is trustworthy when it speaks of Jesus)*
7th Grade	**0%**
8th Grade	**11%**
9th Grade	**6%**
10th Grade	**7%**
11th Grade	**17%**
12th Grade	**12%**

Figure 1.8

▶ Bible Belief Paradigms of Christian Teens (by Gender)

	Female	*Male*	*Total*
Unshakeable Teens *(Believe the Bible is "completely trustworthy" in what it says about Jesus)*	17%	14%	31%
Uncertain Teens *(Unsure about the trustworthiness of the Bible, but not willing to dismiss it either)*	17%	14%	31%
Unsettled Teens *(Feel conflicted and/or confused about the issue of the Bible's trustworthiness)*	15%	13%	28%*
Unbelieving Teens *(Do not believe the Bible can be trusted in everything it says about Jesus)*	4%	6%	10%
Total	53%	47%	100%

* Note: This percentage is different from the corresponding one in figure 1.3 due to rounding principles. Combined in figure 1.4, it rounds up to 29%; separated into female and male data sets here, it rounds down to 28%. Go figure.

2

JESUS—MERELY GREAT, OR SIMPLY DIVINE?

You are the Christ, the Son of the living God.
Matthew 16:16 NIV

The thing is, the signatures were *different*.

I couldn't help but frown as I laid them side by side. Yep, definitely not the same. That was frustrating.

After years of thinking about it, I'd finally decided to spend the money to buy an autograph of one of my heroes, comic book legend Stan Lee. (Yes, I'm a nerd. Get over it.) So I did what any collector with more money than sense does: I hit eBay and started trolling through the autographs for sale.

Then I found it. It was a Captain America comic (my favorite superhero) with a white cover and Stan Lee's autograph in black Sharpie pen clearly written across the front. According to the seller, Stan Lee had signed the comic for the seller's brother at a regional comic convention. Perfect.

I put in my bid (more than I wanted to pay, but not unreasonable) and waited for the auction to end. Meanwhile, I also saw a Spider-Man card with Stan the Man's signature. Not nearly as cool as the comic . . . but selling at a bargain price. On a whim, I went ahead and bid on that autograph as well.

I won both auctions, and a few weeks later the two autographs arrived in the mail. As expected, the comic book was very cool—collectible and signed. Nice. The card was actually in better shape than I'd expected, but I didn't look too closely at it because I was trying to decide whether to frame the signed comic or just display it in a clear plastic cover.

That's when I noticed the difference. Sure, both comic and card had a signature in black Sharpie pen. And yes, "Stan Lee" was clearly handwritten across both items. But even a surface glance at the two together revealed the problem: the signatures were not the same. It was obvious that two different hands had written Stan's name on these collectibles.

One was a forgery! But how could I know which was the fake and which was authentic?

I contacted both sellers. Suddenly the comic book guy couldn't remember exactly where his "brother" had gotten the autograph. And the card owner? She didn't even try to cover. "I don't know where it came from," she said. "I bought it from someone else."

So I was stuck. The next few days were spent in a dogged pursuit of handwriting analysis and comparing multiple authentic Stan Lee signatures to the ones I now had in my possession. Pretty soon it was clear which was which.

The near-throwaway card I'd bought on a whim, at a bargain price? It was the real deal—and worth at least double what I'd paid for it. The fancy comic book for which I'd paid top dollar? A forgery, a complete fake.

And I'd learned a few lessons the hard way: truth matters. Authenticity holds real value. And you can't trust everything you read on the internet!

Interestingly enough, those same lessons are true when tackling the question of Jesus's identity. And, much the same way many eBay sellers competed for my money, there are many forgeries of truth that vie for the currency of your teenagers' faith.

Is He or Isn't He?

When it comes to Jesus, all arguments about him eventually boil down to one of these two viewpoints:

1. Jesus is God.
2. Jesus is not God.

Like the autograph on my pretty-n-shiny Captain America comic book, one of those views is a forgery of truth. Determining which one is the difference between here and eternity.

For Christian teens, and indeed for Christians of all ages, that question of Christ's deity (or "un-deity," if that's a word) is the heart of faith. As I said before, all major religions acknowledge Jesus as a historical figure, a good man somehow associated with God and enlightened thinking. But only Christians assert that Jesus is, in some mysterious way, both the Son of God and God himself.

I have, on more than one occasion, heard a well-meaning intellectual (both teen and adult) make the absurd statement that "Jesus himself never claimed to be divine." They tend to (figuratively) pat me on the head with a knowing smile and speak to me in that condescending voice reserved for explaining toilet habits to children. I (being the obnoxious jerk that I am) return the favor by telling them they are full of toilet habits expressed by children. The only way anyone could even begin to believe that Jesus never claimed to be God would be to first claim unequivocally that Scripture cannot be trusted in what it says about Jesus. (Hmm . . . sound familiar?)

If the biblical account of Jesus is trustworthy (and I believe it is), then the people who drove Jesus to his execution on a cross certainly had no question that Christ claimed to be God. In fact, that was the reason for his execution! He was convicted in the Jewish courts of that time for blasphemy—"the crime of assuming to oneself the rights or qualities of God."[1]

Even before his crucifixion, that claim to godhood almost cost Christ his life. John 10:22–33 reveals a time when Jesus was speaking at the temple and was actually interrupted because the crowd decided to kill him for blasphemy. As they were gathering rocks to use in pummeling him to death, Jesus said to the crowd, "I have shown you many great miracles from the Father. For which of these do you stone me?"[2]

"We are not stoning you for any of these," replied the Jews, "but for blasphemy, because you, a mere man, claim to be God."[3]

Seems pretty clear, doesn't it? But if that's not enough, Matthew 26:57–67 documents Jesus's trial before the Jewish Sanhedrin—the body that passed the judgment of death and proceeded to see it enforced by the Roman government. At this trial, the Jewish high priest demanded to know whether or not Jesus thought himself "the Christ, the Son of God." Jesus responded with a colorfully emphatic and defiant yes. That alone was enough to convict Christ and seal his execution.

"He has spoken blasphemy!" the high priest said. And the rest of the Sanhedrin declared in response, "He is worthy of death."[4]

So, the idea that this condemned, blasphemous criminal who so enraged the religious leaders of his time could also be a benign, benevolent "good man" who never claimed to be God is simply horse excrement. Regardless of that truth, many people have spent millennia trying to create and propagate forged identities of Jesus that can somehow gloss over or dismiss the idea he could actually be God.

What I wanted to know from our Christian teenagers, then, was whether or not they'd bought these mass-media and intellectual forgeries of truth surrounding Jesus's godhood, or if they'd been able to see past those to discern the biblically authentic Christ of the faith they claim.

Enter *The Jesus Survey*.

Jesus: Merely Great, or Simply Divine?

In this portion of the content section of *The Jesus Survey*, I presented teens with two questions regarding their beliefs about Jesus's deity. As with all questions, I listed a one-sentence statement as though it were a fact and then asked kids to indicate whether they agreed or disagreed with the statement.

First, in question 9 I asked kids to react to this statement:

> Jesus, in some mysterious way, is both the Son of God and God himself.

Next, for question 10 I asked the same basic question ("Is Jesus God?") from the opposite perspective:

> Jesus was a good man, a righteous teacher, and a noble person, but he was not God.

That meant, to be consistent, a student who answered "somewhat agree" or "strongly agree" on question 9 should have also answered "somewhat disagree" or "strongly disagree" on question 10. Likewise, a "somewhat disagree" or "strongly disagree" response on question 9 should have been paired with "somewhat agree" or "strongly agree" on question 10. However, if you read chapter 1, you can probably guess that's not exactly what happened.

Question 9: "Jesus Is Both the Son of God and God Himself."

There is some encouraging news at this point: the initial reaction by Christian teenagers to the question of Jesus's divinity is to say overwhelmingly that they believe he is God. More than half (56%) strongly support that idea, and nearly 9 in 10 (87%) at least somewhat agree. On the other end, more than 1 in 7 (13%) of Christian teens expresses doubt that Jesus could be both the Son of God and God himself. That represents a significant contingent of unbelief in our youth groups and Christian homes—but still, those who express initial doubts about Jesus's deity are a clear minority.

Figure 2.1

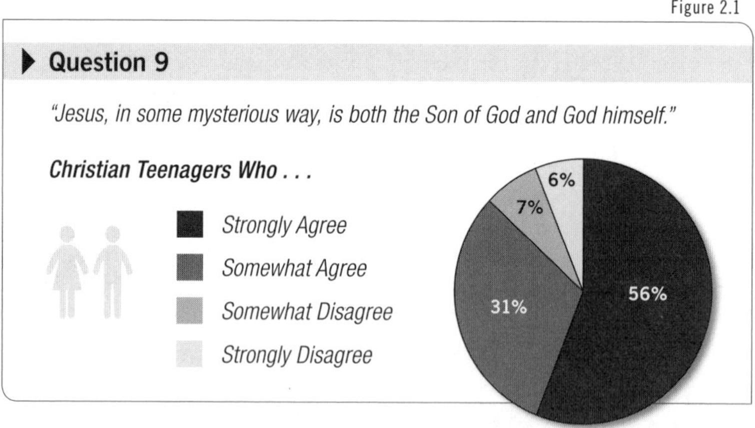

In denominational terms, the numbers are more varied. All denominations represented in this survey indicated initial agreement with the belief that Jesus is God by large margins—but for many of these teens that assertion of belief is tempered by misgivings. This is seen clearly when separating out the number of Christian kids who "strongly agree" that Jesus is God from the number of kids who indicated they only "somewhat agree" with that idea.

Figure 2.2

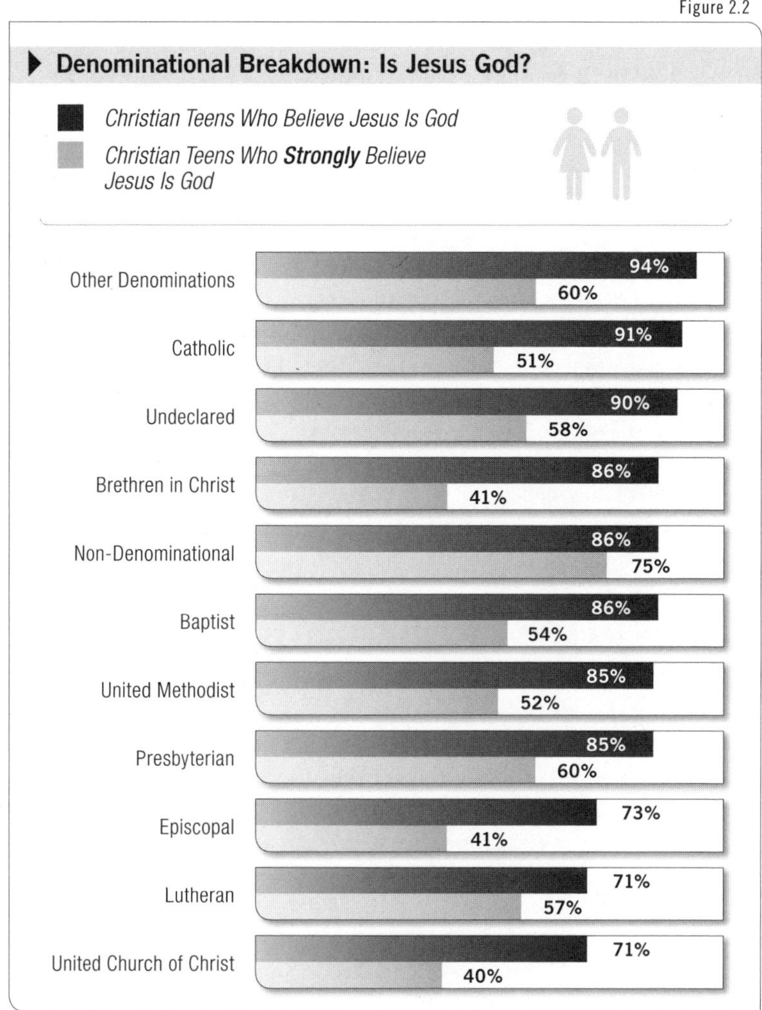

Once again, the Catholic Church is the enigma among the denominations. On the one hand, more than 9 of 10 (91%) Catholic students indicate that they believe Jesus is God. That's an overwhelmingly high number of kids, particularly in light of the professed disbelief in Scripture that showed up among a sizable portion of our Catholic teens in chapter 1. That a belief in Jesus as God is so ingrained in Catholic Christian thinking is heartening.

On the other hand, just barely half (51%) of Catholic teens say they can "strongly agree" to the core belief of Christ as God. Theirs is the second-widest margin of variance (40 points of difference) that shows up in the denominational breakdown on this question, and this should be cause for alarm for any Catholic parents or youth leaders. This "confidence gap" seems to indicate that a significant number of these kids hold more to a cultural, or familial, belief in Christ than a grounded, personal, and unshakeable faith in him as God.

Other denominations that appear to have canyon-sized confidence gaps in this area include Brethren in Christ (a 45-point variance between general agreement and strong agreement), United Methodists (a 33-point variance), Baptists and Episcopalians (a 32-point variance each), and United Church of Christ (31-point variance). United Church of Christ also holds the dubious distinction of being dead last in the number of Christian teens who strongly agree that Jesus is God (only 40%) and tied for dead last in the number of Christian teens who agree in general to the same thing.

Non-denominational churches seem to be doing the best job of helping teenagers grasp the godhood of Jesus Christ, with 86% indicating they favor that belief, and 75% (fully 3 out of 4) saying they strongly favor it.

The trouble here, as we learned in chapter 1, is that many of our teenagers don't reveal exactly what they believe when asked only once. Rewording the question of Jesus's deity so that it requires a negative response has a direct impact on what our kids say they believe in this matter. Case in point? Question 10 on *The Jesus Survey*.

Question 10: "Jesus Was Not God."

After digging through the contradictory data of chapter 1, I was not quite so naive about kids' initial statements of belief this time around. Yes, I was encouraged to see the way an overwhelming majority of Christian teenagers responded to question 9, but I have to admit I was waiting for the other shoe to drop when it was time to look at question 10. I'd learned to expect that the broader context afforded by multiple questions on the same topic would provide a clearer understanding of teen perceptions. Once again, that proved to be true.

Based on the way 87% of our kids responded to question 9, the practical response for the overwhelming majority on question 10 should have been "strongly disagree" or "somewhat disagree." However, when asked to weigh in on the same basic question from the negative perspective, fully 1 in 4 (25%) of Christian teens switched views on the issue of Jesus's deity (see figs. 2.3 and 2.4).

In fact, more than double the number of Christian teenagers *strongly* denied Jesus's deity when asked the question a second time. Only about 1 in 17 (6%) took that view in answer to question 9, but when answering question 10, about 1 in 7 (15%) confidently disavowed this core Christian belief. Combined with those who were somewhat in agreement with them, the number of kids who agreed to the nonbiblical belief that "Jesus was not God" engulfed more than one-third of the entire survey sample.

Figure 2.3

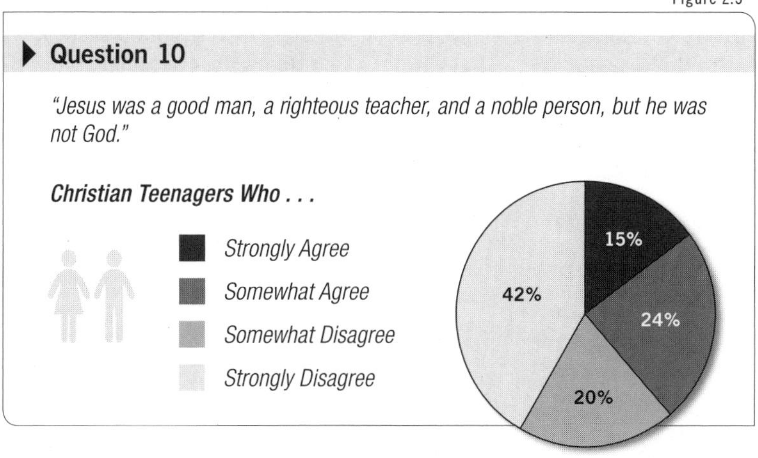

Figure 2.4

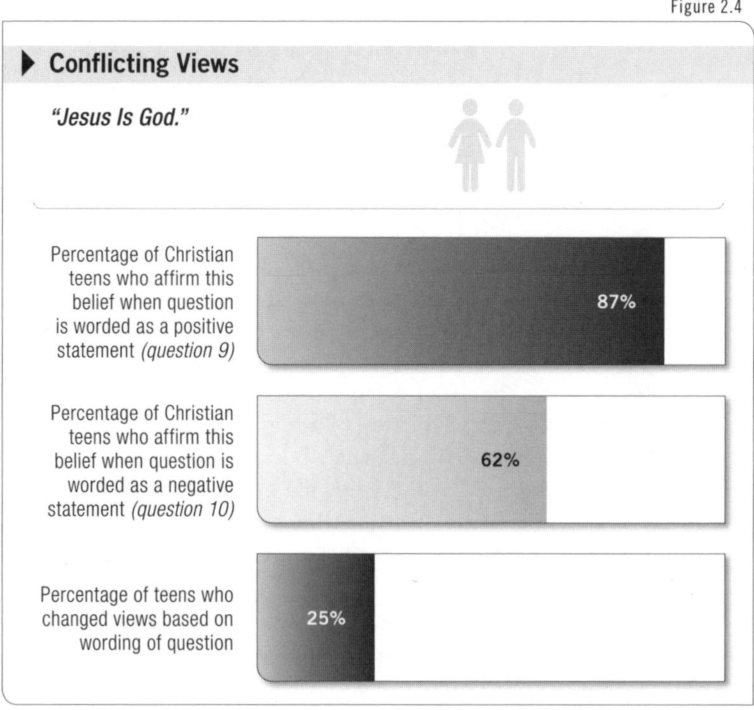

In trying to explain this consistent contradiction of belief, one youth leader from a Brethren in Christ church in Pennsylvania told me, "It seems like a lot of kids today know what they should say . . . but cannot bring themselves to believe what they are saying. This is especially true for kids who have grown up in church."

Figure 2.5

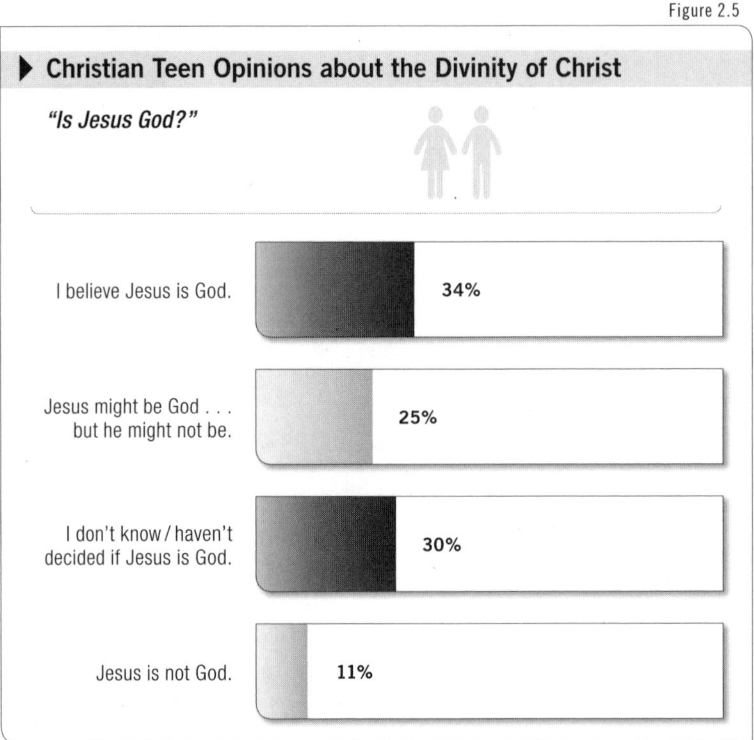

When we cross-correlate the data from question 10 with the data from question 9, we get a clearer, more contextual picture of what teenagers actually think about Jesus and his claims of godhood. In this snapshot of faith, kids break down into four general camps characterized by the following opinion statements:

I believe Jesus is God. These are the teens who answered with identifiably strong consistency on this issue. For instance, they responded to question 9 ("Jesus is both the Son of God and God himself") by marking "strongly agree," and question 10 ("Jesus was not God") by marking "strongly disagree." This group of believers accounts for only about 1 in 3 (34%) of the teens in our churches.

Jesus might be God . . . but he might not be. These teens hedged their bets when answering questions 9 and 10, saying they "somewhat agree" to 9 and only "somewhat disagree" to question 10. Like the Uncertain teens in chapter 1, they're giving Jesus the benefit of the doubt—for now—but haven't yet reached the point of confidence in their belief about Jesus as the Lord of all. These uncertain teenagers fill about a quarter (25%) of our youth groups.

I don't know/haven't decided if Jesus is God. Like the previous group, this segment of Christian teens has measurable doubts about the deity of Jesus—but they aren't willing to rule out Jesus's godhood completely. These are the kids who vacillated between the two options on questions 9 and 10, giving contradictory answers, to varying degrees, on those two survey queries. This group of conflicted/undecided Christian teenagers is significant: 3 out of 10 (30%) teens in our churches fit this description.

Jesus is not God. These teenagers call themselves Christian. They're active in a local church. And they even participated in a weeklong workcamp designed to help teenagers live out a Christian lifestyle of service. In spite of that, they consistently express disbelief in the basic Christian doctrine that Christ is God. And they seem quite comfortable with the ongoing dissonance between their lifestyles and their beliefs. About 1 in 10 (11%) of our students adheres to this viewpoint.

The good news here is that significantly more than half (59%) of Christian students affirm (either strongly or with limited skepticism) the cornerstone belief that Jesus Christ is indeed, in some mysterious way, both the Son of God and God himself.

This number is also reliably consistent with the way teens responded to question 10, which indicates our teenagers may be more comfortable identifying what they *don't* agree with than articulating what they do agree with. Given the polarizing political climate our kids have grown up in, where negative "attack ads" dominate the media every two years, that kind of negative reasoning skill may be something ingrained by societal forces. Of course, that's just conjecture at this point, but it could be a question worth pursuing by future researchers.

Interestingly enough, the number of students who fall into the 59% cohort splits evenly along gender lines. When the data is separated into male/female categories, both guys and girls who believe, at least somewhat, that Jesus is God come in at almost exactly 50%. That would seem to go against the common perception that teen boys are disinterested in authentic faith and that teen girls are more likely to be committed followers of Christ. The truth is, both young men and young women in our churches appear to be equally committed to a relationship with God through Jesus Christ.

The only place this gender equity fades is among those who indicate they don't know, or haven't yet decided on, the truth about who Jesus is. Among those kids, young women are by far more skeptical, by a margin of almost 2 to 1 (61% to 39%). As with beliefs about the Bible that we discussed in chapter 1, that may simply mean these ladies are just postponing the decision until a future time . . . but again, the longer these teens tolerate no decision, the higher the probability they will eventually arrive at a "no" decision.

And that brings us to the bad news: Did you see how many of our *Christian* kids simply can't bring themselves to commit wholeheartedly to the idea that Christ is indeed God? That number is 66%—fully 2 out of 3 of the kids in our youth groups. Yet these kids, apparently, have no trouble going to church to learn about Jesus, singing worship songs to him, and participating in service projects done in his name. In a follow-up interview, I asked one 11th grade girl from Virginia for more insight here. She said, "I mean, it's my understanding that Jesus is God's Son. I can understand if people think God is Jesus in person form. Either way I have doubts about their relationship. I question how God could have had a child if he was in heaven?"

Kenda Creasy Dean, associate professor of youth, church, and culture at Princeton Theological Seminary, calls these wavering teenagers "almost Christians." And she places the blame for their state squarely on people like you and me. She says:

> The hot lava core of Christianity—the story of God's courtship with us through Jesus Christ, of God's suffering love through salvation history and especially through Christ's death and resurrection . . . has been muted in many congregations, replaced by an ecclesial complacency that convinces youth and parents alike that not much is at stake.[5]

With an unblinking eye on both Christian parents (teen influencers at home) and Christian youth workers (teen influencers at church), Dean paints a startling picture. Listen to more of her heartbreaking assessment:

> What if the blasé religiosity of most American teenagers is not the result of poor communication but the result of excellent communication of a watered-down gospel so devoid of God's self-giving love in Jesus Christ that it might not be Christianity at all? What if . . . we are preaching moral affirmation, a feel-better faith, and a hands-off God instead of the decisively involved, impossibly loving, radically sending God of Abraham and Mary, who desired us enough to enter creation through Jesus Christ? . . . If this is the case—if theological malpractice explains teenagers' half-hearted religious identities—then perhaps most young people practice Moral Therapeutic Deism not because they reject Christianity, but because this is the only "Christianity" they know.[6]

I wince when I read Professor Dean's withering words, not because I am offended by them but because I fear she is probably right. After all, how else do you explain the finding that *2 out of 3 "Christian" kids* in our care are unwilling to acknowledge unreservedly that Jesus is exactly who he claimed to be: God incarnate, the Creator who entered his own creation, the embodiment of eternity in human form—both the Son of God and God himself.

The implications of that kind of bland faith-life on the everyday world of a teenager are difficult to think about, but we'll explore them further in part 2 of this book.

Did Jesus Sin?

The last part of this section of *The Jesus Survey* dealt with a natural—and vitally important—corollary to the question of Jesus's deity: Did Jesus sin? Or, by virtue of his godhood, was he truly the only perfect human and therefore uniquely capable of becoming the sacrifice that takes away our individual sins and the sins of the world?

The theological consequences of this simplistic question are far-reaching. If Jesus sinned, then he cannot be God, because God is incapable of sin. And if Jesus sinned, then he himself needed a savior and was therefore unfit to be our Savior.

Scripture is clear on this point: *Jesus did not sin* (see John 8:45–46; 2 Cor. 5:20–21; Heb. 4:15; 9:14; 1 Pet. 2:21–24; 1 John 3:4–5). Classic theologian Louis Berkof describes this central article of faith this way:

> This means not merely that Christ could avoid sinning (potuit non peccare), and did actually avoid it, but also that it was impossible for Him to sin (non potuit peccare) because of the essential bond between the human and the divine natures . . . While Christ was made to be sin judicially, yet ethically He was free from both hereditary depravity and actual sin. He never makes a confession of moral error; nor does He join His disciples in praying "Forgive us our sins." He is able to challenge His enemies to convince Him of sin. Scripture even represents Him as the one in whom the ideal man is realized.[7]

Joshua Harris puts that orthodoxy into more contemporary terms when he says,

> Jesus is like us in every aspect of our humanity—in all the mundane, glorious, and impolite aspects of the human existence. He had all the weakness and desires that make us human; he was tempted in every respect as we are. The difference is that Jesus was without sin. And it was his sinless perfection that made it possible for him to pay for our sins.[8]

With that theology in mind, then, I asked teenagers to respond to these two statements:

> When Jesus walked the earth he never sinned, not even in a small way (question 11).
>
> Jesus was a great, great man, but he was not 100% perfect so he may have sinned (question 12).

Christian teenagers were much less certain of their belief in this natural extension of the godhood of Christ—but for the first time in *The Jesus Survey*, they demonstrated reasonably close consistency when answering the two related questions.

The negatively framed response question again showed a clarifying influence on kids, but this time fewer switched their opinions. That seems to indicate a more settled, concrete decision on this issue—though, unfortunately, a large number of Christian teenagers don't appear confident of biblical orthodoxy regarding the sinlessness of Jesus.

For instance, one Catholic girl from New Jersey affirmed that Jesus was both the Son of God and God himself in response to question 9, but then in questions

11 and 12 she adamantly disagreed with the idea that this Son of God could be sin-free. Her explanation for that seeming contradiction was simply this: "He is *human*." For this Christian 9th grader, then, the doctrine of original sin trumped the incarnation of God. Christ had become a man, and every human being is inherently sinful; therefore, Christ must have sinned. An adult leader from Pennsylvania offered the same reasoning for justifying her prediction for this question. "He was human," she said. Therefore Christ was a sinner like the rest of us.

Still, in spite of those kinds of theological misconstructions, this part of the survey does deliver some good news for us.

As before, I used two survey slots to ask one basic question (Did Jesus sin?), using wording that required a positive response on one and a negative response on the other. A solid majority (54%) of teens spoke confidently of Jesus's sinless character when presented with the positive option. Most of those students (49%) maintained that belief by also strongly disagreeing with the same question in the negative format. Likewise, 7 out of 10 teenagers (71%) overall said, to at least some degree, that "Jesus never sinned," while nearly 2 out of 3 (61%) rejected the idea, to a degree, that "Jesus may have sinned."

According to other studies, this affirmation of Jesus's sinlessness among our Christian teenagers is markedly higher than what the general population of teens and young adults (Christian and non-Christian) would say. According to a recent "Millennials" survey conducted by Thom and Jess Rainer, among the general population barely half (50%) of teens and young adults affirm the belief that Jesus did not sin.[9]

This higher incidence of belief among Christian teens is, I think, good news for youth leaders and parents. Yes, it'd be better if 100% of our Christian teenagers believed the truth about Christ, but these current numbers show an opening for leading our teenagers back toward orthodoxy in the central view that Christ is God. It also represents a positive generational trend that's, no doubt, directly related to the diligent efforts of Christian families and their local churches.

For instance, in the year 2000 George Barna and the Barna Group surveyed over six hundred teenagers (both Christian and non-Christian) and asked their opinion on this statement: "When Jesus Christ lived on Earth He committed sins like other people." For that previous generation of teens, the majority (53%) answer was yes, and only 1 in 3 (33%) disagreed strongly with that error of belief.[10]

Fast-forward ten years to 2010, when I conducted *The Jesus Survey* with the younger brothers and sisters of the generation Barna studied. Results from *The Jesus Survey* suggest that, in our churches at least, true belief about Jesus's sinless nature has increased considerably—even reversing the popularity of faulty theology left behind from the previous generation of teens.

Finally, some good news, eh? Well, whatever it is we're doing in this area, we should keep doing it—and keep working to continue this generational trend toward truth among our Christian teenagers.

Figure 2.6

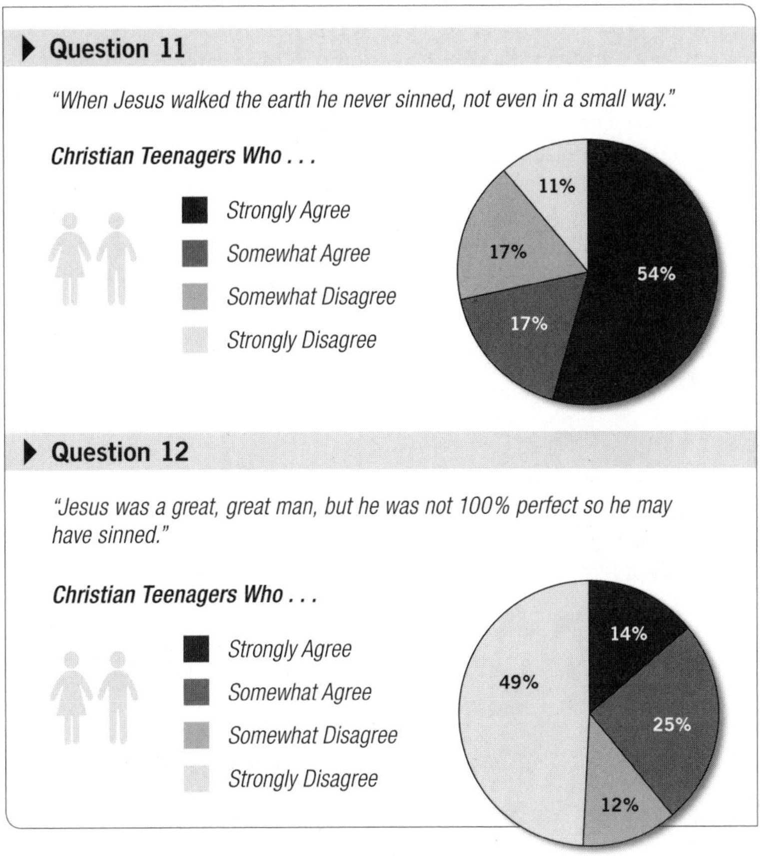

Question 11

"When Jesus walked the earth he never sinned, not even in a small way."

Christian Teenagers Who . . .

- *Strongly Agree* 54%
- *Somewhat Agree* 17%
- *Somewhat Disagree* 17%
- *Strongly Disagree* 11%

Question 12

"Jesus was a great, great man, but he was not 100% perfect so he may have sinned."

Christian Teenagers Who . . .

- *Strongly Agree* 14%
- *Somewhat Agree* 25%
- *Somewhat Disagree* 12%
- *Strongly Disagree* 49%

Putting It Together

As you surely noticed while looking over the four questions in this section of the survey, it's clear that they all are different ways of asking the same thing: Is Jesus merely great, or simply divine? That is, was Christ just a good man, an enlightened teacher, a role model for all of history? Or was he—and is he—God, deserving of worship and holding all authority in heaven and on earth?

The Bible speaks clearly on this issue, affirming Christ's unique status as both the Son of God and God himself. As such, we who are Christian leaders and parents should also be speaking clearly to our teenagers that same truth—and I think it's safe to assume many of us are doing just that. So, are our kids listening? Are they taking that truth to heart, with confidence and commitment?

Obviously, a definitive answer on that can't be delivered until we arrive at eternity. But from the perspective of *The Jesus Survey*, we can at least get a hint of the depth of belief on this issue by combining and cross-correlating responses to questions 9, 10, 11, and 12 from this study. A teen who demonstrates unshakeable belief and clarity of understanding in the idea that Jesus is God can easily be identified simply by tallying his or her answers to those questions. In this case, that person could reasonably be expected first to answer "strongly agree" on question 9 ("Jesus is both the Son of God and God himself"). Next, that student would answer "strongly disagree" to question 10 ("Jesus was not God"). For question 11 ("Jesus never once sinned"), the answer would again be "strongly agree." And the final response in this quartet of questions ("Jesus may have sinned") would be "strongly disagree."

So, how many Christian teenagers answered all four of those questions that way? Well, not many.

Figure 2.7

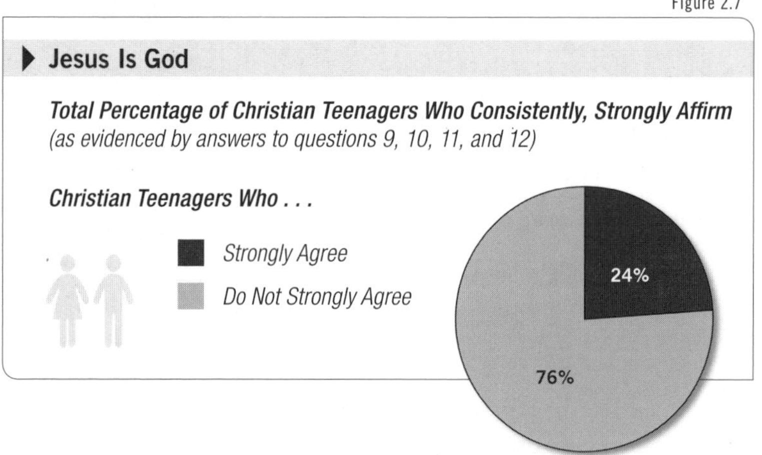

Only about 1 in 4 (24%) of Christian teenagers was able to respond with a dependable, confident affirmation of the belief that Jesus is indeed God. That number seems remarkably low for a doctrine as essential to the Christian faith as this one is. I'd hoped for at least 50% or more in this category, but that hope was apparently unfounded.

Ironically, among the denominational breakdowns, only those who affiliate with non-denominational churches see more than half (55%) of their kids consistently affirm a biblical belief in Jesus. And those who refuse any affiliation at all (Undeclared) rank dead last in this category, with only 3% of Undeclared kids reliably acknowledging that Jesus is Lord. Other denominations do better, but taken in context it mostly looks as though all are really just operating at slightly different levels of failure.

Kenda Creasy Dean's hard-hitting comments notwithstanding, it's hard to say, ultimately, who should be held accountable for this lack of confidence in Christ among our teenagers. The easy thing to do is to point fingers at the way we order our priorities in our churches, or at our programming for youth ministry, or at the inconsistent faith example and conversations that happen in our Christian homes—or to fault teenagers themselves for being so woefully blasé about the faith they claim to own. One could even point to heaven, to the Author and Finisher of our faith, and suggest that if he wanted more teens to believe in him, he'd call more of them to himself in unmistakable ways.

Truth is, I have no real answers to explain this finding from this section of *The Jesus Survey*, and certainly not enough fingers to start pointing. I think that perhaps all and none of the ideas mentioned previously may be accurate.

Figure 2.8

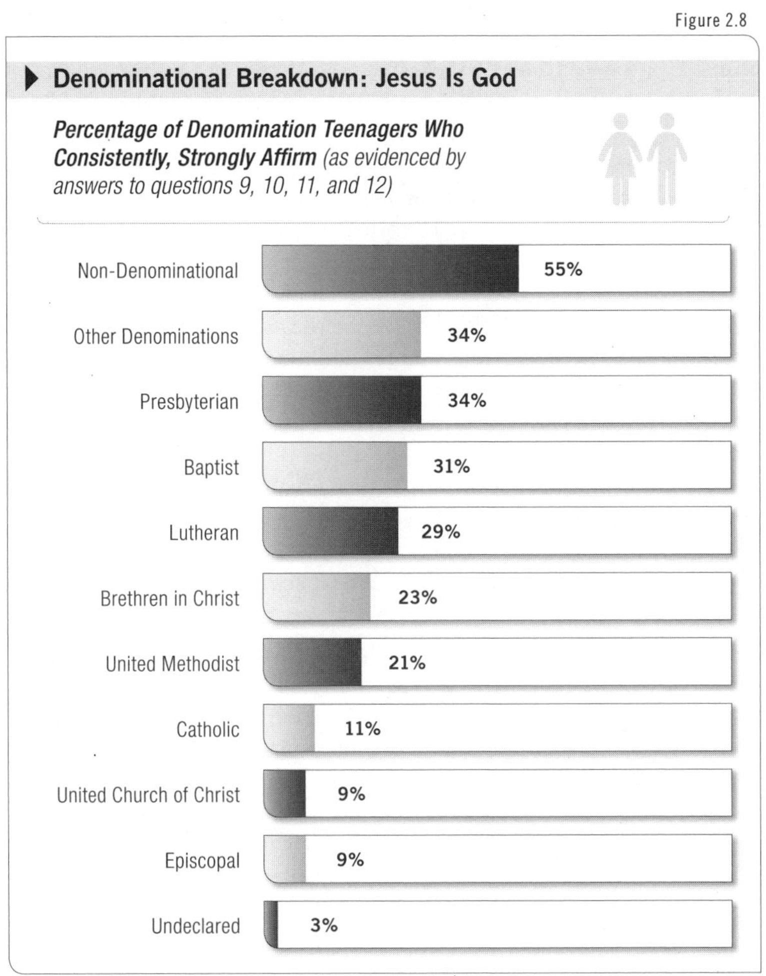

So I pass the baton to you, here and now. To all you parents, youth leaders, pastors, educators, and the like who are reading this book, this challenge is now set before you. The data indicates that 3 out of 4 of our teenagers who call themselves Christian simply are not grounded, or secure in, the belief that Jesus is God. This doctrine of Jesus's deity is the critical belief on which all of Christianity is founded, for which martyrs have been tortured and killed, and by which all of our faith stands or falls—and most of our kids have yet to grasp it in a measurable, consistent way.

So what should we do about that? Talk amongst yourselves . . .

Summary

Once again, I feel as though I was only able to linger at the water's edge of the findings in this data set—and was barely able to address the implications associated with those numbers. Still, every chapter must end somewhere, and this seems like a good place for a few summary thoughts.

• *As with their viewpoints on the veracity of Scripture in the last chapter, Christian teenagers are reliably unreliable when talking about their beliefs surrounding the deity of Christ.* It's often said that we need to teach our kids *why* they believe—and that's certainly a noble goal. However, we may also be overlooking a key assumption: that Christian teens know *what* they believe. It appears that we'd be wise to start being more proactive in helping our kids comprehend the *what* of their faith—particularly as it relates to the doctrine of Jesus and his godhood.

• *Only about 1 in 3 (34%) Christian teens expresses a confident, consistent belief in Jesus as God.* My hunch here is that, again, this has to do more with ignorance than with outright denial. Is it possible we simply are assuming that teenage Christians already know and believe this pillar of Christian orthodoxy, when in fact no one has ever spelled it out clearly for them? Again, that's only a hunch, but it may be worth exploring.

• *Belief that Jesus is God splits evenly across gender lines.* In fact, this 50/50 split was almost exact in the data (only one response separated them). That's good news, especially for those who have worried that guys are being left out of any spiritual awakening among teens today. One caution, though: teen girls are more likely to be conflicted about this issue and more likely to postpone a decision on this issue. If trends proceed as expected, that means we could see significant numbers of young adult women exiting the church in the next ten to twenty years.

• *Although definitely in the minority at 11%, a considerable number of Christian teenagers in our youth groups indicate outright that they don't believe Jesus is God.* It's unclear how these kids can call themselves Christian and yet deny the central issue of the Christian faith, but there it is. Again, could this have more to do with an incomplete doctrinal education than with aggressive denial? It's a question worth studying further.

• *Roughly 2 out of 3 of our churchgoing teenagers consistently reject the idea that Jesus may have sinned.* In my opinion, this is the first solidly good news to show up in *The Jesus Survey*. It indicates that our teenagers are reversing a faulty perception of Christ that their older brothers and sisters largely accepted as fact.

• *Other than non-denominational churches, not a single denomination represented in this survey could show a majority of Christian teens who reliably expressed a belief that Jesus is God.* This is a failure of our local churches and of youth ministries nationwide. If we expect to truly impact teenagers for Christ, then this single issue is absolutely the most important aspect of youth ministry we must change. Of course, if we don't care about eternity, we can just keep doing what we're doing . . . and continue failing an entire generation of teenagers placed in our care.

Bonus Survey Results

Figure 2.9

Question 9

	Adult Leaders Predicted Christian Teenagers Would . . .			
"Jesus, in some mysterious way, is both the Son of God and God himself."	*Strongly Agree*	*Somewhat Agree*	*Strongly Disagree*	*Somewhat Disagree*
	53%	**33%**	**7%**	**7%**

Question 10

	Adult Leaders Predicted Christian Teenagers Would . . .			
"Jesus was a good man, a righteous teacher, and a noble person, but he was not God."	*Strongly Agree*	*Somewhat Agree*	*Strongly Disagree*	*Somewhat Disagree*
	12%	**16%**	**18%**	**54%**

Question 11

	Adult Leaders Predicted Christian Teenagers Would . . .			
"When Jesus walked the earth he never sinned, not even in a small way."	*Strongly Agree*	*Somewhat Agree*	*Strongly Disagree*	*Somewhat Disagree*
	55%	**20%**	**14%**	**10%**

Question 12

	Adult Leaders Predicted Christian Teenagers Would . . .			
"Jesus was a great, great man, but he was not 100% perfect so he may have sinned."	*Strongly Agree*	*Somewhat Agree*	*Strongly Disagree*	*Somewhat Disagree*
	8%	**26%**	**12%**	**54%**

Figure 2.10

Regional Breakdown: Christian Teen Opinions about the Divinity of Christ

Is Jesus God?

	I believe Jesus is God		*Jesus might be God . . . but he might not be*		*I don't know / haven't decided if Jesus is God*		*Jesus is not God*	
	% of Region	*% of Total*	*% of Region*	*% of Total*	*% of Region*	*% of Total*	*% of Region*	*% of Total*
Northeast	**34%**	**17%**	**23%**	**12%**	**33%**	**17%**	**10%**	**5%**
Southeast	**40%**	**7%**	**30%**	**5%**	**19%**	**3%**	**11%**	**2%**
North/Central	**29%**	**6%**	**27%**	**6%**	**32%**	**7%**	**12%**	**3%**
South/Central	**22%**	**2%**	**27%**	**2%**	**33%**	**3%**	**19%**	**1%**
Northwest	**55%**	**1%**	**0%**	**0%**	**36%**	**1%**	**9%**	**<.05%**
Southwest	**79%**	**1%**	**7%**	**<.05%**	**7%**	**<.05%**	**7%**	**<.05%**

3

WHAT ABOUT THE CHRIST CONSPIRACIES?

Part One: The Cross

We preach Christ crucified.
1 Corinthians 1:23 NIV

It's said that during the 4th century AD, St. Martin of Tours once had a fantastical vision of Christ.

In this vision Jesus stood before Martin, radiant with glory. The humbled saint was at first overjoyed by his apparition, and immediately began to kneel down at the feet of this Jesus. A split second before he did so, however, he inexplicably paused to look at the outstretched hands of the Savior—and saw no scars.

"Where are the nail prints?" Martin demanded.

At that moment the glorious apparition was revealed to actually be Satan in disguise. When Martin demanded to see the nail scars, the vision abruptly vanished.[1]

Of course, there's no way of knowing whether this story actually happened or if it is simply legend. But it does illustrate a persistent desire on the part of some to rewrite the history of faith so that Christ was never crucified. Why? Because the cross of Jesus is, and always has been, offensive to those who oppose the Christian faith.

The apostle Paul once declared, "We preach Christ crucified: a stumbling block to Jews and foolishness to Gentiles, but to those whom God has called, both Jews and Greeks, Christ the power of God and the wisdom of God."[2] The apostle's assessment still rings true today: people who adhere to Judaism continue to "stumble" over the death of the Messiah, and Gentiles (non-Jews) still see the brutal, atoning execution of Jesus as a great tragedy—or worse, as something that never happened.

Jewish apologist Dr. Robert Schoen explains his faith's perspective this way:

> Most modern Jews would agree that Jesus was a great man, a teacher, and even a prophet who traveled the land performing wonderful, miraculous deeds and preached love and kindness.

The problem? When Jesus died without bringing an end to world suffering, he invalidated his claim on the title of Messiah, Son of God, and Savior. "When the Messiah comes," Schoen continues,

> the world will no longer be a place of hunger, hatred, and injustice, and the wolf, lamb, lion, and calf will all live together. Jews do not believe, therefore, that the Messiah has come, and they do not recognize Jesus as their savior.[3]

In short, Jesus was a failure because he got himself killed before he could usher in paradise on earth. The Jewish religion can't get past that "failure," and thus stumbles on its way to true faith in God.

Meanwhile, among non-Jews, the cross remains foolishness—even to the point of embarrassment. Among Muslims, for instance, the idea that God (or even a prophet of God) could be killed by humans isn't simply foolish, it's insulting.

In the Qur'anic view, according to Sura 3:54–55 and Sura 4:157–58, God schemed against Jesus's enemies, the Jews, to make sure Christ escaped his execution. Thus, Jesus was never killed nor crucified, but escaped death on the cross and was raised up to Allah instead.

This has led Islamic scholars to put forth some absurd theories about the historical event of Jesus's death. Dr. George Braswell, an expert on Islam and former professor at the University of Tehran, reveals:

> Muslim scholars give differing explanations of these passages. Some say that Jesus hid in a niche [in] the wall, and one of his companions died in his place. Others say that God sent angels to protect Jesus, and Judas Iscariot was made to look like Jesus and die in his place. Some believe that Simon of Cyrene was substituted while he was carrying Jesus' cross.[4]

Thus, Islam has invented new fictions to protect Christ's reputation from that debasing event—the cross—rewriting history in a way that unfortunately paints Jesus as either a coward or a liar, or both.

Muslims are not alone in their wish to rescue Jesus from the indignity of his suffering. Even in the lifetime of the apostle John, people were uncomfortable with the prospect that God would submit himself to human suffering. "Ironically," says theologian Charles Swindoll, "few false teachers in John's day doubted the deity of Christ; they challenged the reality of his being human!"[5]

Accordingly, some in history have claimed that Jesus was not actually a physical being, but instead a "divine apparition." Since Jesus was merely a sophisticated ghost, then, crucifixion couldn't have actually killed him. Likewise, other ancient philosophers denied Jesus's death on the cross by suggesting that he only "swooned," or fainted, on the cross, was presumed dead, and then regained consciousness after being taken down.[6] The real-life practicality of that far-fetched circumstance notwithstanding, variations of this swoon theory still persist today. For instance, as recently as 2007 prominent Hindu leader K. S. Sudarshan declared that Jesus never died on the cross. "He was only injured," Sudarshan said, "and after treatment returned to India where he actually died."[7]

And, of course, our American pop culture loves the romance of a "Jesus Hero" who somehow escapes execution on the cross, gets the girl, and lives happily ever after as royalty. The villains in this kind of story arc are, of course, Jesus's closest friends, power-hungry followers, and the hegemonic Catholic Church. This tidy little plot shows up often, but most noticeably in the recent worldwide bestselling novel and box office hit movie *The Da Vinci Code*, which uses fiction to promote the fiction that Jesus skipped the cross in favor of marrying Mary Magdalene and starting a political dynasty. Other pop fictions, such as *The Last Temptation of Christ*, have regurgitated that story line.

Even in our Christian churches, the cross is often deemed distasteful, something to be avoided or explained away whenever possible. Seattle megachurch pastor Mark Driscoll reports that among what he calls "our dysfunctional Christian family," many "are routinely decrying the concept that Jesus paid the penalty (death) for our sin in our place on the cross. They say it is too gory, too scary, too bloody, too masculine, and too violent." Pastor Driscoll goes on to say:

> Sadly, some Christians and some Christian leaders, while not denying the cross, prefer to keep it out of plain view because they wrongly believe that nice, decent people hate to have their sensibilities offended by such violence and gore.[8]

Timothy Keller, founding pastor of the noted Redeemer Presbyterian Church in Manhattan, New York, adds, "Jesus dies so that God can forgive sins. For many, that seems ludicrous or even sinister. . . . 'Why couldn't God just forgive us?' they ask. 'The Christian God sounds like the vengeful gods of primitive times who need to be appeased by human sacrifice.'" Keller goes on to note that the "doctrine of the cross confuses some people, it alarms others" and that Jesus's death has even been branded "divine child abuse."[9]

Yes, the cross is awful. It is bloody and macabre, and is a sadistic tragedy of human history. But it is also the physical embodiment of the atoning power of God. As Keller eloquently illuminates:

> It is crucial at this point to remember that the Christian faith has always understood that Jesus Christ is God. God did not, then, inflict pain on someone else, but rather

> on the Cross absorbed the pain, violence, and evil of the world into himself . . . this is a God who becomes human and offers his own lifeblood in order to honor moral justice and merciful love.[10]

And so, in the cross of Jesus we finally fully see the redemption of the world encapsulated in the bleeding, disfigured sacrifice of the Creator of everything.

Where are the nail prints?

They are fixed eternally and inalterably in the hands and feet of God. And because of the great violence that put them there—physically and painfully—we can be redeemed from the awful power of sin that demands a punishment greater than our very lives. Without the cross, we are lost. Without hope. Without life.

Still, as you can clearly see, there has been much shouting over the centuries—and particularly in the last decade—that declares Christ's crucifixion was either a sham or an insult unworthy of Jesus. In fact, some say it's offensive to civilized humanity. Has all that noise been enough to drown out the truth for our Christian teenagers today? Or has the bloody, awful, wonderful event of Jesus's death been suppressed by Christian adults to the point that Christian teenagers also shy away from its violent, life-giving truth? That's what I wanted to discover through the questions in the next section of *The Jesus Survey*.

Jesus: A Dead Man?

In this portion of the content section of *The Jesus Survey*, I asked teens to respond to several questions concerning their beliefs about Jesus's death on a cross. As with all questions, I listed a one-sentence statement and then asked kids to indicate whether they agreed or disagreed with the statement.

First, I wanted to get a perspective on their beliefs in regard to the idea of Jesus's physicality in suffering and death. Did our kids believe the bloody, true version of the gospel? Or had they been influenced by the teaching of Gnostics, Muslims, and others, and assumed Christ had somehow escaped the cross due to his divinity, immateriality, or some other miraculous circumstance?

So, in question 13 I asked kids to react to this statement:

> It's a fact that Jesus died physically when he was executed by crucifixion.

Next, I wanted to get a glimpse of how some of the currently popular "conspiracy theories" had influenced teen beliefs about Christ's crucifixion. And because, without exception, those "hoax" theories have been attributed directly to the avarice of early leaders within the church, I went ahead and named the Catholic Church as a conspirator in those historical scams.

So, in question 14 I asked teenagers to respond to this statement:

> It's a fact that Jesus's "death" on a cross was actually some kind of hoax that was later covered up by his followers and the Catholic Church.

Finally, I wanted to assess the "Da Vinci" impact on our teens' perception of Jesus's execution. After all, when responses to *The Da Vinci Code* were being churned out with remarkable frequency, the general assumption in most Christian circles was that it was our young people who were most likely to be taken in by the insidiousness of propaganda packaged in a thriller novel. So had they been swayed by Dan Brown's poetry? I wanted to know.

In question 17, I challenged teenagers to react to this statement:

> Jesus actually escaped death on the cross, married Mary Magdalene, and started a political dynasty—but the church hid this information to keep itself in power.

Taken both individually and as a group, answers to these questions revealed some interesting glimpses into teens' overall perceptions of Jesus—and the influence that popular media has in regard to the question of Jesus's death.

Question 13: "It's a Fact That Jesus Died Physically."

Boxing great Muhammad Ali was once asked what he would do if he could travel through time. A devout Muslim, Ali answered, "If I could go back in time, I'd like to be there . . . with Jesus on the day of the Crucifixion to see if it was really him on the cross, because Muslims believe it was someone else."[11]

Among the Christian teenagers in our churches, that kind of doubtful curiosity about the identity of the Crucified One seems mostly irrelevant.

Figure 3.1

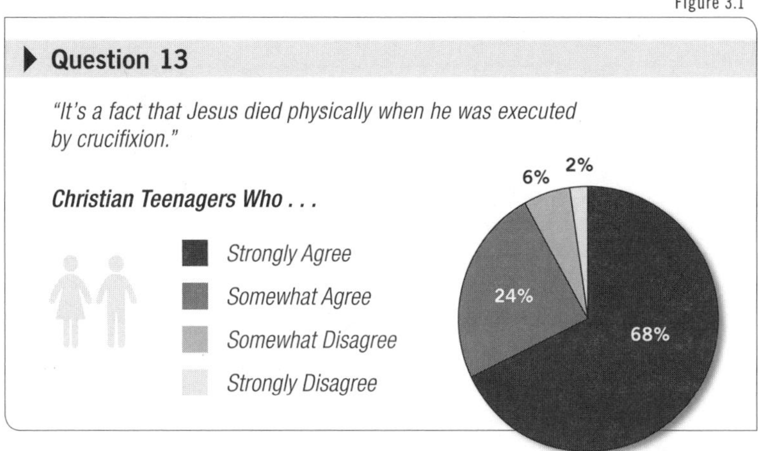

By enormous margins, our kids seem to readily accept the historicity of Jesus's death on the cross. Fully 2 out of 3 (68%) report that they "strongly agree" with the gospel accounts in this regard, and 1 in 4 of those remaining at least "somewhat agree." In total, those who agree that Christ did indeed experience a physical death on the cross number almost the entire youth group (92%) in a typical local church. Given kids' previously demonstrated reservations about the trustworthiness of the Bible and the deity of Jesus, this response is both surprising and encouraging.

As I mentioned before, a number of outsized theories seeking to remove Christ from the cross have been popularized, both in this generation and in the generations before ours. Teens' responses to this question on *The Jesus Survey* seem to indicate that our media-savvy young people have turned a deaf ear to those wild reconstructions of history. Of course, it's unclear whether or not these teenagers also fully understand the implications of Jesus's death on the cross, or the theology of blood atonement that was changed forever when Christ breathed his last . . . but hey, this is a solid foundation on which to start.

Looking at these strong numbers in support of a belief in Christ's actual, physical death, I was curious to see how they corresponded to teenagers who (a) believe the Bible is trustworthy, and (b) believe Jesus is God. So I went back to the categories that earlier cross-correlations revealed among teenagers and compared results.

Figure 3.2

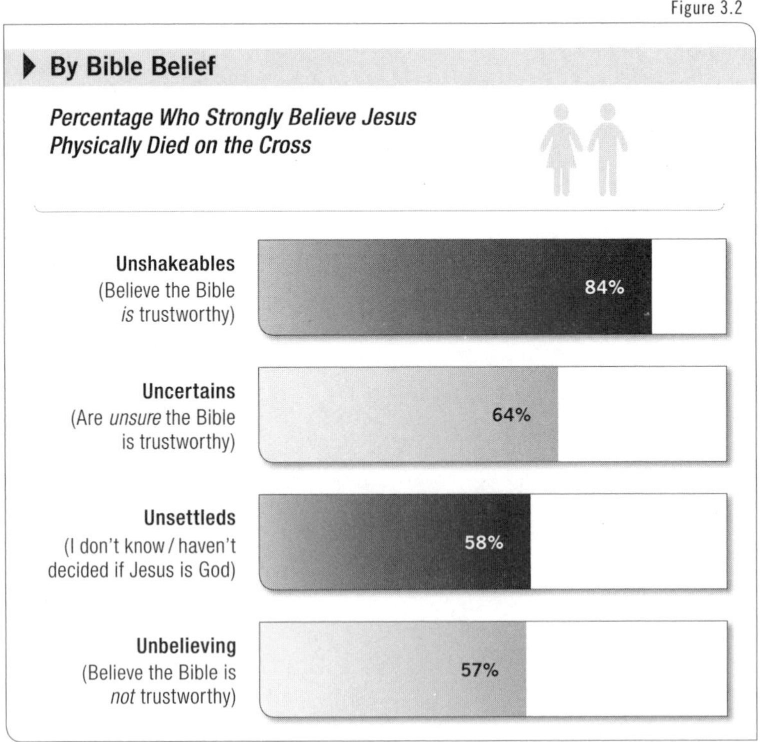

First, I looked at how trust (or distrust) in the Bible affected whether or not students "strongly agree" with the statement that Jesus died physically on the cross. In every instance, no matter whether kids had unwavering belief in Scripture or no faith in the Bible at all, more than half (minimum 57%) still affirmed faith in Jesus's physical execution. There was, however, dramatic variance in teen opinions based on their correlating degrees of belief or disbelief in God's Word.

Among Unshakeable teenagers, more than 8 out of 10 (84%) also affirmed belief in Jesus's physical death by execution. For Uncertain teens, that number drops a full 20 percentage points, with less than 2 out of 3 feeling strongly that Jesus actually died on the cross.

Those who are Unsettled or Unbelieving feel even more skeptical about the gospel's history of Christ's death. Among those self-proclaimed Christian students, only 58% and 57%, respectively, say they "strongly agree" that Jesus died a physical death on the cross.

This appears to indicate, again, that a teen's confidence in the trustworthiness of Scripture is both foundational and a *huge* factor in that same teen's faith development—particularly as it applies to facts about Jesus and his redemptive work.

Next, I looked at how belief in the deity of Jesus affected whether or not students "strongly agree" with the statement that he died physically on the cross. Again, the good news is that, regardless of their views on Christ's divinity, more than half (minimum 51%) of *all* students still strongly affirmed that Jesus was a physical being who experienced a real death at his execution.

The numbers of students who affirmed Jesus's physical death and who also either believe "Jesus is God" (83%) or believe "Jesus *might* be God" (63%) are nearly identical to the corresponding numbers of those who are Unshakeable or Uncertain, respectively, in regard to their views of the Bible. Teens who are as yet uncommitted about Jesus's deity actually are slightly more likely to affirm Jesus's death than those who are Unsettled about the Bible (61% to 58%).

The largest discrepancy is between Christian teens who are Unbelieving about the Bible and also do not believe Jesus is God. Those who disbelieve Jesus's godhood are also the most likely of any of these groups to disbelieve Jesus's physical death on the cross, with only 51% saying they "strongly agree" it actually happened.

What's striking here is the degree of difference between those who believe Jesus is God and those who choose not to believe that. Nearly 1 in 3 fewer teenagers (32%) disbelieves Jesus's physical death is a fact if they also doubt that he is God—even though the issue of Jesus's divinity, in terms of historicity, is irrelevant to the issue of how he died.

History records that Christ died on a cross. Even Roman historian Tacitus mentions the crucifixion of Jesus,[12] and non-Christian Jewish works such as the *Toledot Yeshu* also acknowledge Christ's death without question.[13] Whether one believes he is God or not, that historical fact should be a belief-neutral opinion, much the same way someone accepts that Abraham Lincoln was assassinated regardless of whether or not he or she believes Lincoln was a good president. But that's not the way our

Christian teenagers see it. Their belief (or lack of belief) in Christ as God clearly colors their view of the facts surrounding Jesus's death. As they say, perception of the one creates the reality of the other—even if that new reality simply isn't based in fact.

In short, skepticism about Jesus's divine identity translates significantly into skepticism about any facts associated with Christ. Once again, this should be a wake-up call for those of us who are Christian parents and/or church leaders. If we intend our teenagers to have a thriving, grounded Christian experience, we'd better be diligent in helping them understand and believe the truth about Jesus's eternal reality.

Figure 3.3

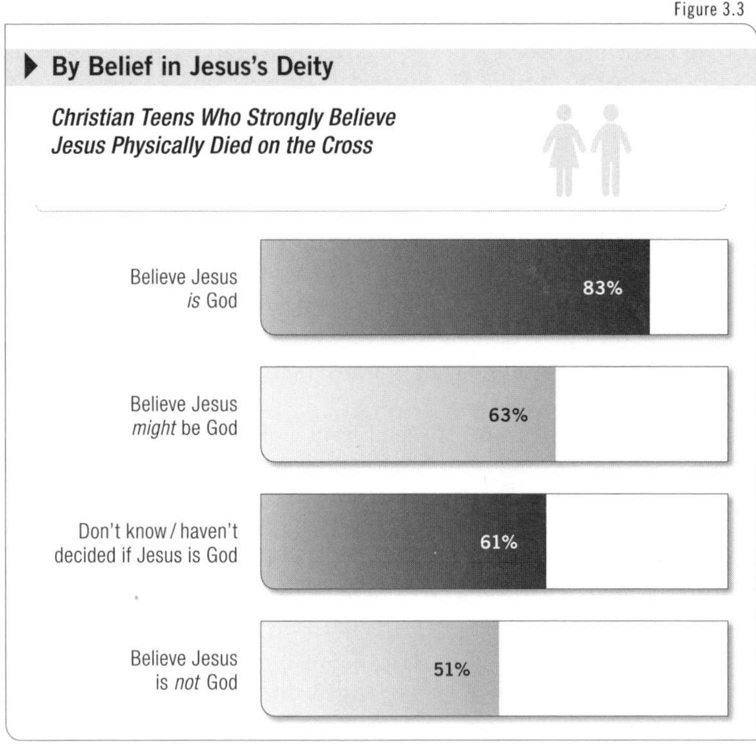

Question 14: "It's a Fact That Jesus's 'Death' on a Cross Was Some Kind of Hoax."

As with other couplets on *The Jesus Survey*, question 14 (Jesus's "death" on a cross was some kind of hoax) offered a clarifying aspect in discovering what teenagers actually believe about Jesus's death on a cross, particularly in relation to their answers to question 13. In order to demonstrate a reasonably consistent belief in regard to Jesus's physical crucifixion, our teenagers' answers to this question should have been to "disagree" or "strongly disagree" in large numbers.

After the experience of chapters 1 and 2, that kind of measurable consistency of belief was not a given! In fact, if our teenagers were to continue to respond according to their demonstrated personalities thus far, consistent results would be *inconsistency* when responding to two questions within a topic-related couplet.

Surprise!

For the first time in *The Jesus Survey*, in almost exact numbers, our teenagers gave strongly congruent expressions of a specific belief. When asked if Jesus physically died on the cross, 92% of Christian students agreed that he did. When asked if Jesus's death was actually a hoax, 92% denied that it was.

Even more, the degree of certainty in regard to these two questions actually increased. Just over 2 out of 3 (68%) strongly affirmed Jesus's physical death; at the same time, more than 8 out of 10 (81%) strongly denied that any hoax was involved in Jesus's crucifixion. Among Unshakeable teens, fully 97% strongly refuted the idea of a hoax surrounding Jesus's death.

Figure 3.4

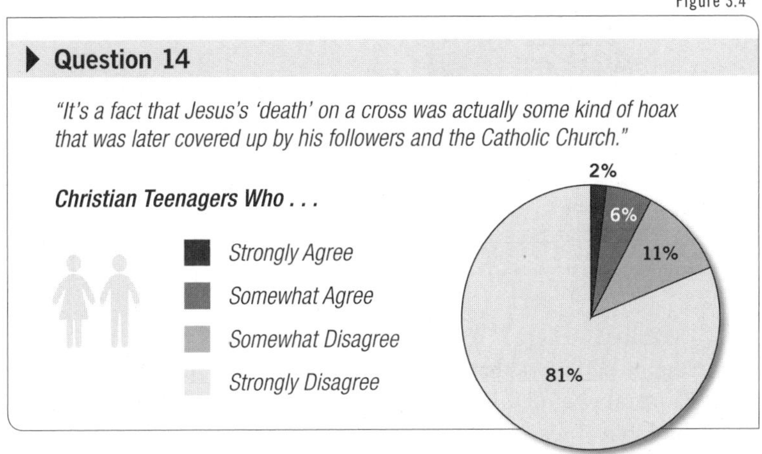

This is not to suggest that none of our kids are susceptible to believing conspiracy theories about the cross, though. Interestingly, it's those kids who are Unsettled about the Bible or who "don't know/haven't decided" if Jesus is God who are most likely to agree with the idea that Jesus's followers and the Catholic Church covered up some kind of hoax in regard to Christ's crucifixion.

Among Unsettled teenagers (those who are confused or conflicted about the reliability of the Bible), roughly 1 in 7 (16%) suspects fraud in relation to our history of Jesus's death. That percentage is actually even higher than the number of teens who profess complete disbelief in the Bible's trustworthiness. Additionally, 1 out of 6 (17%) Christian teenagers who don't know or haven't decided whether or not Jesus is God believes that some kind of hoax was involved. This is more than double the number of Christian teens who don't believe Jesus is God (8%).

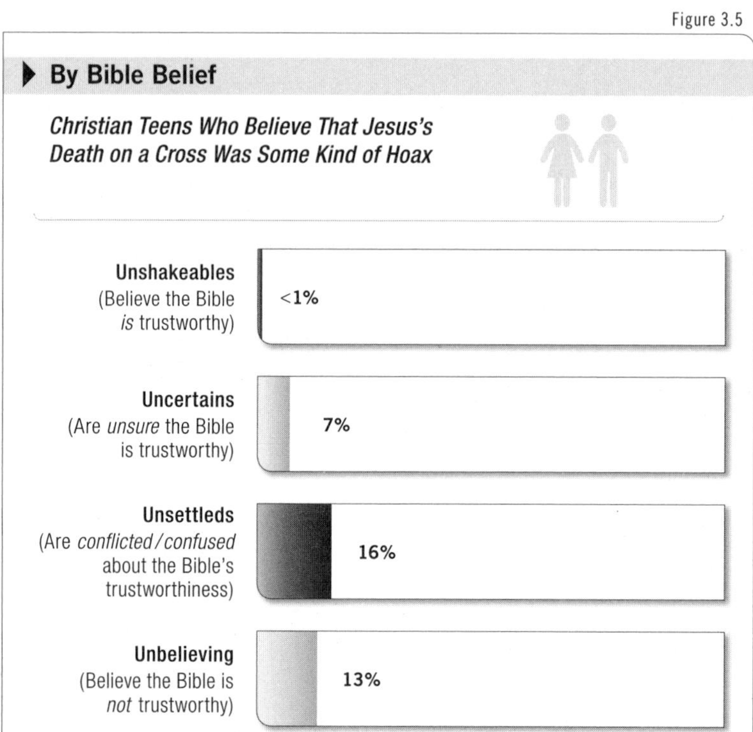

Still, the overall news here is very good, I think, especially when taken in context with the stream of bad news that showed up in chapters 1 and 2. As a general rule, an overwhelming number of Christian teenagers in our youth groups readily accept and affirm the biblical teaching that Jesus, in legitimate human form, physically suffered and died when he was executed by crucifixion.

Now, I do need to mention one last thing about question 14 on *The Jesus Survey*. According to my friends at Reach Workcamps, this question alone caused a minor controversy when the survey was being conducted. Some adults at the camps objected to the fact that it identified by name the Catholic Church as a suspected conspirator in supposed hoaxes surrounding Jesus's death. One Episcopal leader from Alabama in particular vented his anger about this, saying, "This is a disgusting question and not appropriate in this questionnaire." Another leader, a Catholic from Ohio, was adamant with comments that declared, "The Catholic Church did NOT cover up ANYTHING."

Teenagers may have also been upset by the wording of that question, but none included comments to that effect. Instead (as we can see above) they simply denied it by disagreeing with the statement in overwhelming numbers.

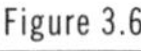

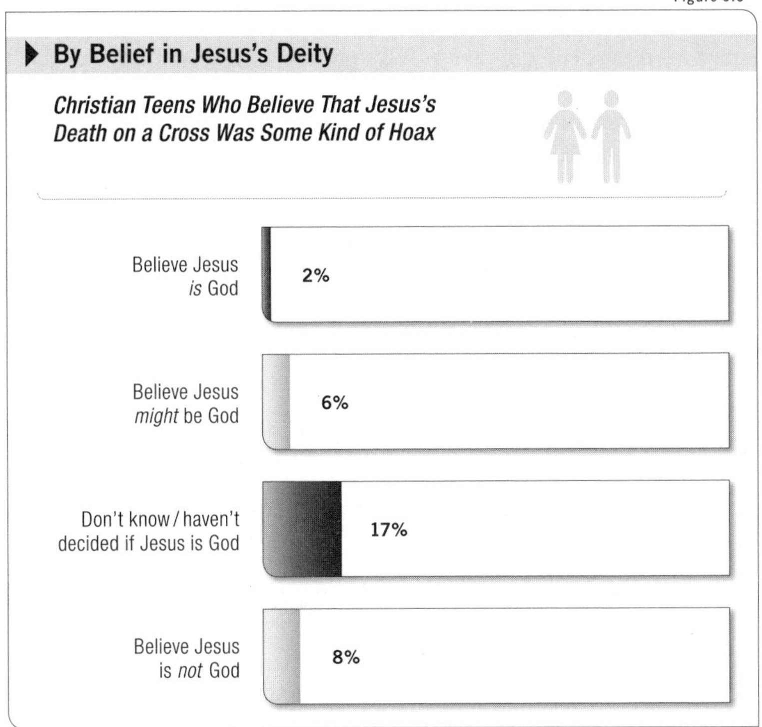

The angry response to this question is interesting. First, it shows that some of our youth leaders, in knee-jerk defensiveness, prefer to let outrage censor dialogue about very serious accusations toward the Catholic Church. That's dangerous—and could account in some measure for the large numbers of Christian teenagers who are confused or conflicted about basics of their faith.

For the record, I agree with that leader from Ohio: I don't think the Catholic Church covered up anything in regard to Christ's crucifixion. But I also know that atheist propagandists—and some liberal theologians—claim very vocally that the Catholic Church is guilty of a multitude of sins in its caretaking of the truth about Christ. Because that's the case, I felt it was imperative to see if kids accepted as truth that kind of anti-Catholic propaganda. Asking the question certainly didn't mean I endorsed the opinion!

Secondly, as you'll see below, question 17 asked a very similar question regarding a crucifixion hoax, but instead of calling the Catholic Church by name, I used generic wording, "the church." The supposedly devious organization behind the hoax in question is exactly the same—the Catholic Church—yet not a single person complained about question 17. That, to my mind, seems a bit hypocritical.

Thirdly, I was impressed that teenagers (who commented freely on other questions in the survey) didn't waste time shouting about how offended they were at being asked to weigh in on popular accusations aimed toward the Catholic Church. Instead, in both question 14 and question 17, they simply answered the question and as a result voiced *overwhelmingly* that they believe the idea of a cover-up/scam in the event of Jesus's execution to be idiotic drivel.

Looking back now, I don't regret naming the Catholic Church in question 14. I was just echoing a popular sentiment of Christianity's enemies and trying to find out how teenagers felt about it. But I do wish I'd included another question that was solely about teen attitudes toward the Catholic Church and its history. That would have been very enlightening. Ah, well. Perhaps another researcher will explore that topic in depth for us all.

Question 17: "Jesus Actually Escaped Death on the Cross and Married Mary Magdalene."

The last question in this topic area of the survey is what I affectionately refer to as "that Da Vinci thing." The worldwide phenomenon of Dan Brown's *The Da Vinci Code* novel is, I'm sure, not unfamiliar to you. In this thriller, Brown posits old, discredited theories that basically boil down to this: Jesus skipped the cross, married Mary Magdalene, and started a political dynasty. The church (that is, the *Catholic* Church) hid this information to keep itself in power.

The Da Vinci Code spawned dozens of "response books" from Christian apologists who (again) ably discredited Brown's mistaken theories—but the truth is that kids will read thriller novels, but they won't often read biblical apologetic works. So I wanted to know, specifically, whether or not our teenagers had bought the conspiracy theory that Dan Brown and his publisher sold to millions and millions of people.

The answer?

Not so much.

In fact, more than 9 out of 10 Christian kids (92%) appear to have shrugged off the media hype and pop culture domination that once was *The Da Vinci Code* and moved on to other, more relevant things. In fact, fully 83% of Christian kids indicated that they *strongly* denied Dan Brown's fantastical theories. Some of the comments teens scrawled on their surveys here were actually entertaining. "Stupid question," said one girl from Michigan. "Say what?!" and "What??!!" said others. And one young lad from New York seems to have missed the whole Da Vinci thing completely. On his survey he wrote, "Where did you hear that?"

The Christian teens most susceptible to the *Da Vinci Code* madness, unsurprisingly, are those Unsettleds who are unsure or conflicted about the reliability of the Bible and Unbelieving teens who don't accept the Bible as trustworthy. Among those teens, about 1 in 8 (14%) thinks Dan Brown might be right.

Still, in the big picture, that whole Da Vinci thing appears to be yesterday's news for today's teenagers. For them, fiction—even about Jesus—is what it always has been: fiction.

Why such a strong, decisive response from teens on this question? Obviously I can only speculate, but here's my thought. When *The Da Vinci Code* was dominating pop culture, it brought one important benefit to churches and to Christians everywhere: it made it OK to talk about Jesus in public. As a result, churches everywhere invested time and money discussing the ideas of *The Da Vinci Code* with people in their congregations. Youth groups took up the topic with regularity and frequency, and teens themselves hit movie theaters and schools armed with talking points about Christ in relation to Dan Brown's book. The result? Pop culture helped our teenagers engage, and understand, at least this aspect of the gospel of Jesus. So thanks, Dan Brown. You might have done us all a big favor after all.

Figure 3.7

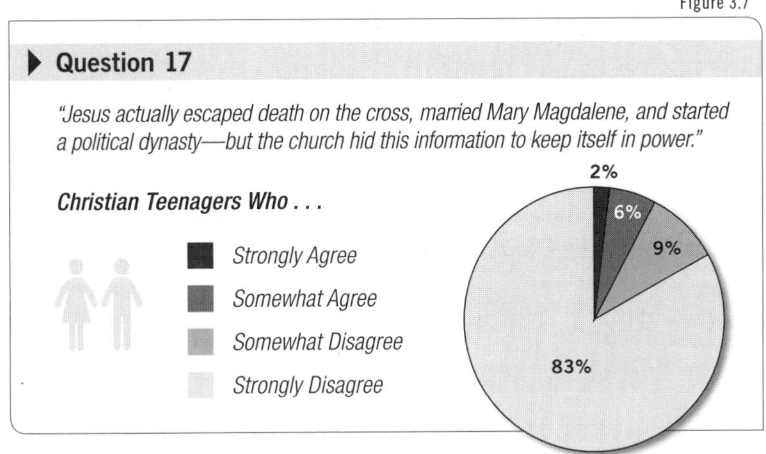

Summary

• *Mainstream attempts to discredit the crucifixion have largely been ignored by today's Christian teenagers.* Pop culture, current media, other religions, and atheists are among the many who've attempted to create and promote a plausible theory that rewrites history so that Jesus didn't actually die on the cross. Teenagers in our youth groups barely noticed. Rather, an overwhelming majority (92%) of Christian kids readily affirm that Jesus died, physically, when he was executed on the cross.

• *Hoax theories are hooey for today's teens.* In an unusual show of consistency in affirming a certain belief about Christ, 92% of Christian teens reject the notion that Jesus's crucifixion was some kind of hoax.

• *There's a significant gap of belief in Jesus's physical death between teens who believe the Bible and those who are unsure or disbelieve the Bible.* More than 8 out of 10 (84%) teens who believe the Bible to be trustworthy also "strongly agree" that Jesus died physically. Among those who are conflicted about or disbelieve the Bible, that number drops dramatically to 58% and 57%, respectively. This reinforces a concern identified in chapter 1. When our teens are unable to trust the Bible, the corresponding result is a lack of confidence that influences just about every area of their faith. This should be a wake-up call for those of us who are Christian parents and church leaders.

• *Da Vinci is dead.* More than 9 out of 10 Christian kids (92%) reject the conspiracy theory popularized by Dan Brown's novel *The Da Vinci Code*. In fact, fully 83% of Christian kids indicated that they strongly denied Brown's fantastical accusations. However, Christian teens who are most susceptible to believing *Da Vinci Code*–style conspiracies are, unsurprisingly, those who are unsure or conflicted about the reliability of the Bible.

Bonus Survey Results

Figure 3.8

By Gender and Grade: Percentage of Christian Teens Who Strongly Believe Jesus Physically Died on the Cross

Girls	**65%**
Guys	**71%**
Junior Highers (Grades 7 & 8)	**63%**
High School Underclassmen (Grades 9 & 10)	**67%**
High School Upperclassmen (Grades 11 & 12)	**69%**

Figure 3.9

By Grade: Percentage of Christian Teens Who Believe That Jesus's Death on a Cross Was Some Kind of Hoax

Junior Highers (Grades 7 & 8)	**6%**
High School Underclassmen (Grades 9 & 10)	**10%**
High School Upperclassmen (Grades 11 & 12)	**8%**

4

WHAT ABOUT THE CHRIST CONSPIRACIES?

Part Two: The Empty Tomb

Why do you look for the living among the dead?
Luke 24:5 NIV

It's not often that pornography mogul Hugh Hefner and the apostle Paul agree on theology. Still, when it comes to Jesus's resurrection, the agnostic founder of the Playboy empire and the first-century church planter echo the same message.

"If one had any real evidence that, indeed, Jesus did return from the dead," Hefner said in an interview with Christian apologist Lee Strobel, "then that is the beginning of a dropping of a series of dominoes that takes us to all kinds of wonderful things. It assures an afterlife and all kinds of things that we would all hope are true."[1]

With a similar line of reasoning, the apostle Paul emphasizes the critical importance of Jesus's resurrection to the Corinthian church. Without it, according to Paul, Hefner's figurative dominoes fall in the opposite direction.

"If Christ has not been raised," the apostle says, "your faith is futile; you are still in your sins. Then those also who have fallen asleep in Christ are lost. If only for this life we have hope in Christ, we are to be pitied more than all men. But Christ has indeed been raised from the dead."[2]

In short, whether or not Jesus actually came back to life after his execution is a big deal. Or as Strobel puts it:

> Everything comes down to that. . . . Nothing is more important in determining the identity of the real Jesus. The cross either unmasked him as a pretender or opened the door to a supernatural resurrection that has irrevocably affirmed his divinity.[3]

Hugh Hefner, the apostle Paul, and Lee Strobel rightly highlight the fact that Jesus's resurrection is the critical testing point for Christianity. For that reason, the resurrection of Christ is often "ground zero" for those who oppose and/or desire to discredit the Christian faith. The result, as expected, has been a proliferation of alternate theories to explain away Easter morning and the empty tomb.

And make no mistake: Jesus's tomb *is* empty.

With extremely rare exceptions, almost no one bothers to contest that fact. Other than allowing for a resurrection, history has never been able to fully account for the absence of Jesus's body. To nonbelievers, then, that empty tomb serves as simply a human mystery to be explained by (what else?) speculative conspiracy theories about Christ.

In the recent past, a number of these speculative theories regarding Christ's resurrection have, at one time or another, gained popularity and press coverage in American society. What are those theories? Have they influenced teen beliefs about Jesus's resurrection? Let's explore the first question to start.

I think my favorite conspiracy theory about Jesus's resurrection is the soap-operatic "Twin Theory" proposed by philosopher Robert Greg Cavin in 1995. It goes something like this: Jesus was actually born to another couple as one of a pair of twin boys. Oops! In some mysterious accident, Jesus got switched with Mary's manger-born baby and was raised as the unknowingly adopted son of Mary and Joseph. Then, thirty-three years later, Jesus's long-lost twin brother (Cavin calls him "Hurome") happened to stumble into Jerusalem just in time to see his identical twin being crucified. Right there on the spot, he decided to perpetrate a Messiah scheme for his now-dead bro. So Hurome single-handedly stole Christ's body and then went around impersonating Jesus to his disciples until they started a new religion.[4]

That an educated, modern person would actually believe—and preach—this kind of hooey would be laughable but for the fact that some have accepted Cavin's "Twin Theory" as a legitimate explanation for the empty tomb. It just shows the lengths people will go to when they desperately *want* to disbelieve the truth.

Still, Cavin isn't the only one wishing for an alternate explanation to erase Jesus's resurrection from history—or the only one whose explanation requires a significant leap of faith. Some decades ago, much like Dan Brown today, Hugh Schonfield dominated bestseller lists with his fantastical theories of a "Passover Plot" that declared Jesus a coconspirator with Joseph of Arimathea and an "unidentified Jew" in a scheme to fool the world into thinking he was the Messiah. Jesus was to be drugged until he appeared dead, removed from the cross alive, and nursed back to health. Alas, he survived only long enough to ruefully command, "Do not let me die in vain. Deceive my disciples into believing I have overcome death and the grave." Thus, the "unidentified Jew" spent the next forty days impersonating Jesus until his disciples bought the lie and started a new religion.[5]

Oh, but wait—that's not all.

For many skeptics and scholars, the story of Jesus's resurrection is dismissed as, presumably, grief-induced mass hallucinations experienced by Jesus's disciples over the course of several weeks following Christ's execution. Apparently they wanted him to be the Messiah so badly that they just went a little nuts and collectively imagined they'd seen, heard, and touched a risen Savior. Then, based on those repeated delusions, they'd gone out and changed the world.[6]

John Dominic Crossan, one of the founders of the influential and widely publicized Jesus Seminar, also has spent the past few decades preaching against the resurrection.[7] His favorite version of events is what's been called the "Carrion Conspiracy." According to Crossan, Jesus was either left on the cross where his body was eaten by carrion birds,[8] or buried in a shallow grave where it was dug up and eaten by wild dogs.[9] Of course, that theory dismisses actual historical evidence in favor of speculation, and—as Dr. Timothy Paul Jones points out—requires governing authorities of Jesus's time to be guilty of public violation of both Jewish and Roman law. Regardless, those issues leave Crossan and his disciples undeterred.[10]

Another explanation for the empty tomb, popular among Jehovah's Witnesses today, is that "Jesus was put to death in the flesh and was resurrected as an invisible spirit creature." In other words, Jesus became a ghost after his execution. And his body that was left behind? Well, it probably just "dissolved into gases."[11]

Honestly, the most realistic conspiracy is "The Jewish Explanation" that circulated at the actual time of Jesus's death. This theory insists that Jesus's disciples stole his body and invented the fiction of a resurrected Christ for their own personal gain. Of course, this theory has long been disproven on many grounds, especially in light of the martyrdom of *all* of Jesus's disciples (except John, who miraculously survived the torture that was intended to martyr him). What the disciples actually "gained" for perpetrating this supposed "myth" of resurrection was lives of suffering, torture, and eventual execution.[12]

If there is one unifying theme in all these alternate explanations for the empty tomb, it is this: *many people have a deep desire to eliminate the intellectual possibility that Jesus actually came back to life after being dead.*

Why such far-fetched fanaticism from anti-Christian circles on this point? Well, Hugh Hefner explained it best. If Jesus was indeed resurrected, then "that is the beginning of a dropping of a series of dominoes" that must be dealt with by every living person.

So, have these conspiracy theories influenced the way our kids perceive the Easter story? Do Christian teenagers hold to the historical Jesus who died and then came back to life? Or has all the propaganda surrounding this issue swayed them toward the perception that Jesus simply could not have come back to life, despite what any "legend" says? I wanted to find out, so I asked them.

Jesus: Alive Again?

In this portion of the content section of *The Jesus Survey*, I asked teens to respond to a few questions concerning their beliefs about Jesus's resurrection. As with all questions, I listed a one-sentence statement and then asked kids to indicate whether they agreed or disagreed with the statement.

The core issue I wanted to pursue here was whether or not Christian teenagers believed that Jesus physically came back to life after his execution. As before, I approached this issue in a question couplet. One question in this couplet required an "agree" response to affirm belief in Jesus's physical resurrection, and the other required a "disagree" response to do the same thing. In previous couplets, I had ordered the questions so that the "agree" statement was first and the "disagree" statement was second. This time, though, I switched the order so that teens might not be lulled into responding to an unspoken survey rhythm.

So, in question 15 I asked kids to react to this statement:

> After his execution, Jesus simply could not have physically "come back to life," despite what the legend says.

Next, for question 16 I asked teenagers to respond to this correlating statement:

> Jesus physically came back to life after his execution.

As with previous questions, Christian teenagers' responses to these two questions delivered both good news and bad news for Christian parents and church leaders.

Question 15: "Jesus Simply Could Not Have Physically 'Come Back to Life.'"

For starters, roughly 4 out of 5 (83%) students in our churches affirm—at least somewhat—a belief in Jesus's physical resurrection. This is demonstrated by their unwillingness to agree with the statement that "Jesus simply could not have physically 'come back to life.'" What's more, fully 2 out of 3 (66%) teens *strongly* disagreed with that statement.

This is encouraging news, particularly in light of the occasional popularity of the never-ending "alternative explanations" for the empty tomb that our teens have been exposed to in the past decade of their lives. It seems to indicate, initially at least, that those conspiracy theories have yet to significantly alter the perception of Jesus's resurrection among our churchgoing teenagers.

At the same time, it should be sobering for Christian parents and church leaders to learn that fully 17% of Christian youth in our churches have measurable doubts about something as fundamental to Christianity as a belief in the Easter story. When we look at these numbers from a human perspective, that concern becomes more pronounced.

For instance, take time right now to think of six Christian students in your church. Go ahead and call them by name in your mind. Now, take a moment to consider that next time those six kids are together—maybe in a small group Bible study or at youth group—it's very likely that one of them simply doesn't believe Jesus rose from the dead.

How does that disbelief affect that teenager's life? How does it influence what you teach as that teen's parent or church leader? And which teenager would you choose to leave out of the miracle of new life found in Jesus's resurrection?

So, yes, I was very glad to see that a considerable majority (83%) of Christian teenagers still affirms, at least somewhat, a belief in the events of that first Easter. But the parent and the former youth pastor in me also feels a tug of concern for the significant number of Christian kids who have lost faith in that eternity-changing historical miracle.

Figure 4.1

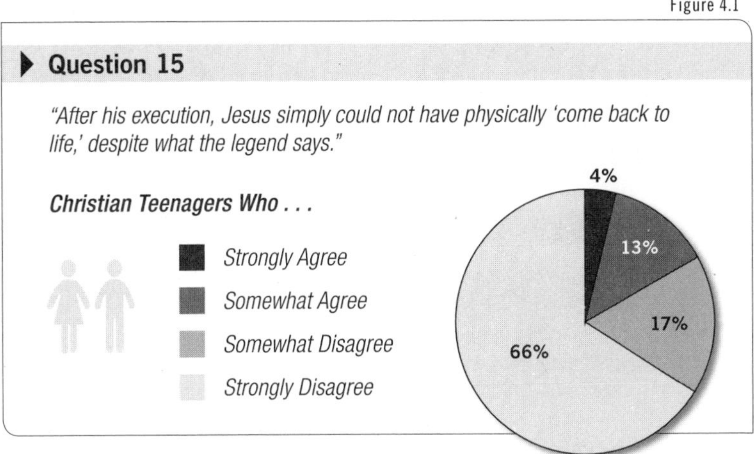

There's another troubling undercurrent within the good news here, and that is the number of Christian teenagers who are unwilling to fully commit to belief *or* disbelief in Jesus's resurrection.

Among non-Christian youth, an attempt to hedge one's bets in this regard could be expected. But remember, the kids who took this survey are ones who first identified themselves as *Christian*—people who supposedly trust in Jesus's death and resurrection as both a way of life today and as a guarantee of future paradise.

In spite of that, nearly 1 in 3 (30%) of the teenagers in our youth groups just *doesn't* have full faith in Jesus's resurrection—but also hasn't fully arrived at a confident point of disbelief either. These are the kids who can only "somewhat" agree or disagree with the statement that Jesus simply could not have physically come back to life.

What's the reason for this phenomenon among churchgoing, Christian teens? Well, the most intuitive explanation could simply be that, hey, these survey respondents are still what we call them: *kids*. They haven't yet matured to the point where it's important for them to make these kinds of firm decisions of faith. As they grow older, they'll begin making more secure commitments.

At least, that was what I thought. Unfortunately, in *The Jesus Survey* at least, that trend never materializes. In fact, just the opposite occurs.

Looking at the data on this question from an age perspective reveals that the older kids are, the less convinced they are of their belief (or disbelief) in Jesus's resurrection. In fact, greater age seems to lead only to greater uncertainty. For instance, nearly 3 out of 4 (71%) of Christian junior highers (grades 7 and 8) strongly affirmed belief in Jesus's resurrection on question 15, while roughly 1 in 4 (27%) expressed measurable uncertainty about that. Among high school underclassmen (grades 9 and 10), the number who strongly affirmed belief dropped to 67%, while the number who were uncertain rose to 29%. High school juniors and seniors moved this trend along even further, with nearly 1 in 3 (32%) showing uncertainty of belief regarding Jesus's resurrection. One can only assume that this kind of drift continues into the college and young adult years.

Figure 4.2

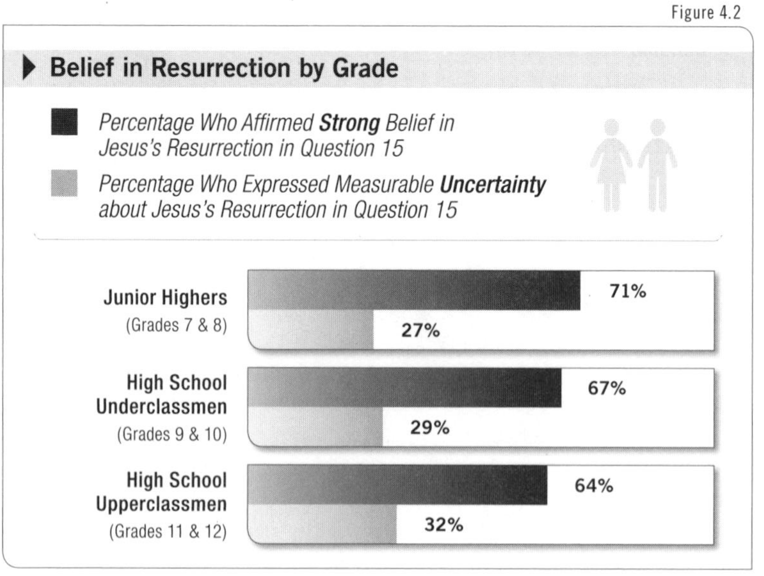

Unfortunately, it appears that as they grow older, more of our Christian kids begin to doubt that Jesus actually, physically rose from the dead. On the plus side, they also have trouble believing that he didn't rise . . . so, you know, we've got that going for us.

Realistically, though, it seems that there is an opportunity for those of us who are Christian parents or youth workers to help our teenagers settle more firmly into the belief that Jesus did indeed die and come back to life. By doing so, perhaps we can help reverse this troubling trend.

Question 16: "Jesus Physically Came Back to Life."

As with other couplets on *The Jesus Survey*, the follow-up question in this section asked teenagers to affirm the same belief as the previous one by responding to a statement from the opposing perspective. So, in question 15, kids who believed that Jesus rose again responded by disagreeing with the statement supplied. In question 16, to affirm the same belief kids would need to respond by agreeing with the statement supplied.

Departing from the trend started in chapters 1 and 2, and continuing a trend begun in chapter 3, this time students remained remarkably consistent in the way they answered these two questions.

When asked to agree or disagree with the statement, "Jesus physically came back to life after his execution" (question 16), again more than 4 in 5 (85%) stated they agreed with that belief. Likewise, about 1 in 6 (16%) expressed measurable doubt about Jesus's resurrection, nearly the exact percentage (17%) that answered similarly on question 15.

This is no doubt good news, because it confirms what students said they believed in question 15, providing repeatable data on the same topic. Additionally, it indicates that teenagers have put at least some thought into belief in Jesus's resurrection—and have (for the most part) come down in favor of it.

At the same time, there are warning bells in this data, particularly when one looks at the depth of belief demonstrated here. When the first followers of Jesus preached that Jesus had risen from the dead, they were routinely beaten, arrested, and even killed. In many parts of the globe—particularly in nations like China, North Korea, and Middle Eastern and African states—believing and preaching that Jesus rose from the dead can result in the same kind of treatment for modern followers of Christ. What keeps these believers going is a deep, abiding faith that what they believe is more than just an abstract assent—it is realistically and eternally true.

Do our Christian teenagers have that kind of deep, abiding faith in Jesus's resurrection? Is theirs a belief that will stand in the face of serious, potentially painful, opposition? Judging by the answer to question 16, many do have that kind of faith—fully 3 out of 5 (60%) indicate that they strongly believe Jesus is risen.

At the same time, a large number of Christian youth just don't. In fact, 41% of these church kids indicated some level of uncertainty about Jesus's resurrection, marking that they either disagree or only "somewhat agree" that Jesus physically came back to life after his execution.

Figure 4.3

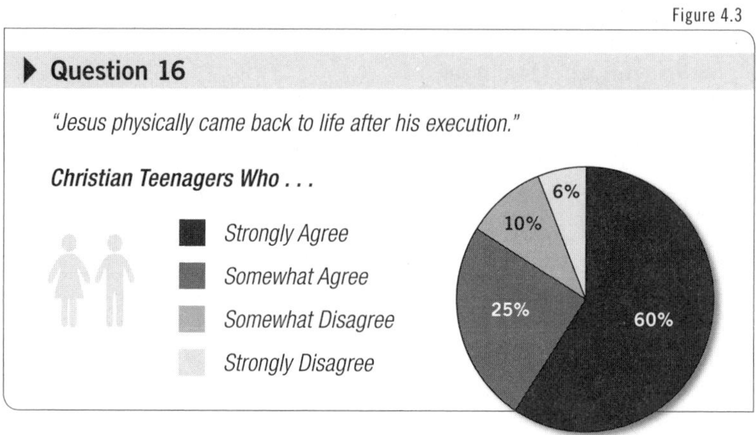

A glimpse at a denominational breakdown of kids' answers to this question reveals some insight into why this is so. It appears there is a denominational divide among teenagers regarding the veracity of the Easter story. Several organizations represented in *The Jesus Survey* seem to have skewed the overall responses in favor of a belief in Jesus's resurrection.

For instance, among Brethren in Christ teens, nearly 9 out of 10 (86%) report that they strongly believe Jesus physically came back to life. Students from what I've lumped together as "Other Denominations" also tip the scales in favor of belief, with a full 80% of those kids strongly endorsing Jesus's resurrection. Lutheran and non-denominational teens add weight as well, with more than 3 out of 4 (76%) of them strongly agreeing here.

A significant drop-off begins when other denominations are added to the mix. The number of Presbyterians, United Methodists, and Undeclared students who strongly affirm belief in Jesus's resurrection falls below 2 out of 3 (from 61% to 64%), while Baptists barely register more than half (53%) who do. Next are the kids from Catholic, Episcopal, and United Church of Christ churches—all with less than half of their teenagers willing to strongly affirm that Jesus is alive. In fact, among those in the United Church of Christ, teenagers who strongly believe in the Easter story are outnumbered by nearly a 2 to 1 margin (36% to 64%).

These numbers are heartbreaking. Yes, I rejoice that several denominations such as Brethren in Christ and Lutheran are doing a good job of reinforcing the truth of

Jesus's resurrection in their youth groups. But my heart also aches for those kids in several of these other churches who, apparently, are not being effectively encouraged with the good news that Jesus died *and rose again*. This, to my mind, can only be a failure of leadership. If we are unwilling to teach teenagers the gospel, then why even bother?

Every teen in every Christian church and in every Christian family deserves to hear, understand, and be encouraged in the belief that Jesus died and came back to life so that we might have eternal life with him. Hey, there's a reason it's called the gospel—the "good news" of Jesus. If we're not sharing that, then what's the point?

Figure 4.4

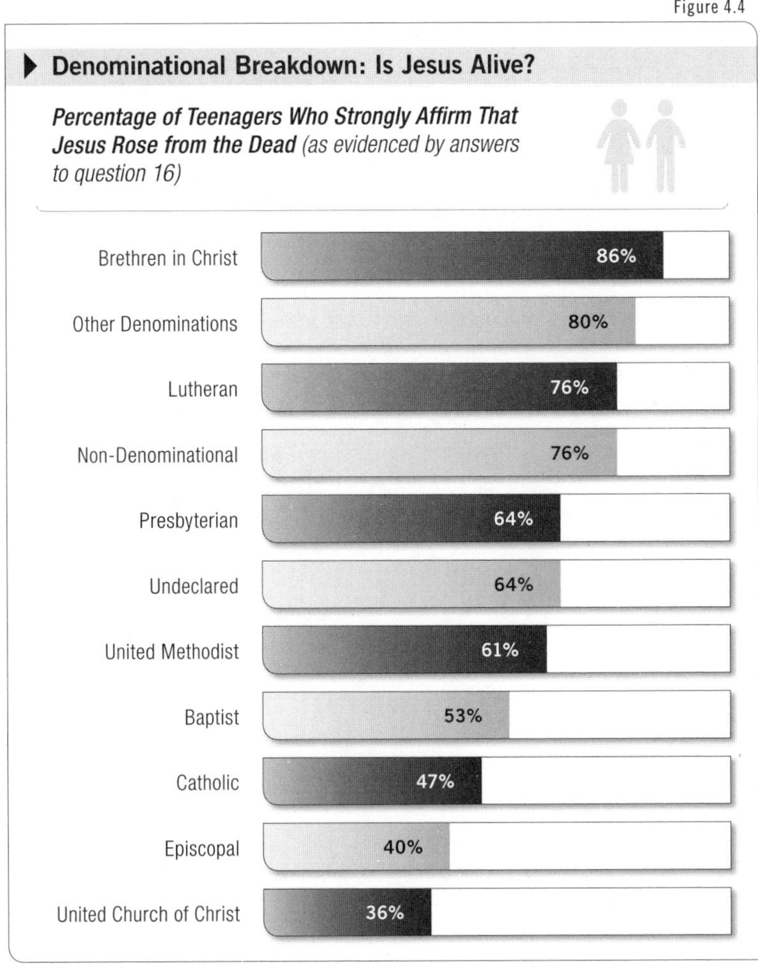

Because it had been so enlightening in previous questions, I decided to take a look at how teen beliefs about the Bible influence, or at least corresponded to, teen beliefs about Jesus's resurrection. So I cross-correlated the data for questions 6 and 7 (the perceived trustworthiness of the Bible) with data from questions 15 and 16 (Jesus's resurrection). Using the four categories first identified in chapter 1, I decided to see what percentages of teens in those categories also believed "strongly" in the physical resurrection of Jesus. For instance, how many of those kids responded that they "strongly disagree" with question 15 while also saying they "strongly agree" with question 6?

The results were illuminating, and unsurprising.

By far and away, the group of teens most likely to believe that Jesus physically came back to life after his execution were those who also strongly believed the Bible is trustworthy—that is, the Unshakeable teens. Fully 4 out of 5 in this group (80%) strongly, consistently affirmed belief in the biblical events of Easter.

After that, no group had even half of its students indicate they strongly believed Easter really happened.

Figure 4.5

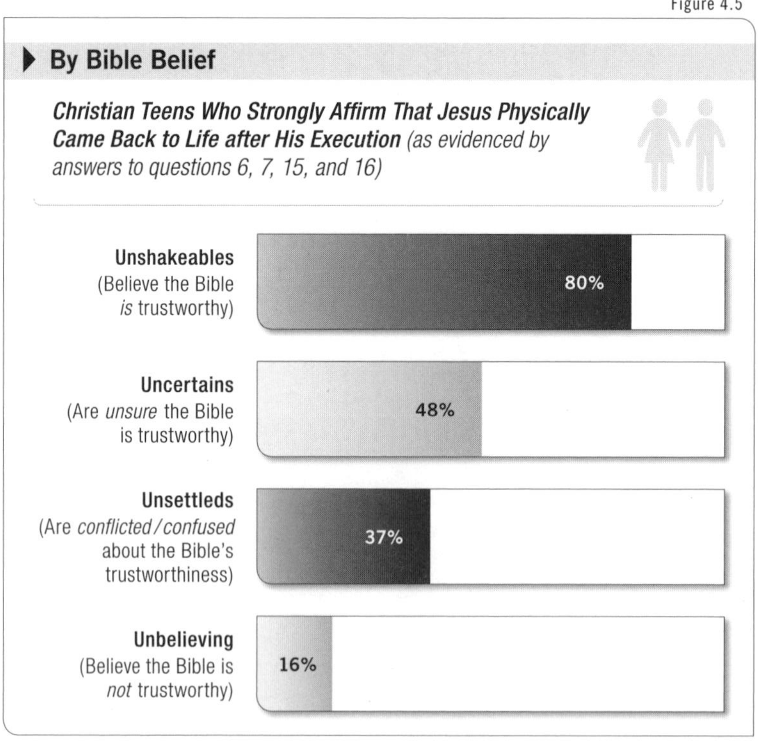

Among teens who were Uncertain about the Bible, only 48% strongly agreed that Jesus physically came back to life. Those who were Unsettled numbered just over 1 in 3 (37%). And, as could be expected, the overwhelming majority (84%) of those who distrust the Bible also distrust, to some degree, the story of Easter as recorded in the Gospels.

It's strange for me to see these numbers imbedded within the same figures that also show as many as 85% of our teenagers affirming a belief in Jesus's resurrection (see question 16). But it also shows that our teenagers may be telling us what we want to hear instead of what is actually roiling around in their hearts and minds.

One youth leader from Pennsylvania offered this insight in his follow-up interview after *The Jesus Survey*:

> It seems like a lot of kids today know what they should say regarding the Bible but cannot bring themselves to believe what they are saying. This is especially true for kids who have grown up in the church. . . . They find it easier to tell us what we want to hear rather than what they really believe. Perhaps their need for love and affection, more today than ever, is causing them to simply tell us what they think we want to hear.

Question 18: "Jesus Was Actually a Fictional Character."

Before I left the topic of Jesus's resurrection in this survey, I felt like it was important to ask one last question of teenagers regarding their view of the historicity of Christ. That's because folks like L. Ron Hubbard (creator of Hollywood's favorite religion, Scientology) and other literary, academic, and atheist thinkers have tried aggressively to make history call a mulligan on Easter and the events thereof. For these people, the problem of the empty tomb is easy to solve: it never existed. Thus, they dismiss it entirely, calling Christ's death and return to life a grand myth that simply didn't occur.

According to Scientologists, this Christ fable was implanted in the human race by deceitful "thetans" (preexistent immortals who continually reincarnate and thus forget their inherent divinity . . . or some gobbledygook like that). Hubbard's sci-fi explanation goes like this: "The Christ legend [was] an implant in preclears millions of years ago. The symbol of the crucified Christ is . . . the symbol of a thetan betrayed." [13]

More serious thinkers among literary and scholarly propagandists don't do much better than Hubbard in their attempts to fictionalize history. According to them, Jesus simply didn't exist, and early Christians fabricated the story of his resurrection by cobbling together ideas from pagan mythology (such as the stories of Osiris or Mithras).[14] Although this viewpoint must deliberately rewrite actual historical events and ignore the brutal torture and death that Jesus's followers endured for persisting to believe in their supposedly self-created myth, this "Jesus is a fairy tale" option has strong appeal for many so-called intellectuals. It has also gained some traction among young adults who are skeptical of religion today.

My friend Timothy Paul Jones tells of a recent visit to his local Starbucks. While there, he conversed with a young man who was also a regular customer at that coffee shop. When he found out Timothy was writing a book about Christ, he made this comment, "I just read some books about Jesus and mythology. I used to be a Christian, you know. Now I can't find enough evidence to make me believe. . . . It seems more likely to me that Jesus never even existed."[15]

If people are talking about this myth theory in casual conversation at Starbucks, that makes me wonder how much influence it might bear in the minds of Christian teenagers in our churches. So, for question 18 of *The Jesus Survey*, I asked kids to respond to this statement:

> Jesus was actually a fictional character invented as an extension of pagan mythology.

I wasn't sure what to expect in teenagers' responses to this question of Jesus-as-myth. Fortunately, they spoke pretty clearly and decisively on this issue:

It's a load of manure.

At least that's the scholarly way I interpreted their responses. Here's why: out of the twenty-five content questions on *The Jesus Survey*, there was no other question where teenagers demonstrated such near unanimity in response. Fully 95% (nearly everybody) disagreed with the idea that Jesus was actually a myth. What's more, 88% strongly disagreed with that idea—the highest single response of any question on this survey.

It appears, then, that our kids are—in this regard at least—smarter than some folks entrenched in either academia or the Hollywood experience. Thank God for small favors, right?

Figure 4.6

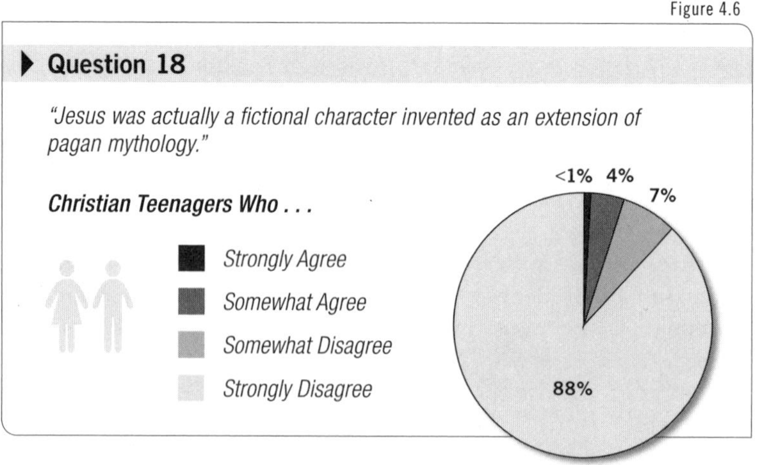

Figure 4.7

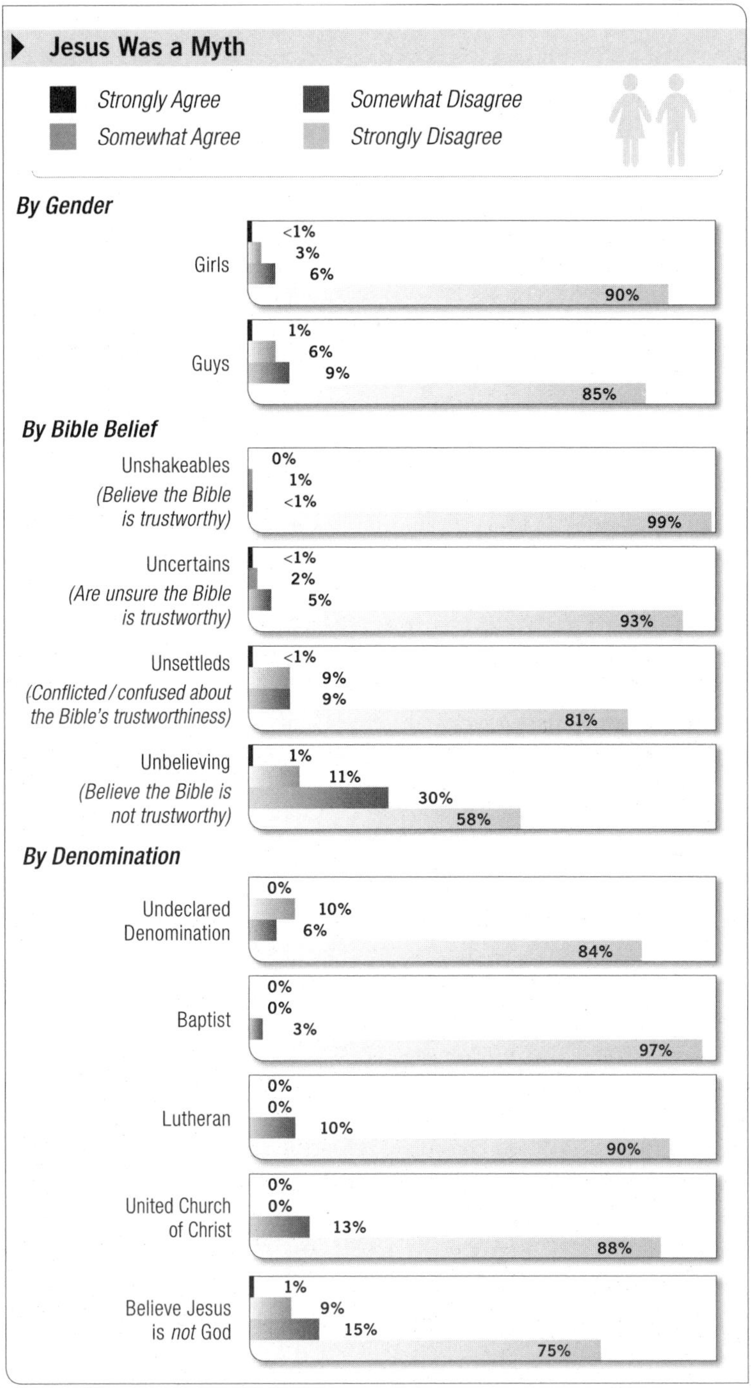

Jesus Was a Myth

	Strongly Agree	Somewhat Agree	Somewhat Disagree	Strongly Disagree
By Gender				
Girls	<1%	3%	6%	90%
Guys	1%	6%	9%	85%
By Bible Belief				
Unshakeables *(Believe the Bible is trustworthy)*	0%	1%	<1%	99%
Uncertains *(Are unsure the Bible is trustworthy)*	<1%	2%	5%	93%
Unsettleds *(Conflicted/confused about the Bible's trustworthiness)*	<1%	9%	9%	81%
Unbelieving *(Believe the Bible is not trustworthy)*	1%	11%	30%	58%
By Denomination				
Undeclared Denomination	0%	10%	6%	84%
Baptist	0%	0%	3%	97%
Lutheran	0%	0%	10%	90%
United Church of Christ	0%	0%	13%	88%
Believe Jesus is *not* God	1%	9%	15%	75%

It is interesting to note that 99% of Unshakeable Christian teens (who believe the Bible is trustworthy) also "strongly disagree" with this Jesus myth idea. Additionally, 100% of Baptist, Lutheran, and United Church of Christ students indicated that they either strongly or somewhat disagreed. Also, teen girls appear slightly less likely than their guy classmates to buy the mythology idea in regard to Jesus and his resurrection (3% to 7%).

The teenagers who appeared to be most open to the possibility that Jesus was a myth were those with Undeclared religious affiliation (10%), those who do not believe that Jesus is God (10%), and those who don't believe the Bible can be trusted (12%). In spite of that, it's encouraging to see that even those kids who don't believe the Bible—the one group that's demonstrated the most skepticism in this survey so far—overwhelmingly reject the idea of Jesus as myth by a 4 to 1 margin (88% to 12%).

Summary

• More than 8 in 10 (83%) Christian teenagers reject, at least somewhat, the negative proposition that Jesus's resurrection couldn't have happened. This seems to indicate, initially at least, that the bulk of conspiracy theories aimed at debunking the traditional Easter story have yet to significantly alter the perception of Jesus's resurrection among our churchgoing teenagers.

• *As they get older, certainty of Jesus's resurrection among Christian teens declines.* For kids who are growing up in church, this is a little surprising. One could expect students to become more grounded—and therefore more confident—of biblical truth the longer they study the Bible in our youth groups and Christian homes. Apparently they are not, which begs the question of why. Church workers and Christian parents would be wise to find the answer to that question.

• *Christian teens' belief in Jesus's resurrection differs sharply among denominational lines.* Affiliations such as Brethren in Christ churches, Lutherans, and even non-denominational churches demonstrate large numbers of teens who hold strongly to belief in Jesus's resurrection. Baptist, Catholic, Episcopal, and United Church of Christ churches show the lowest percentages in this category.

• *By far and away, the group of teens most likely to believe that Jesus physically came back to life after his execution are those who also strongly believe the Bible is trustworthy.* Once again, students who appear most confident of their Christian faith are those who base it on confidence in Scripture. This has now become a recurring theme in *The Jesus Survey*, and may be the most important takeaway from the study as a whole.

• *By almost unanimous consent (92% to 8%), Christian teenagers resoundingly reject the notion that Jesus's resurrection—and Jesus himself—are simply fiction derived from ancient mythology.*

Bonus Survey Results

Figure 4.8

Christian Teen Opinions about Jesus's Resurrection
(Did Jesus come back to life?)

Resurrection Believers *(Strongly believe Jesus died and physically came back to life)*	**52%**
Resurrection In-Betweeners *(Express measurable uncertainty about Jesus's resurrection)*	**40%**
Resurrection Skeptics *(Disbelieve that Jesus died and physically came back to life)*	**8%**

Figure 4.9

By Belief in Jesus's Deity: Christian Teens Who Strongly Affirm That Jesus Physically Came Back to Life after His Execution
(As evidenced by answers to questions 9, 10, 15, and 16)

Believe Jesus *is* God	**77%**
Believe Jesus might be God . . . but he might not be	**41%**
Don't know / haven't decided if Jesus is God	**38%**
Believe Jesus is *not* God	**37%**

Figure 4.10

Jesus Physically Came Back to Life

By Region, Christian Teenagers Who . . .

	Strongly Agree	*Somewhat Agree*	*Strongly Disagree*	*Somewhat Disagree*
East Coast / Near East Coast	**61%**	**25%**	**10%**	**5%**
West of the East Coast	**58%**	**25%**	**9%**	**8%**

5

JESUS—THE ***WAY OR*** *ONE* ***WAY TO HEAVEN?***

Jesus told him, "I am the way, the truth, and the life. No one can come to the Father except through me."
John 14:6

OK, you've stuck with me this far through this book, so I think it's time I tell you a secret: I have a superpower.

No, it's not Kryptonian strength or atomic speed (I wish!), or even a magical green ring that brings to life anything I can imagine. My power is much more dangerous:

I can make people very angry using only my words.

I know. Are you trembling in fear yet?

Trouble is, I don't have any real control over this superpower of mine. Sure, occasionally I know when it's flaring up and can do something about it (like, you know, shut my big fat face), but most times it shows up when I'm least expecting it and I'm completely surprised by its impact. Case in point: several years ago I worked as a book editor for a Christian publishing company. A friend of a friend sent me something he wanted me to publish—a digest-style reference book about the historical and cultural context of Jesus's life on earth. It was interesting, nicely written, and well-researched. I wanted to know more, so I started an email dialogue about it with the author. He responded warmly, and we started talking.

In the book, the writer made no secret of the fact that he was Christian and that he was writing this book as an expression of his Christianity. Then, in one section, he also went to great lengths to say that being Christian didn't really matter in terms of heaven—all religions lead to God, so we should all just show tolerance toward each other, no matter whether we are Muslim, Buddhist, Christian, or whatever.

This is where my superpower blew up in my face. His contradictory beliefs made me curious, so I went ahead and asked him what I was thinking: As a Christian, how do you reconcile the Bible's claim that Jesus is the only way to heaven with your belief that all religions ultimately lead to heaven? He was obviously an educated, intelligent man, and I thought we were simply continuing a conversation about Jesus. Apparently I was wrong.

This author's response toward me was immediate fury.

In his mind, by asking that little question I had crossed a terrible line. I'd insulted him personally and shown myself to be an intolerant, religious bigot worthy of only his contempt. The fierceness of his anger was truly surprising. He told me I was a hypocritical, judgmental jerk who represented all that was wrong with Christians today. Oh, and as such, I was unworthy of publishing his book.

Plus, he never answered my question.

Ta-da! I'd done it again. I'd made this otherwise friendly, articulate, reasonable man so angry that he verbally attacked me in response—and also threw away the opportunity to publish his book with me in order to demonstrate the depth of offense he felt toward my questioning his view that all religions are equally valid.

Still, despite the fact that this author and our society in general find it offensive, the Bible does pretty clearly teach that Jesus alone—not Mohammed, not Buddha, not anything or anyone else—is the sole avenue for reaching heaven and reconciling us to God.

Jesus himself declares unequivocally, "I am the way, the truth, and the life. No one can come to the Father except through me" (John 14:6). The only way that heaven can be attained through faith in Mohammed or Buddha or anyone else is if Jesus is lying or is simply mistaken.

The apostle Peter also declares the same thing when called to the carpet before the Jewish religious leadership not long after Jesus's death. Speaking boldly of "Jesus Christ of Nazareth, whom you crucified but whom God raised from the dead," Peter announces without apology: "Salvation is found in no one else, for there is no other name under heaven given to men by which we must be saved" (Acts 4:10, 12 NIV).

There doesn't seem to be any gray area in those statements. (Other Scriptures that reinforce this view are Matthew 1:21; John 1:28–29; Acts 10:42–43; and Revelation 7:9–10.) Theologian I. Howard Marshall notes that:

> Peter claims that only Jesus can offer salvation. . . . It followed that if God had declared Jesus to be a Saviour, there could be nobody else alongside him.[1]

Now, if it were up to me, I'd say we bring everybody to heaven, regardless of religion or creed or cap size or whatever. Problem is, I'm a big jerk steeped in sin, and an extremely limited, created being—neither capable nor worthy of setting *any* kind of standard in regard to heaven. Same goes for you too (well, except for the "big jerk" part), and for every other man, woman, and child on the planet.

I'm not the creator of heaven and earth and everything in between. I'm not the one who can palm eternity with one hand, who tells the sun when to rise and a child when to be born, who holds every atom together and who forms life out of his very breath. God handles all that stuff, and only he has the authority to decide how humanity may approach and embrace him. If the Bible is true (and I believe it is), that means Jesus—alone—is the way, the truth, and the life. No one comes to God but by him.

In light of *The Jesus Survey*, then, that raises an important question: What do our teenagers believe about this issue of salvation in Christ alone? Hey, they claim to be Christians and to have trusted Jesus for their eternal salvation. And they're being taught regularly about that faith in our churches. At the same time, they live in a culture where tolerance and inclusivity are forcefully demanded—so much so that sometimes simply expressing an unpopular opinion is enough to bring very real punishment. And in that culture, among their peers, more than 2 out of 3 either completely deny or express serious reservations about Jesus's unique saving ability.[2]

So do Christian teens have confidence in Jesus as the only way to heaven? Or, like that Christian author who got so angry at me for asking a question, have they decided that inclusivity trumps Bible truth? That Jesus, Mohammed, Buddha, and other great religious leaders are all the same?

Well, you know me. I tend to talk about whatever it is I'm thinking at the time. So in the next section of *The Jesus Survey*, I went ahead and asked kids to join my conversation.

Jesus: One of Many?

In this portion of the content section of *The Jesus Survey*, I wanted to explore Christian teen beliefs about what theologians call *soteriology*, that is, "the doctrine of salvation."[3] Specifically, I wanted to discover if teenagers in our churches believe that Jesus is the only way to heaven or merely one of many valid pathways to heaven that include Mohammad and Buddha and other great religious leaders.

As with all questions, I listed a one-sentence statement and then asked kids to indicate whether they agreed or disagreed with the statement. Like before, I approached this issue in a question couplet. One question in this couplet required an "agree" response to affirm belief in Jesus as the sole source of salvation, and the other required a "disagree" response to do the same thing. Like the previous set of questions, I ordered these so the negative statement was first.

So, in question 19 I asked kids to react to this statement:

> Jesus, Mohammad, Buddha, and other great religious leaders all have equal standing in leading people to heaven.

Next, for question 20 I asked teenagers to respond to this correlated statement:

> I'm 100% certain that Jesus is the only way to heaven.

Now, before we get into the data on this topic, let's be clear on a few things, just so you know where I'm coming from as I interpret these results.

As I understand it, exalting anything or anyone to a revered status equal with God is not simply a matter of relative opinion; according to scriptural standards, that kind of polytheism is actually idolatry and is in direct violation of the first of God's famous Ten Commandments. Additionally, there's a marked difference between religious tolerance and religious negligence. It is tolerant, and desirable, to allow others to believe differently without fear of reprisal. It is negligent to affirm that all beliefs are equal regardless of whether or not those beliefs are true, even in deference to a desire to promote tolerance.

This is easy to say, not so easy to put into practice.

For instance, I admit that when I was a junior high student I ran with a wild crowd. One day, my best friend (let's maintain his privacy and call him Danny) and I broke into his dad's liquor cabinet. Danny mixed a glass with shots from about a half dozen different bottles and downed it all at once. At first, nothing happened, so we decided to go swimming.

Not long after we hit the pool, the liquor hit Danny's system. In a drunken stupor, he said to me, "I wonder what it's like to drown." Then he exhaled and dropped under the surface. When I saw him start to take in water, I did what anyone would do. I dove under, pulled him out of the pool, and let him cough on the pavement until I could get him safely home.

It would not have been "tolerant" of me to think, *Well, he believes it's a good idea to experience drowning. Therefore, I'll agree that his belief is valid and let him die here in this pool.* Everyone knows that would be absurd—and would in fact be criminal negligence on my part. Why?

Because Danny's *life* was at stake, and my seeking not to offend him by saying his belief in drowning was OK would have been deadly.

And here's the truth about this whole issue of soteriology: if Jesus really is the only way to heaven (and I believe he is), then telling someone that believing in Buddha or Mohammad or anyone else is just as good as believing in Jesus is not tolerance—it's deadly. Why? Because real human lives are at stake—for eternity. Downplaying Jesus's unique saving power is akin to criminal negligence with eternal consequences.

Again, that doesn't mean Christians are free to discriminate or antagonize people who claim another religion. But it does mean we have to be honest with ourselves and with the teenagers in our care and let them know that *salvation is found in no one else but Jesus Christ.*

Judging by the way Christian teenagers responded to questions 19 and 20 in *The Jesus Survey*, we haven't done a good job of communicating that truth to our kids.

Question 19: "Jesus, Mohammad, Buddha, and Other Religious Leaders All Have Equal Standing."

When asked if Jesus, Mohammad, Buddha, and other great religious leaders are all equal in terms of leading us to salvation, fully 1 out of 3 (33%) teenagers who participated in *The Jesus Survey* affirmed that false statement. What's more, less than half of our church kids (48%) were willing to "strongly disagree."

Figure 5.1

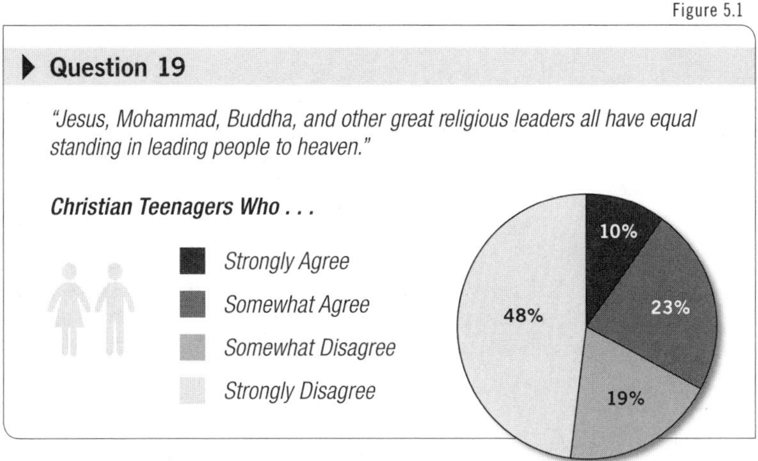

Remember, these are kids who claim to have personally experienced Jesus's salvation—and who are somehow involved with a youth group in a local church. As such, these numbers are tragic, and they reflect a complete misunderstanding of the Christian faith these teens claim to hold. The overarching value of supposed tolerance for other religions has somehow trumped the value of truth, making it natural for our Christian students to actually deny their own beliefs when they may be perceived (whether rightly or wrongly) as intolerant.

I was disappointed by the findings in that regard, but not really surprised. These kinds of trends uncovered in *The Jesus Survey* reflect, and confirm, findings from other recent research studies on religion, most notably in the works of Christian Smith and the Barna Research Group.

According to youth culture expert Christian Smith, this issue of "tolerance over truth" has more to do with social indoctrination than with heresy being preached in our churches. Says Smith:

> Nearly all U.S. teens seem to have adopted a posture of civility and a careful ambiguous inclusiveness when discussing religion. . . . It is also obvious that, in all of this, public schools have served as an effective training ground for teaching teenagers to be civil, inclusive, and nonoffensive when it comes to faith and spiritual matters.[4]

Barna adds that:

> The postmodern insistence on tolerance is winning over the Christian church. Our biblical illiteracy and lack of spiritual confidence has caused Americans to avoid making discerning choices for fear of being labeled judgmental.

This shows up in a marked way among Christian teenagers, and for most of them,

> the idea of love has been redefined to mean the absence of conflict and confrontation. . . . The challenge today is for Christian leaders to achieve the delicate balance between representing truth and acting in love.[5]

Barna further challenges church leaders and parents on this subject with these thoughtful words: "There is a place for tolerance in Christianity; knowing when and where to draw the line appears to perplex a growing proportion of Christians in this age of tolerance."[6]

Although adults seem aware of this problem, they seem just as perplexed on this issue as the teens they lead. It's worth noting that adult leaders who took *The Jesus Survey* with their teens still underestimated the compulsion their teens feel toward this kind of inoffensive inclusivity. Adults predicted that more than half of their teens (51%) would strongly disagree with question 19, and that only about 1 in 4 (26%) of Christian youth would actually affirm this kind of religious syncretism.

Figure 5.2

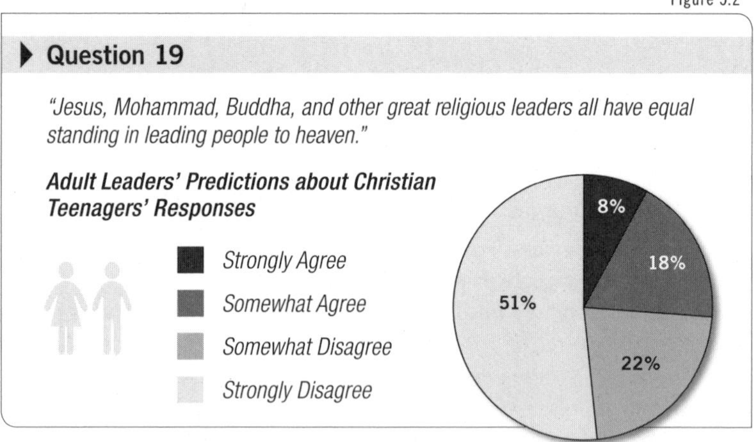

This seems to reflect a casual attitude toward teaching the truth of the gospel to students in our churches—and that has tragic implications. After all, if some other religious leader—be it Mohammad, Buddha, or Stan from the International Church of Fun—is capable of leading people into heaven, then Jesus's incarnation, execution, and resurrection are all worthless. They are redundant at best, and sinfully wasteful at worst. If Jesus is not required *every time* for salvation, then Jesus is not required *anytime*, and our Christian teenagers (along with us) are just wasting our lives by pursuing the Christian faith.

Interestingly, it's the young women in our youth groups who are more likely to reject a belief that all religious leaders are the same. This appears to be consistent with the common assumption that women in our churches are more likely to express commitment to their religious beliefs than men are. As it stands, more than 1 in 3 (36%) young Christian men have adopted, at least somewhat, a multifaith salvation belief. About 6% fewer teen women (30% total) show that same syncretism. Additionally, exactly half of our young women (50%) strongly reject the idea that other religious leaders are equal to Jesus, while less than half (45%) of teen guys feel that way.

Figure 5.3

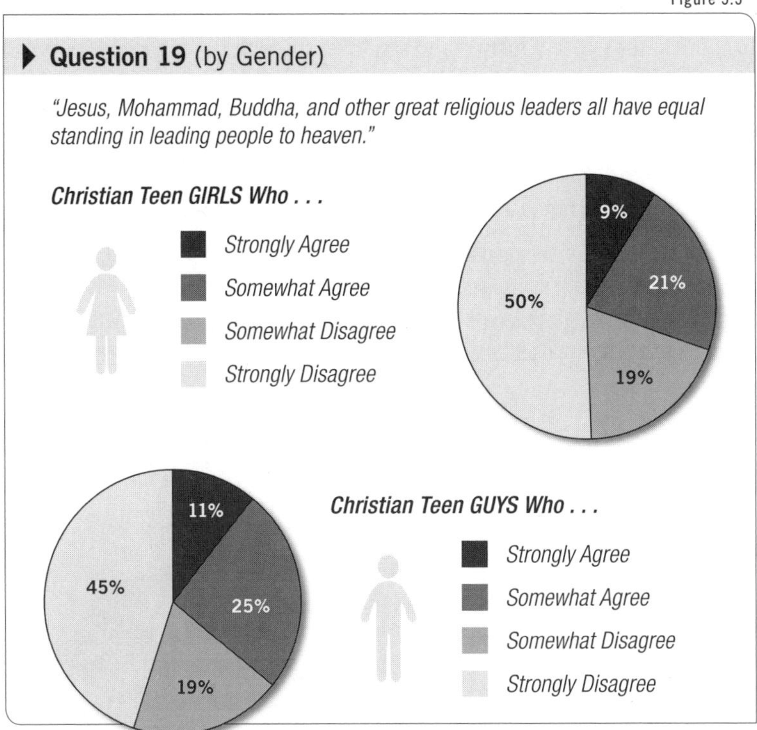

Question 20: "Jesus Is the Only Way to Heaven."

Like other couplets in *The Jesus Survey*, asking the question from an opposite perspective had a clarifying effect on the way teenagers responded to this issue. As a result, when asked in question 20 to affirm that "Jesus is the only way to heaven," more kids indicated that they did believe this to be true. This trend is most noticeable when comparing the number of respondents who strongly disagreed with question 19 and then strongly agreed with question 20. When asked if all religious leaders were the same (question 19), less than half (48%) strongly rejected that belief. Conversely, when asked if Jesus is the only way to heaven, more than half (56%) strongly affirmed that belief.

This could indicate that a good number of teenagers simply are unprepared to think in terms of absolute truth in regard to spiritual matters in general and issues of salvation specifically. One 12th grade girl from New York commented that questions like these were, "Too complex to be able to answer with simple answers. I think that many teenagers are still searching for many of these answers." A junior high student from Pennsylvania simply crossed through question 19 and said, "I don't understand the question." And a 12th grader from a Church of God youth group said the questions here were just too hard for her to answer what she really thought.

Trouble is, when these teenagers do indeed reach the end of their lives, no one is going to stand at the gates of heaven and say, "You thought it was too complex to decide if Jesus saves? Oh, well then. Don't worry your pretty little head about it and come right on in." If our culture shies away from helping teens deal with unpopular issues such as absolute truth, then our Christian families and churches need to do a better job of teaching our kids to think through those issues—including the issue of salvation.

Charles Colson delivers a stinging rebuke in this regard. He says:

> We have come into a postmodern era that rejects the idea of truth itself. If there is no such thing as truth, then Christianity's claims are inherently offensive and even bigoted against others. Tolerance, falsely defined as putting all propositions on an equal footing—as opposed to giving ideas an equal hearing—has replaced truth.[7]

Figure 5.4

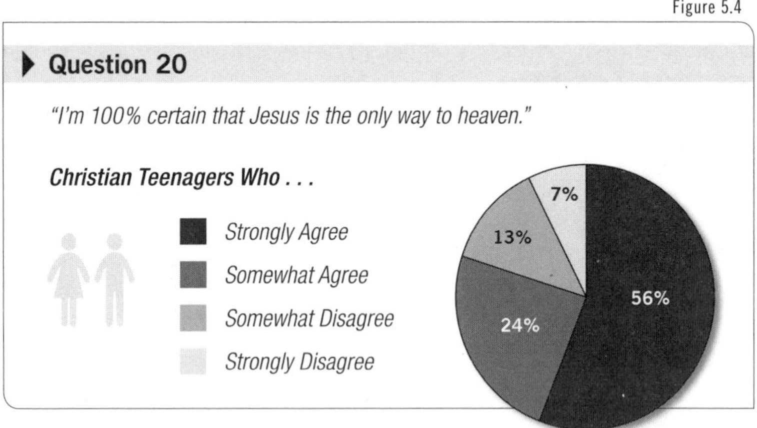

This unwillingness to wrestle with absolute truth in regard to salvation shows up in a unique way in question 20 specifically. You'll notice that the wording of this statement is designed to eliminate, as much as possible, any middle ground in response.

By requiring teens to assert 100% certainty in order to agree with the statement, one would think the majority of responses would naturally fall in the two extremes, either as "strongly agree" or "strongly disagree." In fact, that didn't happen.

More than 1 in 3 (37%) avoided expressing a firm belief either way, choosing instead the emotionally safer middle ground of either "somewhat" agreeing or disagreeing. Perhaps this is due to a desire to conform to societal values in regard to tolerance and/or inclusivity, but how anyone can "somewhat agree" that he or she is "100% certain" about anything is debatable. Regardless, significant numbers of Christian teenagers did just that. As with beliefs about the trustworthiness of the Bible and questions over the deity of Jesus, this seems to suggest that a large number of teenagers in our youth groups and in our Christian families are, realistically, going through the motions of faith, putting off making any real decisions about the Christianity they claim until a future time.

Cross-Correlating the Numbers

As in previous chapters, it was clarifying to cross-correlate student responses to these two questions on the theology of salvation. When I did that, the following three groups appeared in the data:

Teens who believe Jesus is the only way to heaven. In their answers to both questions 19 and 20, these students demonstrated consistent, strong affirmation of Jesus's unique status as the sole means of eternal salvation.

Teens who are unsure or unwilling to fully acknowledge that Jesus is the only way to heaven. These students hedged their bets in answer to questions 19 and 20, choosing middle ground (somewhat agreeing or disagreeing) or even confused/contradictory responses to the two questions.

Teens who believe Jesus is not the only way to heaven. These Christian students consistently denied, in both questions 19 and 20, that Jesus held a unique status as the sole means of eternal salvation.

Figure 5.5

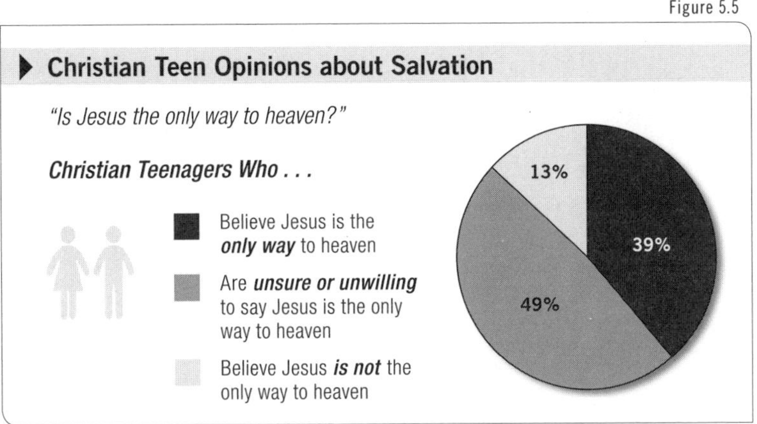

The clear picture here is not pretty. Christian teenagers who firmly hold to the biblical and historical belief that Jesus alone is the only way to heaven are significantly in the minority in their youth groups. In fact, not even 2 out of 5 students (39%) demonstrate confidence in Christ's exclusive saving work. The largest group of Christian kids are those who just don't know or are unwilling to say with certainty that Jesus alone saves. These students number about half of our youth groups (49%). And, tragically, 1 in 8 Christian teenagers (13%) actually holds to a firm belief that Jesus is *not* the only way to heaven.

Denominationally speaking, it appears that groups like Brethren in Christ and non-denominational churches place significantly greater emphasis on Jesus's saving work than do affiliations such as Catholic and United Church of Christ churches. The rest of the church groups represented in *The Jesus Survey* run the gamut in between those four.

Fully 3 out of 4 (75%) teens from non-denominational churches express strong confidence in the belief that Jesus alone is the way to heaven. Nearly that same amount (73%) of students from Brethren in Christ churches report that trusting solely in Jesus is essential to salvation.

Other denominations (Anglican Church, Christian Church [DOC], Church of God, Christian & Missionary Alliance, Evangelical Congregational, Mennonite Church) also show a high number of teens who believe salvation is in Christ alone. About 2 out of 3 (66%) teens from these churches demonstrate that viewpoint consistently across both questions 19 and 20. From there, the numbers get a little shaky.

Among both Baptists and Undeclared teens, barely over half (51% and 55%, respectively) show firm belief in Jesus as the only Savior. Less than half of Christian students in Presbyterian, United Methodist, Lutheran, Episcopal, United Church of Christ, and Catholic churches see Jesus as the sole source of salvation. In fact, among Catholic teens, the number of students who strongly believe Jesus is *not* the only way to heaven (25%) is more than double the number of those who believe he is (11%).

Our Christian youth are certainly not alone in pluralizing—and therefore denying—their religion in this way. Clearly they're adopting what our society has modeled for them since their preschool days. Researcher Robert Putnam surveyed over three thousand adults on this question and revealed that even more adults fall into this line of thinking. According to Putnam:

> Notwithstanding this scriptural injunction [John 14:6] (and many more like it), most Americans who belong to Christian faiths told us that they believe non-Christians can go to heaven.

Among Catholics in Putnam's study, more than 8 in 10 (83%) held this belief, and almost the same number (79%) of mainline Protestants did as well. Evangelicals, known for their conservative theology, weren't that much better, with more than half (54%) ascribing to the belief that there are many paths to heaven besides Jesus.[8]

Figure 5.6

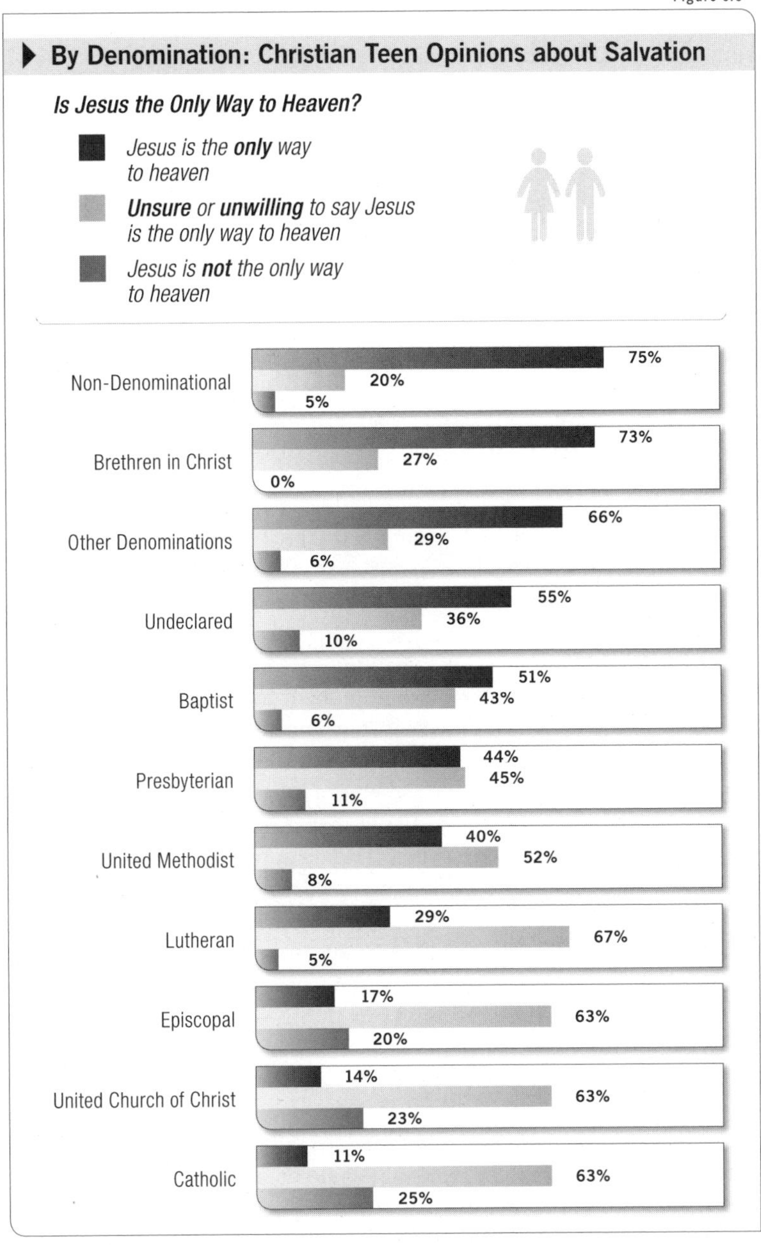
By Denomination: Christian Teen Opinions about Salvation
Is Jesus the Only Way to Heaven?
Jesus is the only way to heaven
Unsure or unwilling to say Jesus is the only way to heaven
Jesus is not the only way to heaven
Non-Denominational
75%
20%
5%
Brethren in Christ
73%
27%
0%
Other Denominations
66%
29%
6%
Undeclared
55%
36%
10%
Baptist
51%
43%
6%
Presbyterian
44%
45%
11%
United Methodist
40%
52%
8%
Lutheran
29%
67%
5%
Episcopal
17%
63%
20%
United Church of Christ
14%
63%
23%
Catholic
11%
63%
25%

Additionally, Lisa Pearce and Melinda Denton report that as teens move through adolescence, they become more likely to adopt a buffet-style approach to belief. After surveying teens in 2002 and then again in 2005, they found that:

> In the first survey 53% of youth said that it is not okay to pick and choose beliefs from a religious tradition; only 37% of these youth (20% of the total sample) still agreed with this statement in 2005. The change in their responses seems to indicate a shift toward greater acceptance of individualized religious beliefs.[9]

The consequences of nurturing this kind of any-religion-fits belief system within our church youth groups and Christian families are far-reaching. Charles Colson advises that:

> Millions acquiesce to the all-beliefs-are-equal doctrine for the sake of bettering their social position in our values-free, offend-no-one culture. But to succumb to this indifference is not to accept a tolerant or liberal view of Christianity; it is to embrace another religion, a belief in some supreme value—perhaps tolerance—but not in the God who is and who has spoken.[10]

Among the three groups of students delineated above, it should come as no surprise that those who believe Jesus is the only way to heaven also overwhelmingly believe the Bible is trustworthy in what it says about Jesus. Among these kids, 99% agreed with the statement of question 6: "The Bible is 100% accurate." Likewise, Bible-believing teens were least likely to buy the popular, politically correct notion stated in question 8 that, "Other highly regarded religious books, such as the Qur'an and the Book of Mormon, are just as important as the Bible." Still, about 1 in 8 (14%) was open to that fallacy.

Among the other two groups, as one would expect, trust in the Bible's unique authority declines significantly. A good number (83%) of those who are unsure or unwilling to say Jesus is the only way to heaven support the Scriptures, but only 29% "strongly agree" that the Bible is trustworthy. Meanwhile, more than half (58%) rank other religious books as being on par with God's Word. For those who reject the idea that Jesus alone saves, the number who also trust the Bible drops to 59% (with a mere 5% strongly agreeing the Bible is trustworthy), and the number of students who think all religious books are equal rises to nearly 4 out of 5 (79%).

It seems obvious that Christian adults in both our churches and in our homes are doing a poor job of effectively communicating biblical truth regarding the way one can be brought into an eternal relationship with God. This appears to be a deliberate decision among us, and one that could literally cost our teens everything.

We must improve at helping our Christian teenagers understand the difference between tolerance and negligence as it concerns the issue of soteriology (the doctrine of salvation). It is indeed possible to be a tolerant, inclusive person without rejecting this one core eternal truth: *to the utmost, Jesus saves.*

Figure 5.7

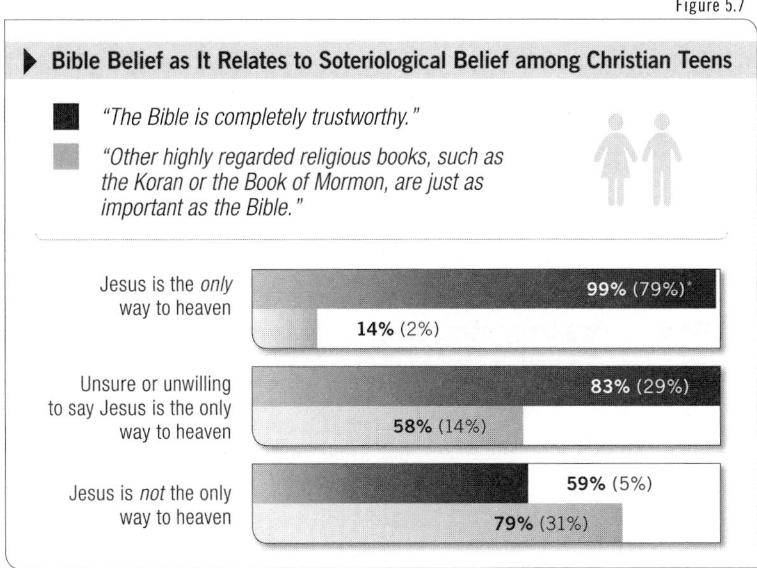

*Percentages in parentheses reflect teenagers who "strongly agree" with the quoted Bible belief statement.

Summary

• Fully 1 out of 3 (33%) Christian teenagers believes that Jesus, Mohammad, Buddha, and other great religious leaders all lead to heaven. This suggests two things: (1) as Christian Smith says, "public schools have served as an effective training ground for teaching teenagers to be civil, inclusive, and nonoffensive when it comes to faith and spiritual matters,"[11] and (2) a significant number of Christian teenagers are operating under a complete misunderstanding of the Christian faith they claim to hold.

• *Teen girls are slightly less likely than teen boys to believe all religions lead to heaven.* Exactly half of Christian young women (50%) reject the idea that other religious leaders are equal to Jesus, while less than half (45%) of Christian teen guys feel that way.

• *Not quite 2 out of 5 students (39%) demonstrate confidence in Christ's exclusive saving work.* As such, Christian teenagers who hold firmly to the biblical and historical belief that Jesus alone is the only way to heaven are significantly in the minority in their youth groups.

• *Among the organizations represented in* The Jesus Survey, *teens from Brethren in Christ and non-denominational churches are most likely to believe Jesus alone saves.* By large margins, teenagers from Catholic and United Church of Christ churches are least likely to believe that.

• *Belief in the trustworthiness of the Bible is directly related to belief that Jesus is the only way to heaven.* Among "Jesus only" kids, 99% also agreed with the statement that "The Bible is 100% accurate." If we haven't learned it yet, this finding again drives home the point that raising youth with strong Christian faith means first raising kids who have strong faith in God's Word.

Bonus Survey Results

Figure 5.8

Belief in Jesus's Deity as It Relates to Soteriological Belief among Christian Teens

	"Jesus Is Both the Son of God and God Himself"	*"Jesus Never Once Sinned"*
Jesus is the *only* way to heaven	**90%** (72%)*	**89%** (82%)
Unsure or unwilling to say Jesus is the only way to heaven	**86%** (49%)	**66%** (42%)
Jesus is *not* the only way to heaven	**74%** (31%)	**40%** (20%)

* Percentages in parentheses reflect teenagers who "strongly agree" with the quoted Bible belief statement.

Figure 5.9

By Grade: Soteriological Belief among Christian Teens

	7th Graders	*8th Graders*	*9th Graders*	*10th Graders*	*11th Graders*	*12th Graders*
Jesus is the *only* way to heaven	**27%**	**45%**	**40%**	**41%**	**32%**	**40%**
Unsure or unwilling to say Jesus is the only way to heaven	**57%**	**47%**	**50%**	**48%**	**53%**	**45%**
Jesus is *not* the only way to heaven	**15%**	**9%**	**10%**	**11%**	**15%**	**15%**

INTERMISSION

WHERE WE'VE BEEN, WHERE WE'RE GOING

At this point in this book, I think it'd be wise to stop for a moment.

Take a deep breath.

Glance back at where we've been so far, and then cast our eyes forward to see where we're headed next.

That's what this brief intermission is for—if not for you then for me. After all, I've been living and breathing the minutia of this data, and riding a roller coaster of emotions along with it, for much too long. It's time to pull back a bit and try to look at the big picture again. So let's do that now.

Where We've Been

Joshua Harris says, "We're all theologians. The question is whether what we know about God is true."[1] It was this kind of thinking that drove the content sections of *The Jesus Survey*, particularly questions 6 through 20. Realistically, all our teenagers are theologians in that they're working through eternal truth in order to arrive at beliefs with immediate lifestyle impact. The question, then, is whether or not what they know about God is actually true.

As is likely obvious to you, questions 6 through 20 of *The Jesus Survey* were designed to help us discover what Christian teenagers know about Jesus regarding a few core issues of the Christian faith. With that in mind, these questions, in varying ways and to varying degrees, tried to clarify just what Christian kids in our churches believe about four key doctrines of historical Christianity. These doctrines are (in my own words):

1. The Bible is completely trustworthy in what it says about Jesus.
2. Jesus is God.
3. Jesus physically lived, died, and came back to life.
4. Jesus is the only way to heaven.

Teens were given opportunity to consistently affirm each of these beliefs in at least two separate questions, through both positive and negative statements. That sometimes produced confusion and/or conflicting results when survey responses were taken individually, but also produced more reliable clarity of viewpoints when taken in context with each other. This gave a better glimpse of students' true beliefs when their answers seemed to conflict—and revealed that many self-proclaimed Christians in our youth groups simply don't know, or haven't yet decided, what they believe about Jesus.

Up to this point, I've been measuring student beliefs according to one key doctrine at a time—for instance, chapter 1 explored teen beliefs about the trustworthiness of Scripture; chapters 3 and 4 examined beliefs about Jesus's life, death, and resurrection; and so on. But here, at the midway point in this book, I felt it was time to take at least one look at all four doctrines and how they relate to each other in the minds and hearts of Christian teenagers.

Because of the way *The Jesus Survey* was created, it was a fairly easy (though tedious) process to isolate the data and discover how many, and which, teenagers expressed a confident, consistent affirmation of the four doctrines I was studying. Basically, it meant tabulating and cross-correlating all of the "strongly agree" and "strongly disagree" responses for questions 6 through 20, and identifying whether those responses affirmed or denied a key historical belief. By doing that, I could see clearly which respondents strongly believed—that is, held a firm, confident belief—in all four doctrines.

So that's what I did, cross-correlating questions to identify just how many "Confident Christian" youth claimed these four simple truths about Jesus Christ. Here's what I discovered:

It's not many.

In fact, only 9% (just under 1 in 10) of Christian teenagers indicate a confident belief in all four doctrines covered thus far. If even one of these key beliefs were an unusual orthodoxy (say, for example, asking kids to affirm belief that Jesus died for animals as well as humans), then that low percentage might be more easily explained. But all four of these doctrines are basic tenets of Christianity—and have been for millennia. Yet over 90% of self-proclaimed Christian teenagers associated with a local church simply don't have full faith in one or more of the ideas that (a) the Bible is trustworthy, (b) Jesus is God, (c) Jesus died and came back to life, and (d) Jesus is the only way to heaven.

I was surprised—and disappointed—by this finding. But I shouldn't have been. It simply brings to light in Christian teenagers what other researchers have already identified in the church as a whole. As the Barna Research Group has reported:

> The Christian church is becoming less theologically literate. What used to be basic, universally known truths about Christianity are now unknown mysteries to a large

> and growing share of Americans—especially young adults. . . . As the two younger generations (Busters and Mosaics) ascend to numerical and positional supremacy in churches across the nation, the data suggests that biblical literacy is likely to decline significantly. The theological free-for-all that is encroaching in Protestant churches nationwide suggests the coming decade will be a time of unparalleled theological diversity and inconsistency.[2]

Additionally, Thom and Jess Rainer recently conducted a study similar to *The Jesus Survey*, polling twelve hundred "Millennials" (teens and young adults) about matters of religious orthodoxy. Whereas *The Jesus Survey* focused on four key beliefs, the Rainer study asked respondents to affirm seven statements of core Christian doctrine. Their findings? "Only 6 percent of Millennials could affirm the statements."[3]

These findings indicate that the results showing up in *The Jesus Survey* are not isolated anomalies, but in fact are part of a larger, identifiable trend. And that raises a few questions for me.

First, who is responsible for this overwhelming lack of belief in Christian teenagers?

Does blame fall on church leaders? Christian parents? Our secularized and often religiously antagonistic society? Teenagers themselves? Jesus, who in the end is the author and finisher of faith? A general lackadaisical attitude toward matters of eternity by people of all ages? The politically correct movement in schools that indoctrinates teens with uneven definitions of tolerance and inclusiveness—and demands obedience to those definitions? "Right-wing" extremists who play out Christianity like it's both a drug and a cult for mentally unbalanced bigots?

Me?

You?

I don't have an answer. But we all need to be asking the question.

Second, at what point does mistaken, or immature, belief actually become *dis*belief?

Or, to put it another way, how much does God overlook when it comes to eternity and his relationship with the teenagers in our churches and Christian homes?

When I shared a bit of this information with youth leaders in follow-up interviews, one articulate Presbyterian man responded this way:

> To reject core Christian beliefs is to reject the Christian identity as a whole. If it is the case, those who reject it themselves might not even be Christian at all, but need to be treated as non-Christians who need to be evangelized and witnessed to with the gospel.

Another youth worker, a woman from a United Methodist church, had a softer response. She recommended that Christian parents and church leaders should, "Respond with love and understanding; try to figure out why they believe like this. Is it them rebelling against their parents' belief? Help them have that God moment." For her, teens' inaccurate beliefs could be attributed mostly to immaturity, not so much to bad theology.

Realistically, none of us is a true authority with full understanding of the workings of God and Christian faith. With his disciples, Jesus often showed great patience in helping them understand previously mistaken beliefs. At the same time, Jesus was also relentless in his rebukes of the religious leaders of his time who denied truth and led others to do the same.

So, at what point does the supposed faith of our teenagers actually become a false religion that's more idolatry than genuine relationship with God?

For instance, if a teen has asked Jesus for her personal salvation but also believes she could have asked Buddha or Mohammad or Joseph Smith or the Dalai Lama or some other religious leader for that salvation, does God overlook that mistaken assumption of faith and honor the sincerity of the original request instead? Or if a teenager believes that Jesus never sinned but also disbelieves that Jesus is God, does God honor the first act of faith and overlook the second denial of truth?

Again, I have no answers.

It is clear, however, that only a remnant of the teenagers who come to our youth groups, claim to be Christians, and even spend time and money in a lifestyle of Christlike service actually adhere to the basics of the Christianity they claim.

That's where we've been so far in *The Jesus Survey*.

Figure Int.1

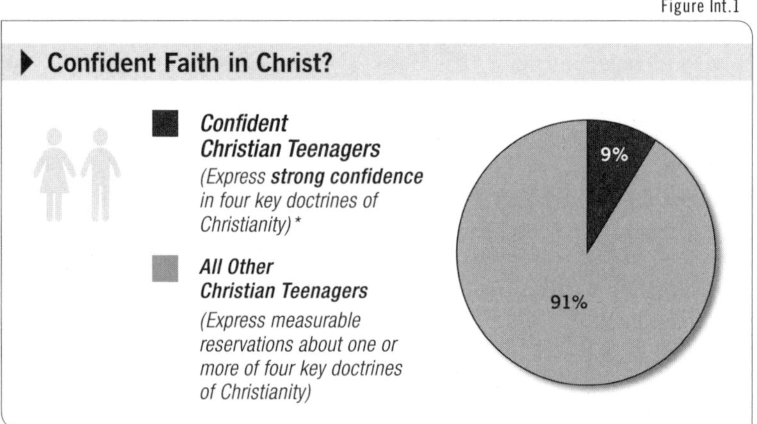

*The four key doctrines are: 1) the Bible is trustworthy, 2) Jesus is God, 3) Jesus died and rose again, 4) Jesus is the only way to heaven.

Where We're Going

As we move into the second portion of *The Jesus Survey*, the focus shifts just a bit. In part 1 we asked kids to tell us about who they believe Jesus is. Part 2 asks Christian kids to tell us what difference (if any) Jesus makes in their lives.

The real goal here, targeted in questions 21 through 29 of the survey, is to see if we can get a glimpse of how belief (as indicated in questions 6 through 20) impacts experience for Christian teenagers. As such, the next set of content questions explores topics such as the Holy Spirit's presence, Bible study, prayer, evangelism, and even attitudes about the second coming of Christ.

So, what difference does Jesus make for young people in our churches and Christian homes? Let's turn the page and find out.

Bonus Survey Results

Figure Int.2

By Denomination: Confident Faith in Christ?

	Confident Christian Teenagers *(Express strong confidence in four key doctrines of Christianity)**	***All Other Christian Teenagers*** *(Express measurable reservations about one or more of four key doctrines of Christianity)*
Non-Denominational	**36%**	**64%**
Other Denominations	**26%**	**74%**
Baptist	**17%**	**83%**
Presbyterian	**12%**	**88%**
Brethren in Christ	**5%**	**95%**
United Methodist	**5%**	**95%**
Undeclared	**3%**	**97%**
Catholic	**1%**	**99%**
Episcopal	**0%**	**100%**
Lutheran	**0%**	**100%**
United Church of Christ	**0%**	**100%**

* Express strong confidence in four key Christian doctrines: 1) the Bible is trustworthy, 2) Jesus is God, 3) Jesus died and rose again, 4) Jesus is the only way to heaven.

Part Two

WHAT DIFFERENCE DOES JESUS MAKE?

Anyone who belongs to Christ has become a new person.

—The apostle Paul, to Corinthian Christians[1]

6

THE HOLY SPIRIT AND CHRISTIAN TEENS

I will ask the Father, and he will give you another Helper.
John 14:16 NASB

If you happen to be in the US Patent and Trademark Office later today, go ahead and ask to see patent number 4,151,613. When the paperwork is presented, you'll see (no, I'm not making this up) formal plans for a Butt Protector.

Yep, some helpful genius out there has actually registered a patent for a "resilient, shock-absorbing plastic and foam" shielding device for your buttocks. Apparently this particular product is meant to help people prevent injuries while skateboarding. It probably works because wearing a hard plastic diaper in public is so embarrassing those people quit skateboarding pretty soon after first being seen wearing one of these contraptions.

If, perhaps, you're more the indoorsy, bookish type, take a peek at patent number 4,249,712: the Adjustable Headrest. This helpful, cantilevered boom device with an attached forehead cradle clamps right to your desk, relieving you of that pesky need for holding your head up while you look at words. A warning though: this one will likely leave a fat, red mark above your eyebrows if you use it too long.

Other helpful inventions you might want to consider are the Diaper Sensing Device that tells whether or not, you know, *something's* in your kid's pants (patent number 4,205,672); the Floating Shade invention to keep you sun-free (and date-free) at all times (patent number 5,076,029); and the Motorized Ice Cream Cone that eliminates the tiresome need for spinning a cone while you lick the chocolate off the top (patent number 5,971,829).[1] In fact, in the files of the US Patent and Trademark Office, you'll find millions of inventions designed to help humankind in innumerable ways.

What you won't find there is what every man, woman, and child on earth really needs: *the Helper*. That's because our eternal, everyday Helper comes only from God.

Before his execution and subsequent resurrection, Jesus made this pledge to his followers: "The Helper, the Holy Spirit, whom the Father will send in my name, he will teach you all things and bring to your remembrance all that I have said to you" (John 14:26 ESV).

This is the great promise of Christ for all Christians: his Holy Spirit will inhabit and empower each and every one of us every day, every moment, every atom of our lives (see also John 14:16; 15:26; 16:7–14; Rom. 8:11, 15–17; Gal. 5:22–23). This promise is an ironclad guarantee that our heavenly Helper will change us from the inside out, bringing new life and eternal hope to our physical, emotional, and spiritual beings. It's unbreakable assurance that the Holy Spirit will—in real, tangible ways that are both seen and unseen—transform us into the image of Jesus himself, both now and forever.

One theologian describes the Holy Spirit this way:

> He fills believers, empowering them for service (Acts 2:4, 4:31). He indwells believers, enabling godly living (Rom. 8:1–27). The Spirit produces the fruit of good character (Gal. 5:22–23). He assists us in our prayers to the Father (Rom. 8:26–27). The Spirit's permanent, indwelling presence makes the body of the believer a temple (1 Cor. 6:19), and he is a constant source of inner strength (1 John 4:1–6). The Spirit gives gifts which enable Christians to minister to others (Rom. 12:1, 1 Cor. 12). In brief, the Holy Spirit is the active agent in every Christian's life, the Person through whom the Godhead presently works out the divine will in this world.[2]

It's this kind of all-encompassing experience with the Holy Spirit that our teenagers need—that they often long for—and that, too many times, they just can't find.

For instance, in this weekend's newspaper I read a letter from a junior high girl to Dear Abby. She wrote,

> I have lost people close to me lately and made mistakes I wish I could take back. I love God and the fact that He gave me life, but I don't like myself. . . . I want to change who I am to who I really want to be. Do you have any tips on how to make myself the person I want to be?[3]

Sad to say, no advice columnist can effect the change this young woman craves. Not even an Adjustable Headrest or Motorized Ice Cream Cone, or anything else in the files at the US Patent and Trademark Office can help this girl find the life she desires. Only the one who can bring *new* life can do that—the Holy Spirit of Jesus.

Which begs the question: What about all those millions of Christian teenagers like this junior high girl? Are they finding the Helper they need—the one Christ promised them—to bring heavenly help and transformation into their daily existence? Or are they missing that power and presence in their lives? That's what questions 21 and 22 in *The Jesus Survey* were designed to find out.

The Holy Spirit: Active or Absent in Christian Teens' Lives?

In this portion of the content section of *The Jesus Survey*, I wanted to explore not just Christian teen beliefs about the Holy Spirit but also their *experience* with him. First, I wanted to know if kids were familiar with Christ's promise of his Holy Spirit; next, I wanted to find out if they knew of that promise firsthand.

Like all questions, I listed a one-sentence statement and then asked kids to indicate whether they agreed or disagreed with the statement. So in question 21 I asked kids to react to this statement regarding the *promise* of the Holy Spirit:

> The Holy Spirit of Jesus resides in every Christian today, leading and empowering that Christian to be more like God.

Next, in question 22 I asked teenagers to respond to this correlated statement regarding their *experience* of the Holy Spirit:

> I'm 100% certain that the Holy Spirit of Jesus is present and active in my life today—and I have proof that this is true.

As usual, the answers Christian teens gave in response to these two questions were varied and unique, as we'll soon see.

Question 21: "The Holy Spirit of Jesus Resides in Every Christian Today."

Generally speaking, survey respondents overwhelmingly affirm the belief that Jesus's Holy Spirit resides in every Christian, with more than 9 in 10 (91%) either somewhat or strongly agreeing to the statement in question 21. What's significant here is the number of Christian teenagers who, while agreeing in principle with the statement, also expressed reservations about the presence of the Holy Spirit in believers today.

Fully 1 out of 3 (34%) students were hesitant to assert confidently that God's Spirit resides in Christians today, choosing to "somewhat agree" with the statement of question 21 instead of strongly agreeing with it. This indicates that though they are giving God the benefit of the doubt on this issue, they also have some intellectual and/or emotional reservations about whether or not he truly is present and active in all Christians today. That they would choose this option in light of the premise of the question is a little disconcerting: after all, how does the Holy Spirit only "somewhat" reside in a Christian? Again, as in previous questions, it seems to demonstrate an emotional need to avoid articulating absolutes in terms of faith and belief.

Additionally, nearly 1 of 10 students (9%) do *not* believe, to some degree, that the Holy Spirit is active in the lives of all Christians. Yes, that still leaves a solid majority

(57%) who are fully committed to the truth of Christ's promised Holy Spirit—and that's definitely good news—but it also shows that nearly half (43%) of kids in our youth groups and Christian homes are measurably uncertain of God's transforming presence in their lives today.

Figure 6.1

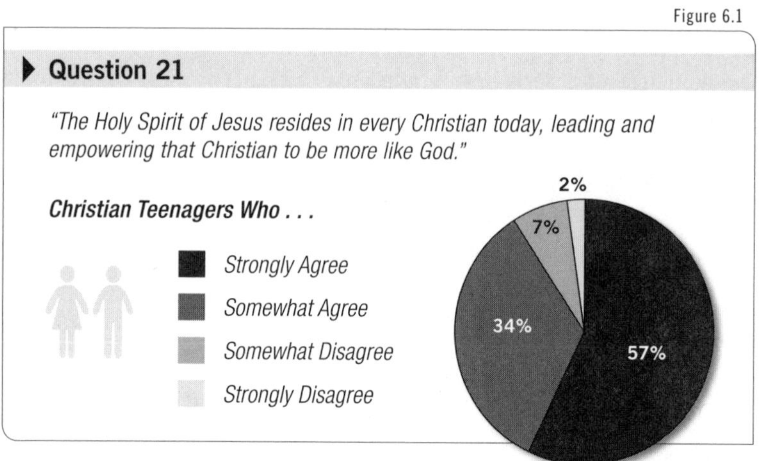

Among the genders, it appears that young women conform to expectations of the status quo that says girls are more spiritually attuned than guys, with 3 out of 5 teen girls (61%) expressing strong faith that the Holy Spirit is present and active in the lives of Christians today. That's nearly double digits (9%) higher than Christian guys who affirm the same belief (52%). When you factor in those who "somewhat" agree, the genders draw closer together, with 93% of girls expressing some measure of faith in the Holy Spirit and 89% of guys doing the same. Still, across the board, girls seem to affirm this belief more consistently than the guys who share their youth group experiences. This finding is in line with what Lisa Pearce and Melinda Denton uncovered through their research in the National Study of Youth and Religion. They report, "Across ages, races, and a wide range of religious traditions, female adolescents report higher levels of religious engagement than males." Pearce and Denton also found that the opposite is true: adolescent males, by a 3 to 2 margin, make up the majority of unbelieving or skeptical teens.[4]

I'm not sure of the reason for these findings. If I say that the female gender, as a whole, appears more receptive to matters of faith, that may seem to be simply stating the obvious, or it may be interpreted as blatant gender bias on my part. And the truth is, I don't ascribe to the belief that God is more successful at drawing women to him than men. But, in this situation at least, it seems clear that young women in our churches are more open to a belief in the Holy Spirit's modern ministry than guys are.

Figure 6.2

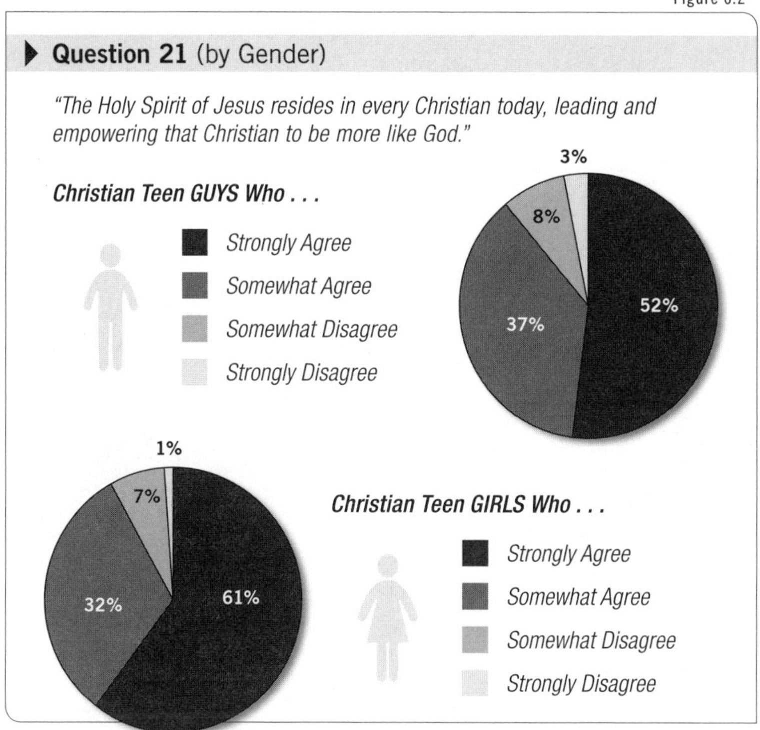

One surprising result in this portion of the survey was the way belief in the Holy Spirit broke down by age. By significant margins, students in middle school demonstrated the greatest hesitation to affirm belief in this promise of Christ. Junior highers were the only age group with fewer than half willing to strongly affirm a belief that the Holy Spirit is present and active in believers' lives today. Only 39% of kids this age chose that response; meanwhile, nearly half (44%) expressed reserved agreement, and about 1 in 6 (17%) actually disavowed this belief.

It is possible that, as the youngest students in *The Jesus Survey*, these Christian kids are operating under limited knowledge and/or understanding in regard to the promise of the Holy Spirit. It's also possible that they simply don't believe that promise as fully as their older brothers and sisters do. Either way, there is cause for concern, and an opportunity for Christian parents and church leaders to do a better job of educating our younger believers on the wonderful presence and power that God has promised to each and every one of them.

Teenagers in grades 9 and 10 appear to be most confident in the Holy Spirit's role in the lives of Christians today, with 3 out of 5 (60%) strongly affirming belief, and more than 9 out of 10 students (94%) giving at least measured support of the same. As they move into the upper grades of high school, that faith in the ministry of the Holy Spirit erodes a bit, dropping to 58% who strongly affirm and 90% who at least somewhat affirm, but those numbers are still well above those of the junior high respondents.

Figure 6.3

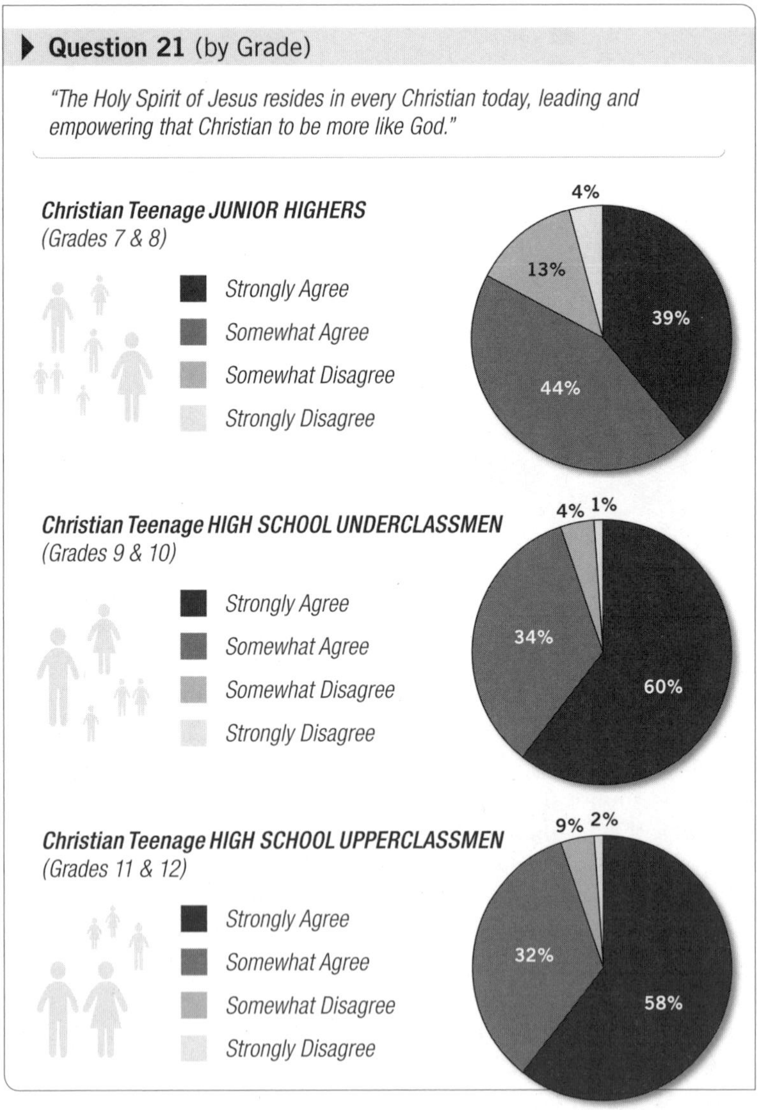

Question 21 (by Grade)

"The Holy Spirit of Jesus resides in every Christian today, leading and empowering that Christian to be more like God."

Christian Teenage JUNIOR HIGHERS
(Grades 7 & 8)

- *Strongly Agree*
- *Somewhat Agree*
- *Somewhat Disagree*
- *Strongly Disagree*

39%
44%
13%
4%

Christian Teenage HIGH SCHOOL UNDERCLASSMEN
(Grades 9 & 10)

- *Strongly Agree*
- *Somewhat Agree*
- *Somewhat Disagree*
- *Strongly Disagree*

60%
34%
4%
1%

Christian Teenage HIGH SCHOOL UPPERCLASSMEN
(Grades 11 & 12)

- *Strongly Agree*
- *Somewhat Agree*
- *Somewhat Disagree*
- *Strongly Disagree*

58%
32%
9%
2%

Question 22: "The Holy Spirit of Jesus Is Present and Active in My Life Today."

Having established their general beliefs about the Holy Spirit, and having gotten these teenagers thinking about the Holy Spirit's work in a Christian's life, I wanted to use the next question on *The Jesus Survey* to take kids out of general, theoretical thinking and toward individual, personal experience. After all, as Professor Kenda Creasy Dean points out, "*Until we have experienced God's engulfing presence with us*—the relationship between faith and other aspects of our lives will seem opaque and meaningless."[5] So, in question 22 I asked each student to report whether or not the Holy Spirit was present and active in his or her personal life.

Figure 6.4

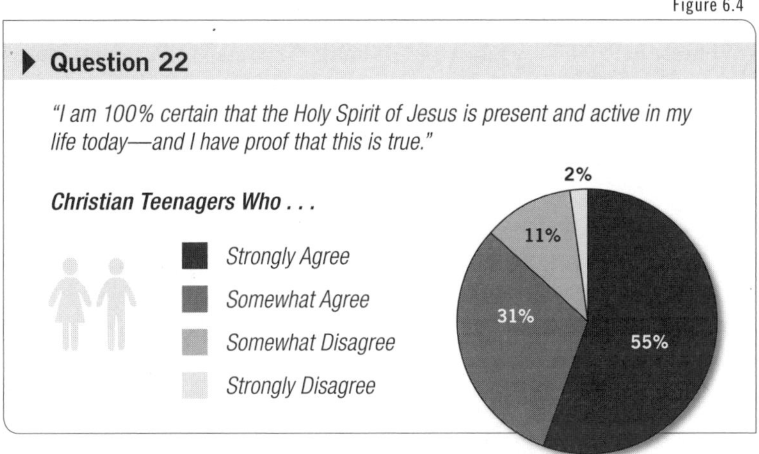

You'll notice that in question 22, I used a few not-so-subtle prompts like "100% certain" and "I have proof" to try to help teens clarify their answers. I wanted to remove the temptation toward default middle ground here as much as possible, and was trying to prod respondents toward a clear yes or no response that could easily be answered with either a "strongly agree" or "strongly disagree." Of course, teenagers don't really care what a researcher is trying to do, and a good number of them happily camped out in the middle ground of "somewhat agree" or "somewhat disagree" anyway. Again, I don't know how a person can be "somewhat 100% certain" and "somewhat have proof that this is true," but that's beside the point. What's relevant is that many of our Christian teenagers report that they *are* uncertain about the Holy Spirit's activity in their lives.

Here's how the numbers added up: just over half (55%) of Christian teenagers said that they were 100% certain of the Holy Spirit's presence and activity in their lives, and that they could back it up with "proof." These were the kids who marked that they "strongly agree" with question 22. At the same time, more than 2 out of 5 Christian students (42%) expressed some measure of reservation about whether or not the Holy Spirit was noticeably active in their lives, marking either "somewhat agree" or "somewhat disagree" to this question. And the number of youth group teens who either somewhat or strongly deny that the Holy Spirit is active in their lives is surprisingly significant: 1 of 8 (13%) Christian teenagers feel this way.

Among guys and girls who do not experience the Holy Spirit, the numbers are disappointing, but fairly equal. For both genders, roughly 1 out of 10 (12% of guys and 11% of girls) fits this category. But for those who express full assurance of the Holy Spirit's active presence in their lives, something of a gender gap appears.

Fully 3 out of 5 Christian young women (60%) "strongly agree" they are 100% certain of the Holy Spirit's presence and activity in their lives—and have proof they can point to in that regard. Among young Christian men, that number drops a full 10 points to barely half (50%) who can speak with the same kind of confidence about their personal experience with the ongoing ministry of the Holy Spirit. Likewise, nearly half (48%) of Christian teen guys express some doubt about the Holy Spirit in their lives, while that number is just over 1 in 3 (38%) for Christian girls.

Figure 6.5

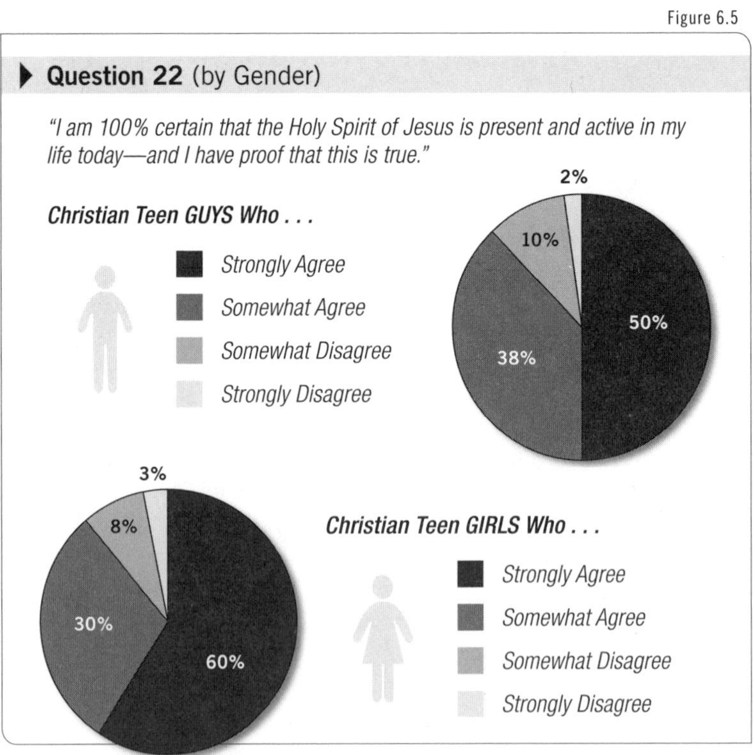

Again, I have no explanation for this gender gap of experience with God's transforming promise. I resist the idea that women are somehow inherently more attuned to God, or that God shows preference for one gender over another in this respect. Yet, clearly, in this instance at least, young women are having more consistently recognizable experiences with Christ's promised Holy Spirit.

Figure 6.6

Question 22 (by Grade)

"I am 100% certain that the Holy Spirit of Jesus is present and active in my life today—and I have proof that this is true."

Christian Teenage JUNIOR HIGHERS
(Grades 7 & 8)

Response	%
Strongly Agree	55%
Somewhat Agree	36%
Somewhat Disagree	6%
Strongly Disagree	2%

Christian Teenage HIGH SCHOOL UNDERCLASSMEN
(Grades 9 & 10)

Response	%
Strongly Agree	55%
Somewhat Agree	36%
Somewhat Disagree	6%
Strongly Disagree	2%

Christian Teenage HIGH SCHOOL UPPERCLASSMEN
(Grades 11 & 12)

Response	%
Strongly Agree	55%
Somewhat Agree	31%
Somewhat Disagree	11%
Strongly Disagree	2%

Interestingly, when asked about their personal experience with the Holy Spirit in question 22, Christian junior highers (grades 7 and 8) reversed the disbelief they indicated in question 21. Even though they expressed the most skepticism of all students about the presence and power of the Holy Spirit in the generic Christian's life, equal numbers of them strongly agreed with the assertion that they, personally, were 100% certain of God's activity in their own lives. In fact, 55% of all three grade groupings (junior highers, high school underclassmen, and high school upperclassmen) made that claim. High school upperclassmen, though, were most likely to report an absence of the Holy Spirit in their lives, with 13% (about 1 in 8) indicating that was the case.

When I brought up this topic with youth leaders in follow-up interviews, one gentleman from Virginia counseled patience and prayer in response. "Until you have a little age and maturity," he said, "it is difficult to see the subtle but nonetheless miraculous ways God works in our lives." Perhaps that's good advice for those of us who are Christian parents or church leaders—but at the same time, it appears that as kids get older, those who are unsure of Christ's daily presence drift away from greater experience with the Holy Spirit rather than toward it. Food for thought for all of us.

The "Confident Christian" Connection

At this point, I wanted to begin cross-correlating some of the questions to see if there were any relationships between belief and experience regarding the promise of Christ's Holy Spirit.

First, I looked at the numbers from the perspective of those teens who (a) believe the Holy Spirit resides in every Christian today and (b) subsequently demonstrate incontrovertible evidence of personal experience with the Holy Spirit. I suspected those teens who said they believed in the promise of Christ's Holy Spirit would also show up in significant numbers as the ones most likely to experience the Holy Spirit's presence and power in everyday life. But once again, I was wrong.

It is true that more than half (57%) of those who said they believed the promise in question 21 also "strongly agree" to the assertion that Christ's Holy Spirit was active in their lives. However, that number is not a significant break from the overall population (see fig. 6.4) and doesn't show a differentiating statistical relationship. What's more, nearly 3 of 10 students who *don't* believe the Holy Spirit resides in every Christian still said they had personally experienced the Holy Spirit's active presence in their lives. In many ways that's good news, because it shows that God is working even in the lives of those who are unsure he's available to work! But it also raised more questions for me, so I went one step further in exploring the data.

Next, I isolated the students I call "Confident Christian" teenagers; that is, those students identified in the intermission of this book. These are the kids who adhere strongly to four core beliefs about Christ: 1) the Bible is trustworthy in what it says about Jesus, 2) Jesus is God, 3) Jesus died and rose again, and 4) Jesus is the only way to heaven.

Figure 6.7

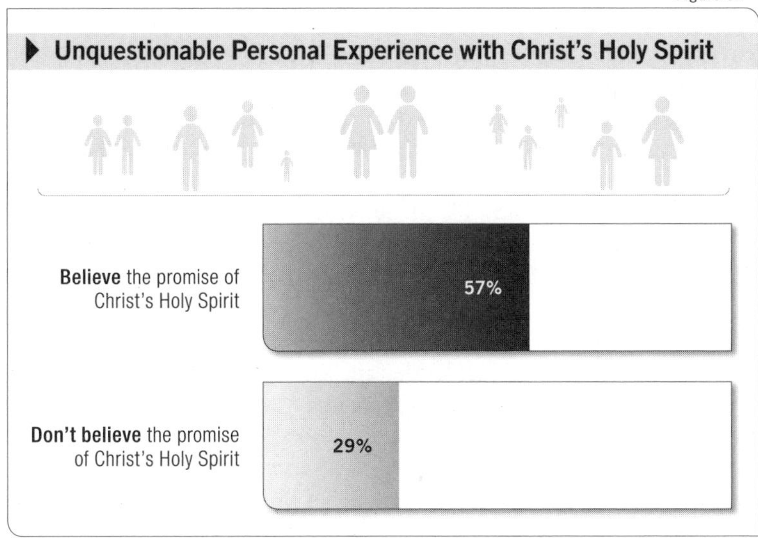

Figure 6.8

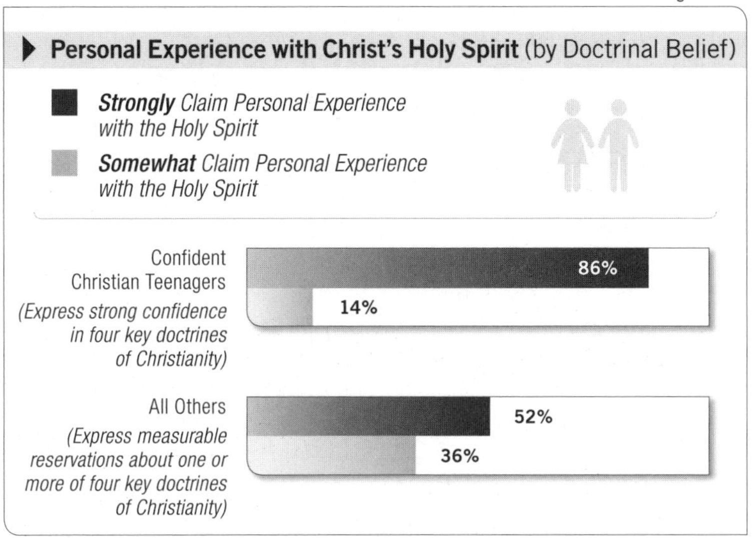

The differences here were staggering.

Among students who did not hold all four of these core Christian beliefs, personal experience with the Holy Spirit was nearly the same as the general survey population, though slightly lower at 52%. However, among the Confident Christian teenagers who expressed full faith in those four core beliefs, nearly 9 out of 10 (86%) strongly asserted they were certain of the Holy Spirit's active presence in their lives—and indicated they could prove that claim (see fig. 6.8).

Additionally, the remaining 14% of this Confident Christian group "somewhat agree" to the claim of Holy Spirit activity, meaning *not a single person* in the Confident Christian category denied personal experience with Christ's Holy Spirit. In contrast, about 1 in 9 (12%) of all other students indicated that the Holy Spirit was *not* present and active in their personal lives.

In a survey of this size, any time an identifiable subgroup within the sample shows 100% agreement on any issue, that's noteworthy. When 100% of these Confident Christian teenagers report that they've personally experienced Christ's Holy Spirit at work in their lives, and when 86% of that 100% strongly make this claim, that seems to indicate something important—and it flies in the face of modern experience as indicated by other research studies.

The Barna Research Group reports that, as part of a larger trend in 2010, belief in the Holy Spirit has waned to near mythological status. "A growing majority," Barna says, "believe the Holy Spirit is a *symbol* of God's presence or power, but not a living entity."[6] For Confident Christian teens, however, the Spirit of Jesus is not simply a symbol of power, but is indeed a living entity of God's power in their lives—and they claim to have experienced that Spirit in personal, undeniable ways. This experience is clearly correlated to these teenagers' depth of belief about core Christian truths. If you'll allow me a moment to make an understatement: *that's significant*.

Interestingly enough, this seems to be a one-way correlation. While *all* students who adhere to the four core beliefs also report undeniable personal experience with God's Holy Spirit (see fig. 6.9), not all who report personal experience with God's Holy Spirit adhere to the four core beliefs (see fig. 6.10). In fact, just a minority do. Only about 1 in 7 (15%) of those who strongly affirm the Holy Spirit's activity in their lives also strongly believe all four core Christian doctrines held by the Confident Christian teenagers.

Clearly, in this regard Christ's Holy Spirit is not limited by wavering belief—or even lack of belief—in the hearts and minds of our Christian teens. God does what he wants, when he wants, and with whomever he wants. Still, judging by youth responses in *The Jesus Survey*, the Holy Spirit is also clearly—or at least noticeably—more active in lives of teens who hold to the four core doctrines of Confident Christian teenagers than in the lives of other Christian teenagers.

This is noteworthy, and deserves attention from Christian parents and church leaders. The data here suggests that *right belief translates into real experience*. If we want our teenagers to have authentic, ongoing relationships with God, we would do well to help them also experience authentic, ongoing growth in matters of Christian doctrine.

Figure 6.9

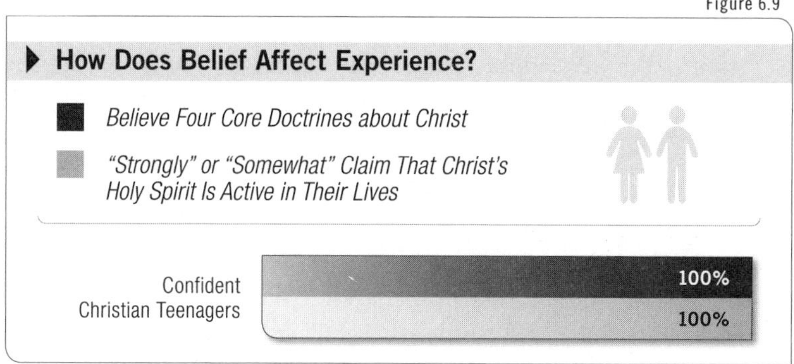

Figure 6.10

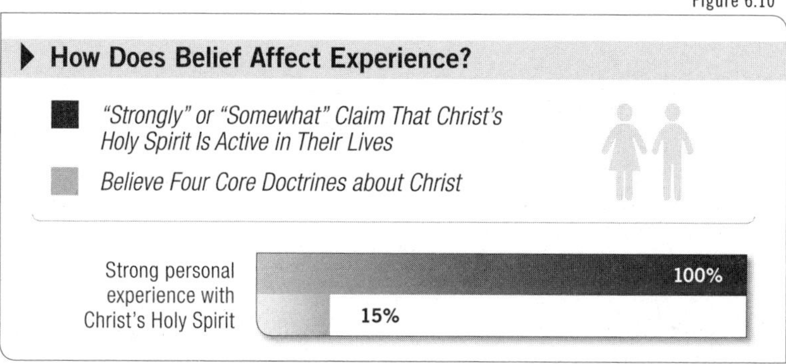

Summary

• Though they generally agree that Jesus's Holy Spirit is for all Christians, a significant number of Christian teenagers express measurable reservations about that promise. A majority (57%) strongly approve this belief, but the rest (43%) indicate that they only "somewhat agree" or actually disagree. Teen girls are most likely (61%) to affirm this promise of Christ, and surprisingly, middle school students are least likely to affirm it. In fact, jnior highers were the only group with fewer than half (39%) willing to strongly affirm a belief that the Holy Spirit is present and active in believers' lives today.

• *Similarly, just over half (55%) of Christian teenagers strongly indicated that they were 100% certain of the Holy Spirit's presence and activity in their personal lives*. Conversely, a surprisingly significant number of youth group teens (13%) report that the Holy Spirit is *not* active in their lives.

• *There's a gender gap among Christian teens when it comes to personal experience with the Holy Spirit.* Among young women, 3 out of 5 (60%) "strongly agree" they are certain of the Holy Spirit's presence and activity in their lives. Among young men, that number drops a full 10 points to barely 50%. The reasons for this type of gap among Christian teenagers remain unclear.

• *Right belief translates into real experience.* Fully 100%—the *entire* subgroup—of Confident Christian teenagers who adhere to four core Christian doctrines about Christ report that they also have personally experienced the Holy Spirit's presence and power. What's more, the overwhelming majority of that group (86%) strongly assert that they have proof of the Holy Spirit's ministry in their lives. Among all other Christian teens, only 52% strongly make that claim—an enormous statistical difference of more than 30 percentage points. This seems to indicate that if we truly want our teenagers to experience God, we would be wise to also teach them true doctrine about God, both at home and at church.

Bonus Survey Results

Figure 6.11

By Bible Belief:
Christian Teens Who Strongly Claim the Holy Spirit Is Active in Their Lives

Unshakeables *(Believe the Bible is trustworthy)*	**82%**
Uncertains *(Are unsure the Bible is trustworthy)*	**49%**
Unsettleds *(Are conflicted / confused about the Bible's trustworthiness)*	**45%**
Unbelieving *(Believe the Bible is not trustworthy)*	**22%**

Figure 6.12

Comparison: Confident Christian Teens and Denominational Groups

	Believe the Holy Spirit Is Active in All Christians	*Strongly Claim the Holy Spirit Is Active in Their Lives*
Confident Christian Teenagers	94%	86%
Non-Denominational	77%	70%
Other Denominations	71%	69%
Brethren in Christ	73%	68%
Baptist	58%	66%
Lutheran	52%	62%
Undeclared	39%	60%
Presbyterian	54%	57%
United Methodist	59%	56%
Catholic	51%	46%
Episcopal	44%	44%
United Church of Christ	49%	34%

7

BIBLE STUDY AND CHRISTIAN TEENS

Your word I have treasured in my heart.
Psalm 119:11 NASB

Pastor Chuck Swindoll tells the story of a student—let's call him Mike—encountering problems in a Bible class.

"I'm having some struggles with Genesis," Mike told his teacher.

The teacher was sympathetic—and also well-educated on the Old Testament. So he helpfully began to explain, as best he could, a few theological and academic insights behind the book of Genesis, digging into the question of authorship and even touching on scholarship like the Wellhausen theory and higher criticism of the text. It was fascinating stuff, well-researched and grounded.

When he finished, Mike nodded thoughtfully and said, "Well, I appreciate that." Then he sheepishly explained the real problem to his teacher:

"I'm having trouble *finding* Genesis."[1]

Unfortunately, conventional wisdom suggests that many today, including our teenagers, are like poor ol' Mikey. They're so unfamiliar with the Word of God that they don't even know where to start—let alone study it, embrace it, and grow in it. And while we may chuckle at Mike's ineptitude with Scripture, recent studies like the September 2010 "U.S. Religious Knowledge Survey" reveal that he is clearly not alone. Most Americans simply don't know basic content from the Bible. Or, as Boston University professor Steve Prothero is quoted as saying in that study, "Americans are both deeply religious and profoundly ignorant about religion."[2]

Meanwhile, the Bible continues to be a source of transformation and hope and power and security and truth and joy and lofty vision and real-world guidance and more. Theologian Henry Thiessen eloquently describes the gift of God's Word this way:

> The Bible . . . has produced the highest results in all walks of life. It has led to the highest type of creations in the fields of art, architecture, literature, and music. Think of the great paintings of Raphael, Michelangelo, Leonardo da Vinci, and the Dutch masters; envision the great cathedrals and sanctuaries of Europe and America; remind yourself of the great Christian writings of the early fathers, of the Protestant reformers, of the British, continental, and American poets and men of letters; recall the great hymns, anthems, cantatas, and oratorios of the church; examine the fundamental laws of the so-called civilized countries; observe the great social reforms that have been made, as the freeing of the slaves and the recognition of the rights of woman; to say nothing of the regenerating effect on millions of individual lives, and you will find everywhere the higher influence of the Bible. Where is there a book in all the world that even remotely compares with it in its beneficent influence upon mankind?[3]

St. Augustine of Hippo, who lived during the fourth century AD, is testament to what Thiessen proclaims. At the age of thirty-one, Augustine had achieved remarkable success in both his career and in academia. One of the finest philosophical minds of his time, he'd been appointed as Public Teacher of Rhetoric in Milan, Italy. Yet in spite of his prestigious career, his dalliances with willing mistresses, and his complete freedom to live and do whatever he saw fit, Augustine found himself miserable and desperate for something more, something real.

In a state of despair one day, he went to a garden nearby and bitterly prayed to God. I'll let him tell you what happened next:

> I heard from a neighboring house a voice, as of a boy or girl, I know not which—chanting repeatedly, "Take up and read. Take up and read." My facial expression changed instantly, and I began to think more earnestly whether children were in the habit of playing any kind of game with such words. I could not remember ever having heard anything like it. So checking the torrent of my tears, I got up, interpreting it to be nothing other than a command from God to open the Book and to read the first chapter I should find. . . . I grabbed it [the Bible], opened it, and in silence read the paragraph on which my eyes first fell: Not in reveling and drunkenness, not in debauchery and licentiousness, not in strife and envying, but put on the Lord Jesus Christ, and make no provision for the flesh to gratify its desires. I read no further, nor did I need to. For instantly, at the end of this sentence, by a light, as it were, of serenity infused into my heart, all the darkness of doubt vanished away . . . You converted me to Yourself, so that I sought neither wife nor any other hope of this world.[4]

The experience of St. Augustine has repeated itself, with different circumstances, millions upon millions of times throughout history—and it continues even today.

Consider Jean: by age eleven, she'd already become addicted to cigarettes. At thirteen, she was on her way to becoming an alcoholic. At her high school one day she received a free copy of the New Testament from a volunteer with the Gideons. Her first impulse was to simply throw it away, but for some reason she stuck it in with the rest of her books and took it home, where she promptly forgot about it.

Months later, Jean found the free Bible she'd received and, curious, began reading about the life of Jesus. She became so intrigued about what she was reading, she asked a friend at school to tell her more about Christ. That led Jean to meet Jesus personally—and to become a Christian. [5]

Or consider Walter: after a life spent in empty personal pursuits, a painful and selfish divorce, and disappointment with Christianity and other spiritual quests, he was ready to give up. He decided to chuck it all and go on a sailing trip through the Hawaiian islands with two buddies, taking along with him several books on religion and philosophy. "As we sailed," Walter says, "I pored over books on Hinduism, Buddhism, ancient Egyptian religions, and Eastern and Western philosophies."

At the bottom of his pile of books, he was surprised to find a little New Testament he'd somehow managed to keep around for years.

"I began to read about Jesus Christ," Walter reports.

> He didn't just talk peace and love and joy like the rest. Here was a man Who loved those who hated Him, forgave those who abused Him and died that I might have life. I said, "Lord, if You will come and take over this mess, I will follow You anywhere"—and He did. The emptiness that I felt inside suddenly felt full and complete. The life that had been falling apart began to come back together.[6]

Or consider Sherry, who discovered a Gideon Bible when she reached for a phone book in a hotel . . . and ended up reading it until she met Jesus. Or Russell, an elementary student who found a relationship with God by reading a "youth testament" version of the Scriptures—just a few months before he was killed in a tragic traffic accident. [7] Or . . . well, you get the idea. And maybe you don't need me to tell you what you already know about the Bible anyway. Maybe, like me, you have your own personal stories, your own private experiences of meeting God in the pages of his Word. I sincerely hope you do.

Still, the point of all this talk is this: *The word of God is alive and powerful. It is sharper than the sharpest two-edged sword, cutting between soul and spirit, between joint and marrow. It exposes our innermost thoughts and desires.*[8]

Our teenagers have at their disposal this same, timeless, life-changing Scripture to help them through life, to guide them toward truth, and—most importantly—to connect them with Jesus himself. The question, then, is whether or not Christian teenagers are turning to this incredible treasure on a regular basis, gleaning from it at least some of what it has to offer. That's what I wanted to find out, so in the next section of *The Jesus Survey*, I asked them.

Teens and Bible Study: Hit or Miss?

In this portion of *The Jesus Survey*, I wanted to explore the values and actions of Christian teenagers in regard to Bible study. Specifically, I first wanted to know if kids thought that daily Bible study was indeed important for Christians; next, I wanted to find out if they studied the Bible daily.

As I have done for all questions, I listed a one-sentence statement and then asked students to indicate whether they agreed or disagreed with the statement. So, in question 23 I asked kids to react to this "values" statement:

> Followers of Jesus should study the Bible daily.

Next, for question 24 I asked teenagers to respond to this correlated statement regarding their personal *actions* regarding the value of daily Bible study:

> I study the Bible daily.

When creating these two questions, I juggled the idea of whether or not to include the word "daily" as a clarifier here. After all, I would assume that the more general term "regularly" would be similarly insightful, or even that the phrase "at least once a week" would have been revealing. Realistically, though, a student who is exposed to Scripture at church once or twice a week could easily, and truthfully, say that he or she studies the Bible "regularly" or "at least once a week" without ever engaging the Bible one-on-one. And what I really wanted to know was whether or not Christian teenagers had *daily* personal experience with the Bible outside of their church experiences. So, in the end, I opted to stick with the limiting word "daily" in this section.

I know some of you who are reading this book will probably disagree with that choice—and to be honest, it also had implications in the way teens answered these two questions—but there are a few privileges with being the guy who writes the survey. This was one of them, and I took it, so let the chips fall where they may. However, I think the issue of Bible study frequency among Christian teens is definitely worth further, more detailed research. I encourage some of you out there in the real world to pursue that with studies of your own.

Meanwhile, how did our students respond to these two questions on *The Jesus Survey*? Let's find out.

Question 23: "Followers of Christ Should Study the Bible Daily."

After their landmark research in the National Study of Youth and Religion (NSYR), one of the key findings that Christian Smith and Melinda Denton articulated was the relationship of teen faith with the traditional practices of Christian faithfulness. According to Smith and Denton, Christian parents and church leaders should be working hard to help young people practice faith skills like reading the Bible and prayer "in the direction of excellence in faith, analogous to musicians and athletes practicing their skills." Why is that so important? Well, as Smith and Denton report,

"Even basic practices like regular Bible reading and personal prayer seem clearly associated with stronger and deeper faith commitment among youth."[9]

My personal opinion is that these researchers are both a little bit right and a little bit wrong in their assessment on this issue. It does seem apparent that basic faith practices like Bible study and prayer are associated with what we would term a deeper, more grounded faith. Smith and Denton's conclusion, however, appears to be that this happens because kids are first taught to read the Bible and pray, and then *voila*! Strong faith results.

Figure 7.1

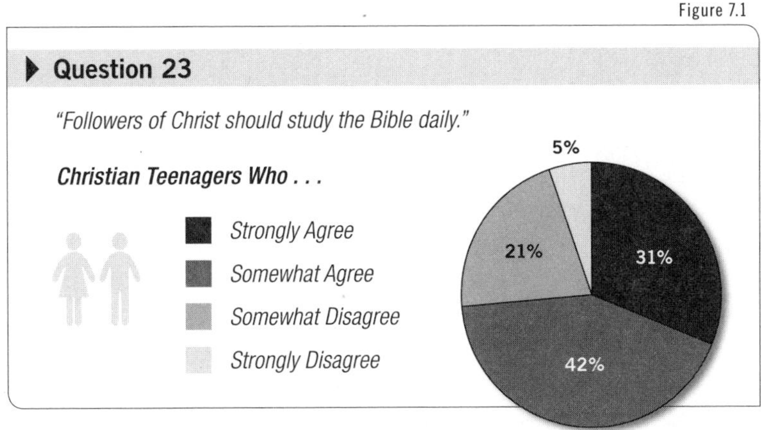

My experience with teens in this regard has been the opposite. I've found that when teens are taught first to outwardly *practice* faith, then that faith expressed—in Bible reading, prayer, or whatever—tends toward a dry, debilitating experience that often falls dangerously close to the territory of legalism. However, when kids are taught first to inwardly *value* faith practice (such as Bible study), then that Bible study and prayer become much more natural expressions of that value and yield refreshing, life-giving spiritual growth—and that's why it then becomes associated with stronger faith in teens.

Yes, I realize that my perspective on this issue could be seen as an exercise in hairsplitting or a "which came first, the chicken or the egg" conundrum, but I need you to understand my viewpoint here because it influenced the way this next portion of *The Jesus Survey* was conducted. In order to get some kind of measure of teens' experience with Scripture, my first inclination was to ask a question that would help determine whether or not our youth group kids inwardly *value* something as basic as daily interaction with the Bible. After all, if Bible study is not important to Christian teens, that's significant.

As with other questions on *The Jesus Survey*, the responses teens gave were mixed. Among all survey respondents, nearly 3 out of 4 (73%) indicated at least somewhat that daily Bible study is an important part of any Christian's life. What was a little unexpected was the number of teenagers who gave only reserved agreement to that faith principle. In fact, just under 1 out of 3 students (31%) was willing to "strongly agree" that followers of Christ should study the Bible daily. Meanwhile, nearly the same number of Christian students (26%) actually rejected the assertion that Christians hold any obligation to study God's Word daily.

Now, to be fair, the inclusion of the word "daily" in this question likely influenced the way students responded. If I'd used an indistinct term like "regularly," I would guess that more kids would have agreed with the statement. But, again, I wasn't interested in assessing vague feelings from kids on this issue; I wanted to know if Christian students involved in Christian churches thought that daily Bible study was important in their spiritual lives. And I got my answer: about 1 in 3 thinks so. For the rest, Bible study is not a daily necessity. No, I wasn't happy with those results, but I appreciated kids' honesty in sharing this information with me.

As might be expected, belief in the trustworthiness of Scripture has enormous impact on whether or not our students place value on studying the Bible each day.

Figure 7.2

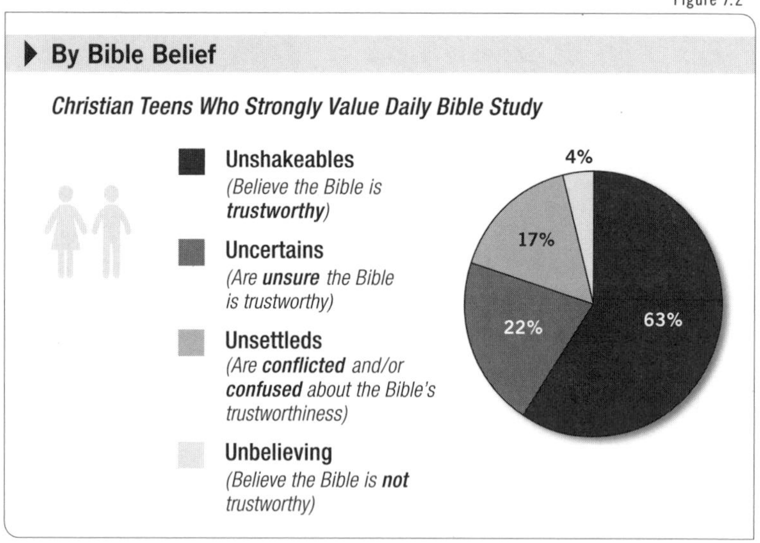

Among our Unshakeable teens (those who believe the Bible is completely trustworthy), nearly 2 out of 3 (63%) "strongly agree" with the basic belief that "Followers of Christ should study the Bible daily." Not even 1 out of 4 of the rest of our youth group kids indicated unreserved belief like that. Among Uncertain students (those who are unsure of the Bible), only 22% express high value in daily Bible study; that number dropped to merely 17% among Unsettled kids (those who are confused or conflicted about the reliability of the Bible). Barely 4%—that is, 1 in 25—of

Unbelieving Christian students (those who think the Bible is *not* trustworthy) are willing to affirm that daily Bible study has strong value for Christians.

The main reason for this seems to be obvious: if the Bible is untrustworthy, it is also irrelevant. So why bother to study it every day?

In the follow-up interviews, one Unbelieving girl from Virginia, an 11th grade Episcopalian, explained that perspective this way:

> The culture and time period when the Bible was written was so different from ours today, in respect to technology and society. This fact makes it hard to compare the situations in the Bible to current everyday life.

An Unshakeable young man from a non-denominational church in Pennsylvania echoed this girl's insight. "Most people find the Bible boring," he said, "or that it doesn't relate to them."

The failure of Christian leaders to demonstrate the authentic relevance of Scripture in their own lives may also play a part in this devaluing of daily Bible study among teens. One youth worker from a United Methodist Church in Alabama mentioned this in a follow-up interview. Echoing sentiments of other leaders, she said:

> There is so much in the news every week about a pastor caught embezzling, cheating on his or her spouse, or making inappropriate statements guised as a message from God, that teenagers have lost trust in religious leaders. That loss of trust . . . gives them the sense that the Bible must not be much of anything.

Kenda Creasy Dean, commenting on Anna Carter Florence's work on the topic, brings this into sharper focus:

> The issue is not whether young people can read the Bible (they can). The real issue is . . . well, really, why would they want to? What have they seen in the church that would suggest that the Bible is a source of power and wonder? When have they seen their parents derive life and joy from reading Scripture? "We have been duped into thinking that the issue is Bible drills instead of instilling a love of reading the Bible," Florence claims. "We have been scared into sharing information about the text instead of our passion for it."[10]

Interestingly, as a whole adult leaders overestimated—sometimes by double digits—how much value their teenagers placed on daily Bible study. When asked to predict how kids in their youth groups would answer question 23, a significant number were wrong.

Whereas only 73% of students noted that they strongly or even somewhat valued daily Bible study, their leaders anticipated near unanimity on that issue, predicting more than 4 out of 5 kids (83%) would respond that way. Additionally, leaders predicted that 2 out of 5 Christian teens (40%) would strongly value daily Bible study, yet less than 1 out of 3 (31%) responded that way. Also, about 1 of 4 kids (26%) actually rejected the value of daily Bible study, while adults predicted that number would be closer to only 1 in 6 (17%).

Figure 7.3

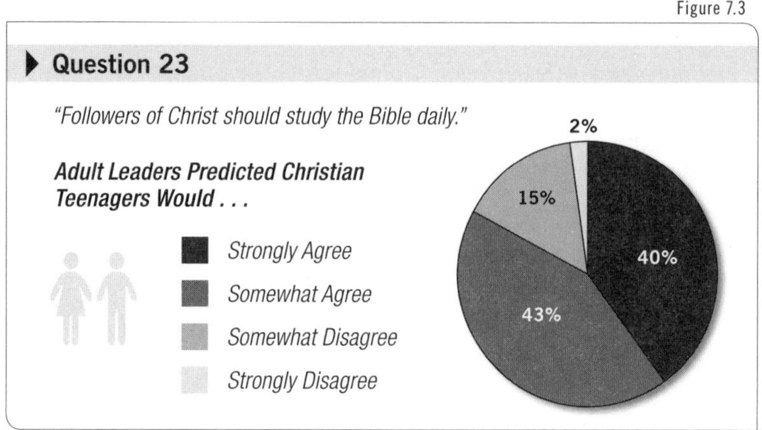

Question 24: "I Study the Bible Daily."

Having established, at least in general, what intellectual value Christian teenagers placed on the issue of daily Bible study, I felt it was time to see how that value translated into kids' real lives. About 1 out of 3 (31%) placed high value on Bible reading, and nearly 3 out of 4 (73%) placed at least some value on it. So how many were actually living out that value? That was what question 24 set out to discover.

Before I dive into the results on this question, I think it's important to note, again, that my decision to use the word "daily" in this question appeared to affect a number of students' responses. This showed up primarily in the "somewhat" answers. For instance, one young woman, a 12th grader from South Carolina, marked "somewhat agree" to question 24, and then noted beside her answer, "It's not like I don't agree, I just don't always have the discipline to do it." Another student, an 11th grade girl from New Jersey, also marked "somewhat agree" here and then wrote, "I try!" next to her answer. And one young man in 12th grade, from New York, agreed that Christians should study the Bible daily (question 23), but then opted to skip question 24 entirely, saying, "I think that it is not possible to answer yes or no to questions such as 24."

While I disagree with that New Yorker's excuse for avoiding an answer to a straightforward question, I understand why it made him uncomfortable. No one likes to be confronted about possible hypocrisy so soon after being asked to affirm what is supposed to be one of your core values. That said, after looking at the responses and the comments, and discussing them with a few trusted colleagues, my impressions led to the following interpretations of the question 24 results.

Students who actually *do* read the Bible just about every day most likely marked "strongly agree" in response to this question. Those like the young woman from South Carolina who *want* to study the Bible every day but don't always live up to that personal expectation most likely marked "somewhat agree" here. Those for whom Bible study is more the exception than the rule likely marked "somewhat disagree." And those who simply don't study the Bible—and aren't afraid to admit it—marked "strongly disagree."

Figure 7.4

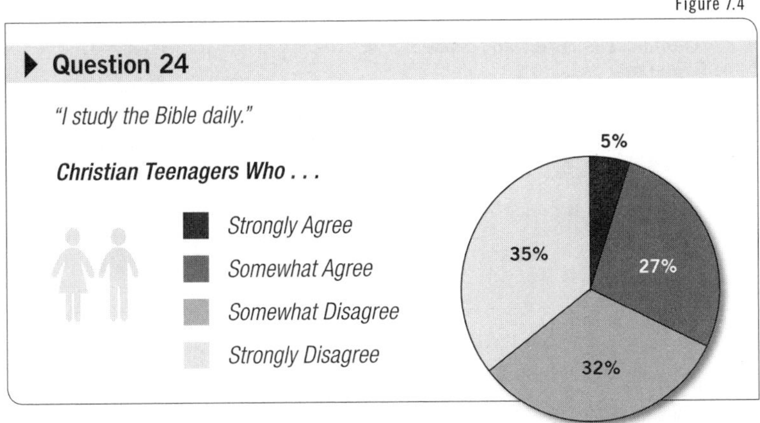

Now, I realize there is an obvious element of subjectivity to the interpretations above, so feel free to ignore my biased assumptions in this regard and assign your own significance as you see fit. But, for the sake of discussion here, it's best that you understand I'll be commenting with these interpretative biases in mind.

Back in 1991, it was reported that 8% of Christian teenagers said they read their Bibles every day.[11] Some twenty years later, we've effectively cut that number almost in half. According to respondents in *The Jesus Survey*, barely 5%—about 1 in 20—study their Bibles on a daily basis. In 1991 more than 1 in 3 (35%) of Christian teenagers indicated they had good intentions in this regard, opening their Bibles "a few times a week or less."[12] Today, barely 1 in 4 (27%) says the same. Meanwhile, more than 2 out of 3 (67%) teens today report that they seldom, or never, study Scripture as a part of their daily lives.

This downward trend among the Christian teen population is troubling, and it reverses a slightly upward trend reported by the Barna Research Group. According to their studies, in 1990 33% of Christian teens "read from the Bible (excluding while at church)" during a typical week; by 2000, that number had slowly risen to 36%.[13] As of 2010, the percentage of teens who turn to the Bible regularly appears to have dropped back to slightly below 1990 levels, at 32%.

These results show a clear disconnect, as it applies to Bible study, between values and actions among the teenagers in our youth groups. Actually, let me rephrase: this shows more than simply a disconnect; this reveals a chasm of inauthentic reality in the ranks of our youth groups. It also indicates that kids don't actually believe what they say they believe, or perhaps they feel exempt from living what they say they believe.

Figure 7.5

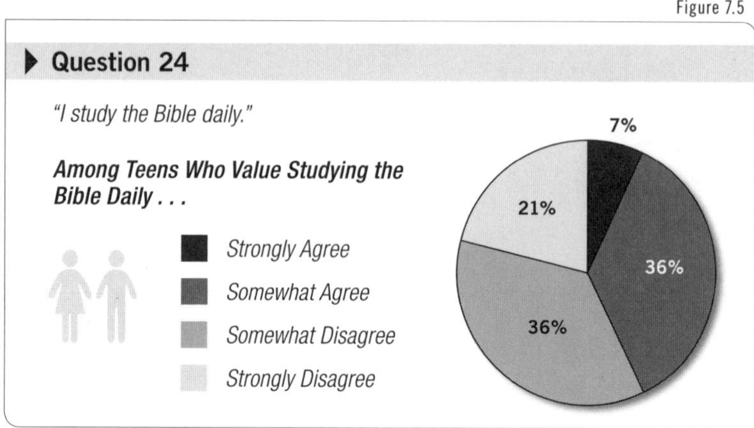

Figure 7.6

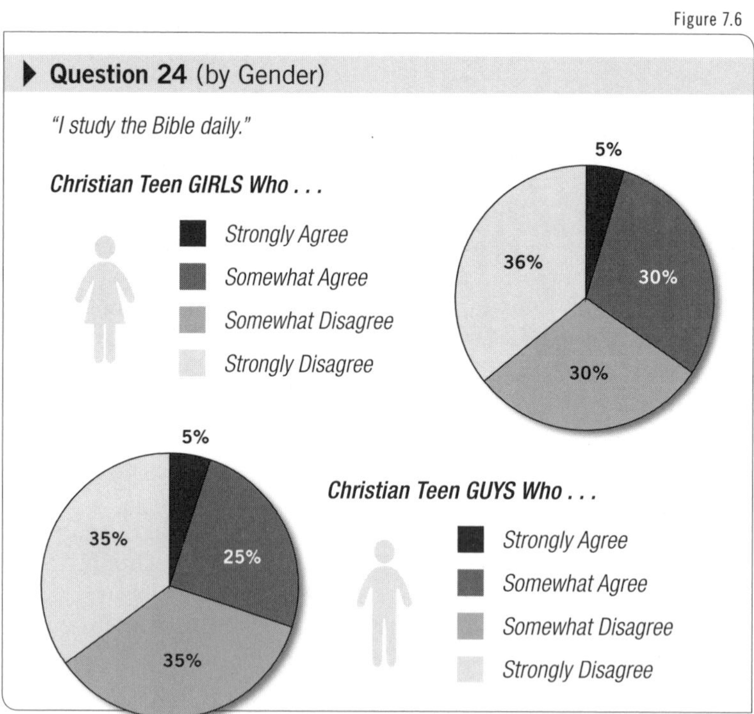

For instance, 73% of Christian teenagers indicate that they value daily Bible study, agreeing to some degree that "followers of Jesus should study the Bible daily." Among this 73% of teens, however, only 7% also indicate that they actually *do* study the Bible daily. And the solid majority of these Christian teens (57%) actually deny making Bible study a part of daily life, even though they just said it was something *all* Christians should do. Additionally, among students who "strongly agree" that studying the Bible daily is something all Christians should do, only 12% of those kids also indicated that they actually do study the Bible every day by answering "strongly agree" to question 24.

Guys and girls are equally likely to be committed to studying their Bibles on a daily basis. Still, obviously the ones who do so (5% of each gender) are overwhelmingly in the minority in their youth groups. Among those who are *least* likely to study the Bible, guys win the slacker title, outnumbering girls 70% to 66%.

Figure 7.7

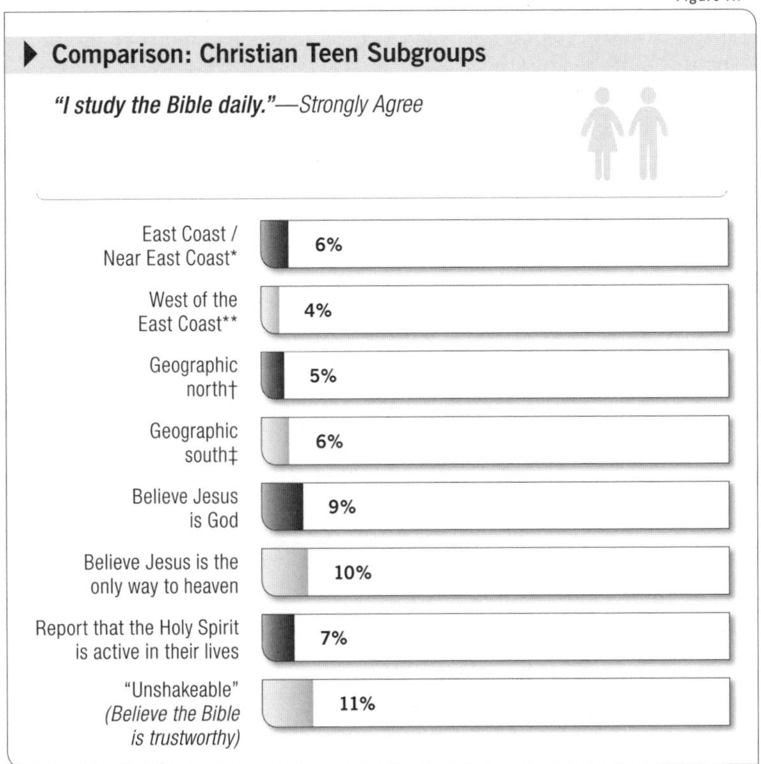

* Roughly from PA east, then down to FL on the map. **Roughly west of PA, then over and across the map. †Roughly from PA and up on the map. ‡Roughly from PA/IL and down the map, including CO and CA.

Generally speaking, the low number of Christian teenagers who claim to study the Bible daily remains remarkably consistent (between 4% and 11%) across a number of significant subgroups within the survey sample, including geographical region, experience with the Holy Spirit, those who hold beliefs like "Jesus is the only way to heaven," or "Jesus is God," and even among Unshakeable teens who believe the Bible is trustworthy. This suggests that avoiding Bible study is not simply an accident or oversight of teen faith, but is instead the normative experience for nearly everyone in our Christian youth groups.

One Unshakeable student, a high school senior from an Evangelical Congregational church in Pennsylvania, attributed that situation to time constraints and lack of relevance for most of today's teens. "They do not want to put the time into studying and learning the Bible," she said in a follow-up interview. "They don't think it is important at this point of their lives" (see fig. 7.7).

The most significant departure from this norm shows up when looking at the data from the perspective of Confident Christian teenagers. These are the kids in our youth groups who adhere to four core Christian beliefs: (1) the Bible is trustworthy in what it says about Jesus, (2) Jesus is God, (3) Jesus died and rose again, (4) Jesus is the only way to heaven.

Figure 7.8

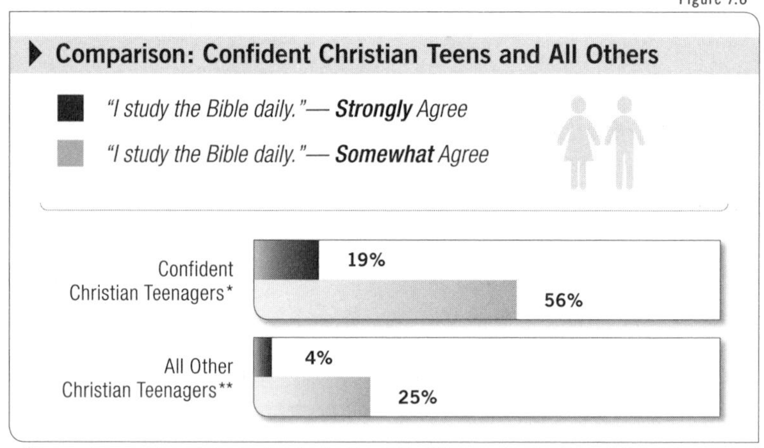

*Express strong confidence in four key Christian doctrines: 1) the Bible is trustworthy, 2) Jesus is God, 3) Jesus died and rose again, 4) Jesus is the only way to heaven.

**Express measurable reservations about one or more of these four key doctrines of Christianity.

Among Confident Christian teens, nearly 1 in 5 (19%) reports that he or she studies the Bible daily, as evidenced by a "strongly agree" response to question 24. While this is still significantly in the minority, it is also nearly five times the rate of the rest of the Christian student population. Additionally, another 56% of these Confident Christians appears to be making an effort toward daily Bible study (as evidenced by a "somewhat agree" response to question 24). That means that, among Confident Christian teens, 3 out of 4 (75%) appear to be at least attempting to study the Bible on a daily basis. Among all other teenagers, that number is only 29%. Once again, this appears to show something we learned in chapter 6: *right belief translates into real experience.*

In general, then, it seems that our teenagers value daily Bible study, but—with the exception of our Confident Christian teens—simply aren't experiencing it and aren't committed to it. This is a serious issue for Christian parents and church leaders, and it deserves some focused attention outside the parameters of this book.

What's preventing Christian youth from finding passion and power in the pages of Scripture? What role do parents and youth leaders play in igniting passion for God's Word? How much of this problem stems from simple lack of education, and how much stems from an institutionalized devaluation of the power of Scripture in our churches and individual lives?

In the end I think those of us who are leaders in Christian families and in churches need to ask ourselves two questions: Should followers of Christ study the Bible daily? What kind of example am I giving my students when it comes to living out the value of Bible study in a Christian person's life? Our answers may just dictate the way our teenagers answer those same questions in the years to come.

Summary

• A solid majority of Christian teenagers (73%) indicate that they value daily Bible study as a part of the Christian life. Of this number, nearly 1 in 3 (31%) "strongly agree" with this view.

• *At the same time, significant numbers of Christian teenagers actually reject the idea that Christians have an obligation to study God's Word on a daily basis.* More than 1 in 4 students in our youth groups hold this viewpoint. This seems an unexpectedly large number, considering that it comes out of a survey sample of teenagers who (a) self-identify themselves as Christian and (b) are at least occasionally involved in a church youth group.

• *Belief in the trustworthiness of Scripture has enormous impact on whether or not our students place value on studying the Bible each day.* Among the general youth group population, only 31% of Christian teens believe daily Bible study is very important. Among Unshakeable teens (who believe the Bible is trustworthy), that number more than doubles to 63%.

• *Despite what they say they value, nearly all Christian teenagers fail to crack open their Bibles outside church.* Barely 5%—about 1 in 20—study the Bible on a daily basis. Meanwhile, more than 2 out of 3 teens (67%) report that they seldom, or never, study Scripture. This reflects a slight downward trend from teen studies conducted only ten years ago.

• *Right belief translates into real experience.* The big exception to the findings here shows up among Confident Christian teens—those who strongly adhere to the four core beliefs outlined earlier. Among those students, nearly 1 in 5 (19%) reports that he or she studies the Bible daily. Additionally, 3 out of 4 (75%) Confident Christian teens appear to be at least *attempting* to study the Bible on a daily basis. Among all other teenagers that number is only 29%—about 250% *fewer* students.

Bonus Survey Results

Figure 7.9

Comparison: Denominational Groups

	"I Study the Bible Daily." — Strongly Agree	"I Study the Bible Daily." — Somewhat Agree
Non-Denominational	16%	35%
Baptist	12%	30%
Brethren in Christ	9%	50%
Other Denominations	6%	31%
United Methodist	6%	28%
Presbyterian	4%	34%
Undeclared	3%	23%
United Church of Christ	3%	11%
Catholic	1%	15%
Episcopal	0%	28%
Lutheran	0%	25%

Figure 7.10

Comparison: Age Groups

	"I Study the Bible Daily." — Strongly Agree	"I Study the Bible Daily." — Somewhat Agree
Junior Highers (Grades 7 & 8)	7%	37%
High School Underclassmen (Grades 9 & 10)	4%	27%
High School Upperclassmen (Grades 11 & 12)	6%	26%

8

PRAYER AND CHRISTIAN TEENS

Come near to God and he will come near to you.
James 4:8 NIV

There was a time in my life when I felt pretty sure God had given up on answering my prayers.

I was working primarily as a freelance journalist, most of my time taken up with writing profile articles and puff pieces about Christian celebrities. At the same time, I had developed a chronic illness that often left me gasping in bed for days, sometimes weeks, on end. I actually managed to move my entire office to my bedroom so I could continue working from within a pile of pillows on my mattress.

When I was facing the daily pressures of constant deadlines, and feeling awful and exhausted day in and day out, it would have been an understatement to say that I spent a lot of time in prayer. I spent almost all my time praying! And I kept saying basically the same thing: "God, why am I this sick? Why can't I get well? Why have you stopped listening to me?"

Finally, I was so discouraged I decided that if God wouldn't answer my prayers, I could at least live vicariously through others' answered prayers. I was doing a lot of phone and email interviews with Christian musicians, authors, and athletes. So, for my own personal benefit, I started adding this question to the end of every interview: "When was a time you felt certain that God had answered one of your prayers?" In some depressing way, I really needed the encouragement that came from other people remembering God's goodness to them.

The results of that silly, greedy little question were wonderful. In every instance, with every person, testimonies of God's faithfulness in prayer came almost instantly. Sometimes people had so many fresh memories of God's responses to their prayers they almost couldn't decide which one to tell me about.

I remember early in this desperate experiment I was conducting a phone interview with gospel music legend Andraé Crouch. In the background I could hear his secretary saying (with a frown in her voice), "Pastor Crouch, your next appointment is waiting for you." I almost didn't ask him the question. In fact, I even turned off the tape recorder and had begun my perfunctory "Thanks for your time today" closing. But, as I say, I *needed* to hear people answer my question, so in a rush of embarrassment, I said, "Um, one last thing. When was a time you felt certain God had answered one of your prayers?"

Pastor Crouch's voice suddenly became animated, and his story spilled out with joy. I quickly turned the recorder back on and drunk it in. In the middle of his story, I heard the secretary calling to him again. "Do you need to go?" I said, feeling a bit guilty. "No, they'll wait," he said. "This is more important."

Turns out that Andraé had been to his doctor for a checkup, and they found bad news in the form of testicular cancer. Three tumors in all; treatment would be painful and immediate. A follow-up appointment was made to begin laying out his regimen for recovery.

A few days later, Andraé was sleeping in his office/apartment at the church he pastors when he heard his phone ringing at 3:30 a.m. He almost didn't answer, but then groggily realized it was his private, unlisted line. He reached over and picked up the receiver.

"Hello?" he said.

A woman's voice, heavy with a Spanish accent, responded. "Is this the Memorial Church?"

"Yes."

The voice on the phone was firm. "I am to pray for the shepherd."

Andraé was wide-awake now. As pastor of Christ Memorial, he was often called the shepherd of his church.

Without hesitation, the woman began to pray. "Father," she said, "in the name of Jesus, I pray for the infirmity of the shepherd, and I curse it. I curse it at the root and it is gone in the name of Jesus." Then she hung up without saying good-bye.

Pastor Crouch lay awake a few moments, wondering how the woman had gotten his phone number, how she knew he had an infirmity, and why she'd called to pray in the wee hours of the morning. He finally returned to sleep, still wondering.

Two days later Andraé reported to the doctor's office. The physician wanted to do more tests to assess how quickly the cancer was growing and to begin making firm recommendations for treatment. After searching for the tumors for about ten minutes, the doctor put a hand on his hip. "Maybe you can find them, Pastor Crouch, because I don't feel anything."

Andraé pointed and said, "Well, they're right here, remember? The big one's right . . . right . . ." Suddenly his eyes filled with tears.

The tumors, all three of them, were gone.

Pastor Crouch's story was only one of many that people told me. *VeggieTales* creator Phil Vischer told me about a time he was flat broke and ready to give up on his "big idea" for children's cartoons. Then, as he was praying, he noticed an unmarked envelope mixed in with his daily mail. Inside it was a generous cashier's check—enough to keep Phil's family going a little while longer. Encouraged by that answer to prayer, he kept working on *VeggieTales* . . . and the rest is history. Christian musician Rich Mullins told me about the joy and power he found when God answered his prayers by providing a place of ministry for him on an Indian reservation. Pro football kicker Todd Peterson shared about the game that started his NFL career. He'd missed a field goal that would have won the game, and the pressure he felt was nearly unbearable. So he prayed for God's peace until he felt Christ's comforting presence with him. (Then he calmly booted the game-winner in overtime.) Truth is, I collected so many of these kinds of testimonies that I eventually published fifty of them in a book called (what else?) *True Stories of Answered Prayer*.[1]

My point (in case you haven't picked up on it already) is this:

Jesus answers prayers.

Even when I was wallowing in self-pity and feeling as if God had given up on me, he was still answering prayers—mine included. Some prayer responses are flashy (healing of testicular cancer, anyone?). Others are more mundane, but still miraculous in their own way. I've seen firsthand that this is true, and heard it from many, many others who've also experienced God's gracious action in response to prayer.

I love the way theologian/radio host Steve Brown describes this privilege of prayer:

> Prayer is not just for experts. It's for people like you and me. It's for people who mess up, who have doubts, and who wonder. . . . It's for those who pretend that they have it together and are afraid others will discover the lie. . . . It's about you and it's about God.[2]

What about our Christian teenagers? Do they believe prayer is for them? That Jesus answers prayers? And have they noticeably experienced answers to their prayers? In this section of *The Jesus Survey*, it was time to find out.

Teenagers + Prayer = ???

In this portion of the content section of *The Jesus Survey*, I wanted to explore Christian teen beliefs about, and experiences with, prayer. I wanted to know if kids believed that Jesus himself actually answered prayer. And I wanted to find out if they could—without a doubt—point to any personal experience that they felt confirmed the power of prayer in their lives.

As with all questions, I listed a one-sentence statement, and then asked kids to indicate whether they agreed or disagreed with the statement. So, in question 25 I asked kids to react to this statement regarding prayer:

> Jesus answers prayers.

Next, for question 26 I asked teenagers to respond to this follow-up statement regarding their *experience* of praying to Jesus:

> I'm 100% certain Jesus has answered one or more of my prayers—and I can prove it.

I deliberately avoided using the more generic term "God" in these questions because I wanted to make it clear that this part of the survey dealt with how teens viewed Jesus in their belief and experience of prayer. For at least one student, a 10th grade girl from a non-denominational church in New Jersey, that was a problem. She made a point of crossing out the name of Jesus and replacing it with "God" in both questions. However, the use of Jesus's name in this context didn't seem to bother any other students.

Question 25: "Jesus Answers Prayers."

Now, it's clear to me, as I'm sure it is to you, that prayer involves so much more than simply a tally of requests and wishes granted. Prayer, at its core, is an ongoing expression of relationship with Jesus. In another book, I describe prayer as "intimate apparel" in the wardrobe of spirituality—the place where we lay ourselves bare before God.[3] I know this. Still, when exploring the aspect of prayer with teenagers in *The Jesus Survey*, I opted to go for the most common denominator among us, asking kids to express how they felt about the idea that Jesus answers prayers.

Like very few of the other questions on this survey, Christian teenagers showed remarkable unity in their response to question 25. Fully 94% (nearly all students) agreed, either strongly or somewhat, that Jesus himself responds to prayer. Furthermore, almost 2 out of 3 (62%) confidently affirmed that belief. That was even more than the number of teens who strongly agreed that Jesus is God (56%) back in question 9.

Interestingly, even among teenagers who previously indicated *disbelief* in Jesus (saying that Jesus is not God), a broad majority, fully 83%, agreed at least somewhat with the statement that "Jesus answers prayers." How does Jesus even hear prayers, let alone answer them, if he's not God? But these students didn't seem fazed by that. This belief in Jesus's ability to answer prayer seems to contradict their otherwise consistent denial of Christ's deity, yet this contradiction meant little or nothing to these kids. This gives us an encouraging sign that, perhaps deep down, even the vocal skeptics of Christ in our youth groups and Christian families at least *want* to believe that Jesus is who he claims to be.

Figure 8.1

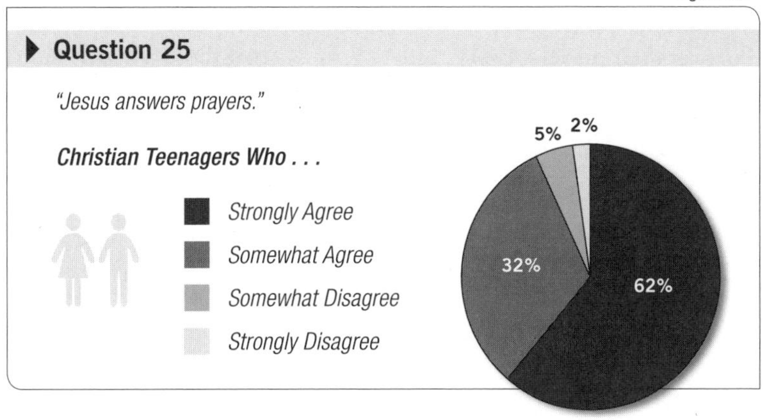

Figure 8.2

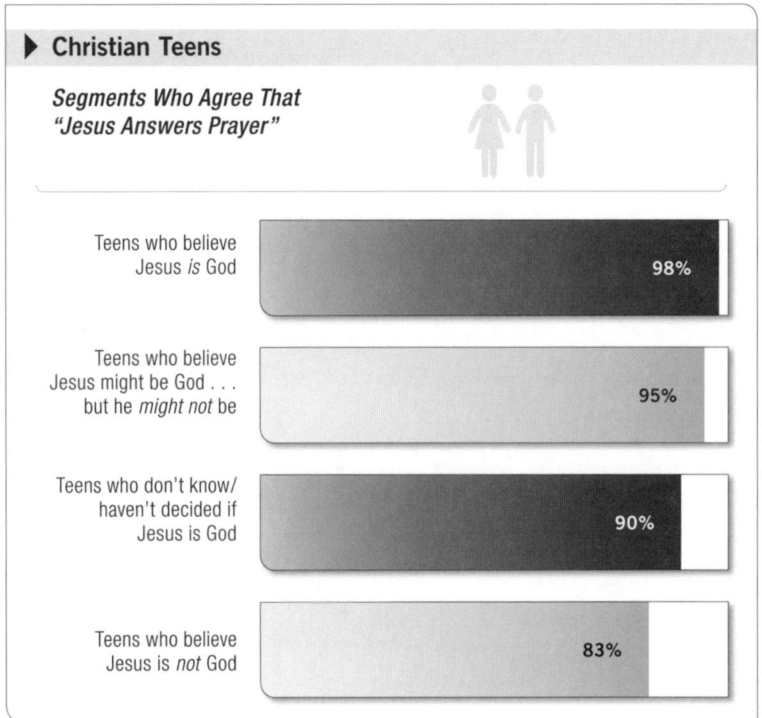

Among the denominations, teenagers with Baptist or Brethren in Christ affiliation are most likely to see Jesus as the omniscient, omnipotent One who can—and does—answer their prayers. Every student representing those two denominations in *The Jesus Survey* agreed, either somewhat or strongly, with question 25. Teens from most denominations represented in the survey produced similar, if not unanimous, results.

Figure 8.3

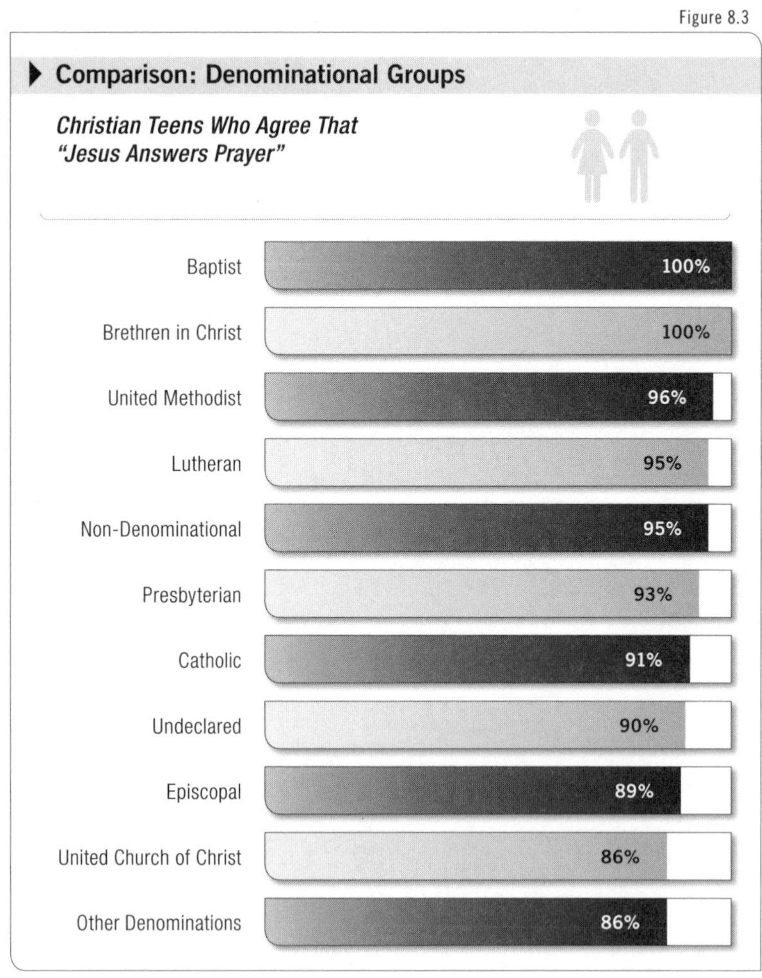

Only three groups dropped below 90% agreement on this issue: Episcopalians (89%), United Church of Christ (86%), and Other Denominations (Anglican Church, Christian Church [DOC], Church of God, Christian & Missionary Alliance,

Evangelical Congregational, and Mennonite Church) (86%). The surprising group here is the Other Denominations. Up to this point, teens in this catch-all group have typically shown themselves to be on the top end of those affirming traditional Christian beliefs, including issues such as the trustworthiness of Scripture, the deity of Jesus, and the question of whether or not Jesus is the only way to heaven. For them to be tied for dead last in terms of this belief about prayer is unusual. Still, like all other denominational groups, kids in the Other Denominations did overwhelmingly agree with the belief that Jesus answers prayer.

Question 26: "Jesus Has Answered One or More of My Prayers."

As with the questions about Bible study in the previous chapter, the aim of this follow-up to the first question on Jesus and prayer was designed to prompt teenagers to go from theory to experience in their thinking. Having established that nearly everyone in our youth groups believes, in general at least, that Jesus answers prayer, the next logical step is to make the question personal and specific.

You'll notice that in the wording of question 26, I used phrasing designed to encourage teenagers to answer with a degree of certainty that would move them away from hesitant, middle-ground responses of "somewhat" agreeing or disagreeing. This shows up, of course, in the phrase "I'm 100% certain" and in the criteria of personal proof added at the end of the question. You'll also notice that, once again, our kids are not easily pushed out of their emotionally safe middle territory, even on issues where personal experience reigns supreme. A good portion—more than 1 in 3 (37%)—still chose to qualify their answers with some reservation by marking either "somewhat agree" (27%) or "somewhat disagree" (10%) on question 26.

Figure 8.4

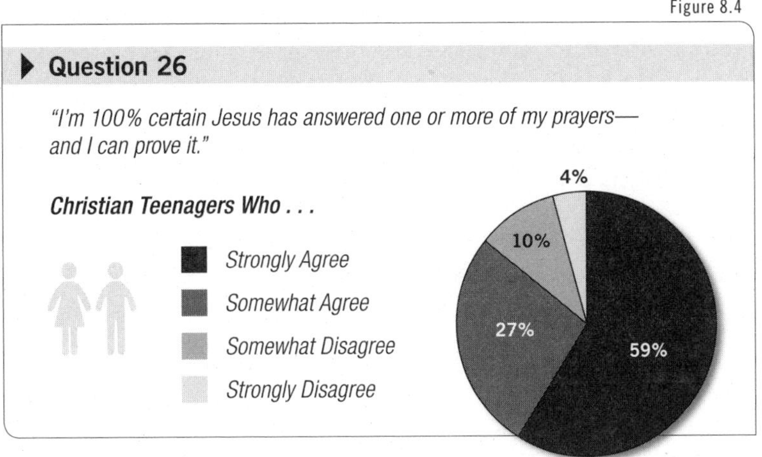

Additionally, some adult leaders actually took offense to this question, and made a point of letting me know about it. While they had no problem asserting that Jesus answers prayer as a general principle, they refused to affirm he would do so in a measurable way for any individual. One Catholic youth worker from New York objected particularly to the "proof" criteria here. "You can't prove faith," he wrote next to the spot where he marked his disagreement to question 26. An adult leader from a Disciples of Christ church in Iowa also expressed a similar viewpoint, telling me plainly, "No one has proof, that's what faith is."

Well, based on Hebrews 11:1, I obviously disagree with the flimsy definition of faith these leaders are operating under—and I suspect that Andraé Crouch, Phil Vischer, and millions of others would too. But, for our purposes here, that's irrelevant. What matters is what our youth group kids believe in this regard. We know that 94% of Christian teenagers believe Jesus *can* answer prayer, but how many have also *experienced* answered prayer from Jesus—and feel they can prove it?

According to the way they responded to question 26, a demonstratively large majority claims to have experienced Jesus's answers to their prayers. More than 8 in 10 students (86%) say they either somewhat or strongly agree to the statement that they are "100% certain" of that claim. Once again, it's difficult to assess how someone can be "somewhat" 100% certain. Perhaps teens shied away from asserting empirical proof but still felt an emotional and/or intellectual connection between their prayer and the way their issue was resolved. Regardless, it does seem clear that even those who marked "somewhat agree" on this question could point to at least one experience where they could see Jesus working in response to a prayer. And the exceptionally large number of teenagers who report answers to prayer indicates that Jesus is indeed working in the lives of teenagers everywhere.

Follow-up interviews with some of the survey respondents lend further credence to this interpretation of the data. One girl, a high school senior from a Presbyterian church in California, could barely contain her enthusiasm in answer to this question. "I prayed that I would one day find a church family that I would feel comfortable around and that would accept me," she said. "God answered my prayer last December. . . . Every week I'm greeted by adults, friends, and pastors who ask how my week was and how I am doing. Now I'm very involved at church and I can honestly say that I have seen God's presence working in my life!"

Another student was more sober but no less convinced of Jesus's answer to her prayers. An 11th grader from a United Methodist church in Michigan shared:

> I know that God answered my prayers when my grandpa was sick. I knew that he was in pain so I prayed to God, asking him to let my grandpa not be in pain anymore. The next day my grandpa passed away. Even though I didn't want him to go, I knew it was God's way of answering my prayer.

Teens told other stories of answered prayer that involved illness, death, grief, dating relationships, friendships, suicide prevention, church community, life, and more. And it appears that very few of them are not experiencing at least some level of answered prayer when they pray to Jesus Christ.

Again, though, answered prayer is not a unanimous phenomenon among Christian teenagers. In fact, more teenagers agree Jesus *can* answer prayer (94%) than agree he *has* answered prayer (86%). And, for about 1 in 8 youth group kids (14%), experience with answered prayer just hasn't happened yet—or perhaps they are simply unaware of Christ's answers to their prayers.

Doctrine vs. Prayer Experience

Up to this point in *The Jesus Survey*, there has frequently been a pronounced correlation between doctrinal belief about Jesus and teenagers' actual Christian experience. So, of course, I wanted to see if that correlation still held true regarding an issue where an overwhelming majority of kids report the *same* Christian experience: answered prayer.

To see if I could get a better glimpse here, I first listed sixteen doctrinal perspectives I'd been able to identify among teenagers thus far, and then sorted survey respondents into these various subgroups. Yes, some of the members of those subgroups overlapped, but I wasn't necessarily trying to exclude any respondent. I was just trying to see how many factors applied to how many respondents in the survey.

Next I limited the data in each subgroup to show how many Christian teenagers answered "strongly agree" to question 26: "I'm 100% certain Jesus has answered one or more of my prayers—and I can prove it." I was looking for kids with full confidence on this issue, ones who didn't shy away from the demand for proof of answered prayer or wanted to hedge their bets by answering "somewhat" on this question. Then I tabulated all the correlated data into a simple graph (see fig. 8.5) and let the numbers fall where they may.

The results were definitely illuminating.

By far and away, the teenagers who most often reported "100% certainty" of experience with answered prayer were those Confident Christian teenagers who also adhere strongly to the four basic Christian doctrines identified in the intermission. In fact, nearly all (94%) of these kids answered "strongly agree" to question 26 on *The Jesus Survey*. That response rate was higher by double digits (11%) than the next closest group, and nearly 40 percentage points (39%) more than Not Confident teens who expressed reservations about one or more of those four doctrines. These are enormous numbers, and simply can't be ignored.

Figure 8.5 (Part 1 of 2)

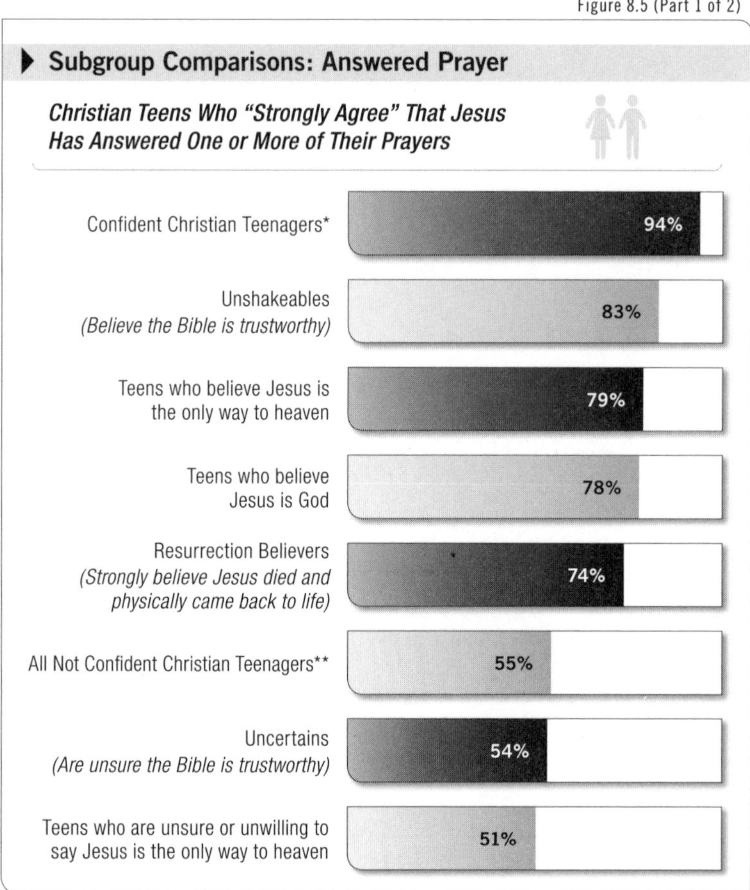

* Express strong confidence in four key Christian doctrines: 1) the Bible is trustworthy, 2) Jesus is God, 3) Jesus died and rose again, 4) Jesus is the only way to heaven.

** Express measurable reservations about one or more of four key doctrines of Christianity.

Unsurprisingly, the next largest group to report unquestioned personal experience with answered prayer was the teenagers I've labeled Unshakeable because they demonstrate steady belief in the trustworthiness of Scripture. More than 4 of 5 (83%) of these Bible-believing teens strongly agreed to the statement that Jesus had answered their prayers—and that they could prove it. From the beginning of this book, these Unshakeable teens have consistently reported higher levels of personal experience with Christ, so this finding here is actually somewhat predictable—but no less significant. Once again, being able to trust that Scripture is true appears to free Christian teenagers to experience a more personal, satisfying Christian life in their everyday world.

Figure 8.5 (Part 2 of 2)

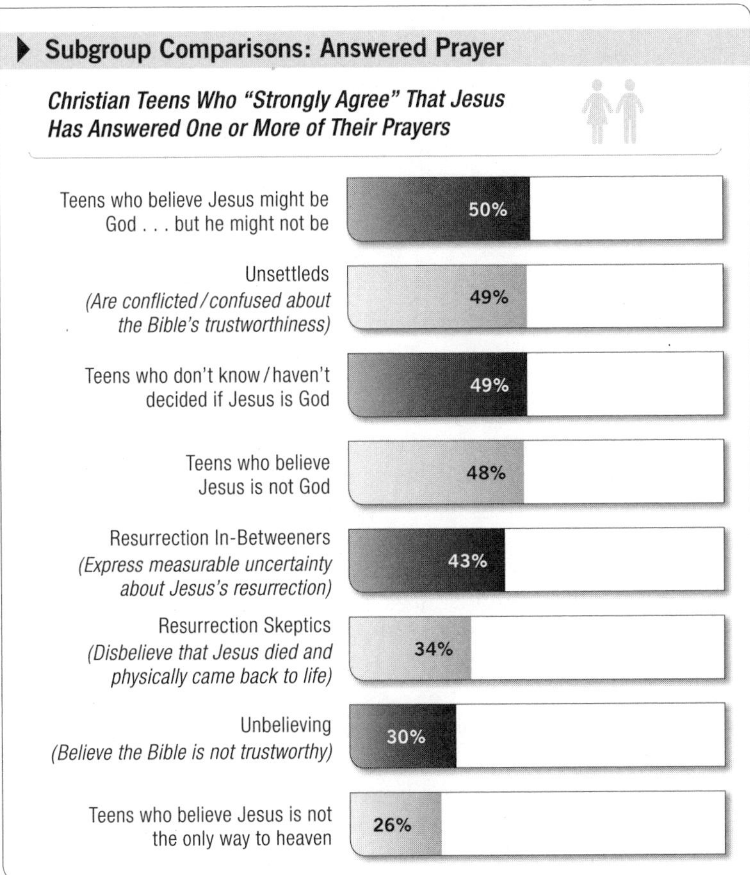

The next three largest groups of teens who report confident experience with answered prayer are those who seem to have "cherry-picked" their favorites from among the four core Christian doctrines. Of kids who believe Jesus is the only way to heaven, nearly 8 of 10 (79%) say they are 100% certain Jesus has answered their prayers. Teens who believe Jesus is God report almost identical experience, with 78% of them saying the same. And about 3 out of 4 (74%) "resurrection believers" also say that Jesus has answered their prayers.

What this means is that Jesus appears to reward right belief with real answers to prayer—or perhaps that teenagers who are more faithful to traditional Christian orthodoxy are also more attuned to God's activity in their lives. Either way, the top five subgroups of our church kids that report answers to prayer are *all* those that adhere wholeheartedly to one or all of the four core Christian doctrines addressed in *The Jesus Survey*. After these five groups, a huge gap in experience emerges, with no other group of teenagers reporting more than 55% who can "strongly agree" to having an experience with answered prayer. Additionally, most of the other groups with wavering or skeptical belief about who Jesus is reported fewer than half confidently experiencing answer to prayer.

I have, on occasion, had church leaders and parents "explain" to me that it's not terribly necessary for Christian teenagers to be doctrinally accurate, or even aware. "They're just kids, after all," they say to me. "And besides, theologians have been arguing these topics for thousands of years. Who's to say, ultimately, who's right and who's wrong on these issues?"

While I agree that some (OK, maybe a lot) of theology is puffery and irrelevant hairsplitting ("seminal transmission of sin" comes to mind), it's almost criminal negligence for church leaders and parents to take an apathetic approach to helping their teenagers understand—and believe—core Christian orthodoxy. We help our children learn every other aspect of life in great detail. Remember the intense weeks (maybe months) we spent potty training? The years refining social discipline? The time spent nurturing emotional health and physical responsibility? The (too many) hours helping with after school homework? The list goes on and on . . . yet when it comes to the most important aspect of existence—eternity with Christ—we too often abdicate our obligation to help our kids develop a grounded, real belief system that will help them in every aspect of every moment of every breath of their lives.

Do you want your teenagers to have a real, life-changing relationship with Jesus? To have a faith that can be seen, felt, heard, and touched in their everyday lives? Then you'd better take the time to help them understand and learn to trust in the basic doctrines of Christ. Judging from what can be seen in the data of *The Jesus Survey*, that kind of right belief translates, over and over again, into a consistently authentic and rewarding personal experience with God.

OK, enough of my little sermon. But before I close out this chapter, it's important to note one more thing: the subgroup of Christian teenagers reporting the lowest incidence of answered prayer is "Teens who believe Jesus is *not* the only way to heaven." Only about 1 in 4 (26%) of these kids can point to an unquestioned experience where they felt Christ responded to their prayer.

That's a disappointingly low number, I admit. But think about it: God, in his great mercy and kindness, still responded in an undeniable way for these teens—even though they themselves have consistently denied a critical aspect of his person and power. Let that be both a lesson and an encouragement for us.

Jesus is active in the lives of all teens. He never gives up on anyone. He never demands a legalistic approach that welcomes some teens and completely disinherits others. Like a father loving *all* his children, he always reaches toward us—and toward our teens—with grace and help. We would be wise to imitate his example.

Summary

• Nearly all Christian teens believe Jesus answers prayer. Unlike most of the other questions on this survey, Christian teenagers showed remarkable unity on this question. Fully 94% (more than 9 out of 10) agreed, either strongly or somewhat, that Jesus himself responds to prayer. Even teenagers who otherwise disbelieve in Christ (saying he is not God) hold this view, with more than 4 out of 5 (83%) disbelieving teenagers also indicating they believe Jesus answers prayers.

• *A large majority of Christian teens believe that they've experienced Jesus's answers to their prayers.* More than 8 in 10 students (86%) claim to have personally experienced Jesus's answers to their prayers. This exceptionally large number indicates that Jesus is indeed working in the lives of teenagers everywhere. Answered prayer is not a unanimous phenomenon among Christian teenagers, though. More of these kids agree Jesus *can* answer prayer (94%) than agree he *has* answered prayer (86%). And, for about 1 in 8 youth group kids (14%), experience with answered prayer just hasn't happened yet.

• *Experience with answered prayer appears to be directly correlated to doctrinal belief among Christian teenagers.* By far and away, the teenagers who most often reported "100% certainty" of experience with answered prayer were those Confident Christian teenagers who adhere strongly to the four basic Christian doctrines we've previously identified. The next largest group to report unquestioned personal experience with answered prayer was Unshakeable teens, who demonstrate steady belief in the trustworthiness of Scripture. In all, the top five subgroups of church kids that report experiencing answered prayer are all those adhering wholeheartedly to one or all of the four core Christian doctrines addressed in *The Jesus Survey*. After these five groups, a huge gap in experience emerges, with no other group of teenagers reporting more than 55% who can strongly point to an experience with answered prayer.

• *The subgroup of Christian teenagers reporting the lowest incidence of answered prayer is "Teens who believe Jesus is not the only way to heaven."* Only about 1 in 4 (26%) of these kids can point to an unquestioned experience where they felt Christ responded to their prayer. While that's a disappointingly low number, it still shows that Jesus is active, in some way and on some level, in the lives of all teenagers—even those who disbelieve in him.

Bonus Survey Results

Figure 8.6

Question 25

"Jesus answers prayers."

Adult Leaders Predicted Christian Teenagers Would . . .			
Strongly Agree	Somewhat Agree	Strongly Disagree	Somewhat Disagree
54%	38%	7%	2%

Christian Teens' Actual Responses			
Strongly Agree	Somewhat Agree	Strongly Disagree	Somewhat Disagree
62%	32%	5%	2%

Figure 8.7

Question 26

"I'm 100% certain Jesus has answered one or more of my prayers—and I can prove it."

Adult Leaders Predicted Christian Teenagers Would . . .			
Strongly Agree	Somewhat Agree	Strongly Disagree	Somewhat Disagree
50%	33%	10%	7%

Christian Teens' Actual Responses			
Strongly Agree	Somewhat Agree	Strongly Disagree	Somewhat Disagree
59%	27%	10%	4%

Figure 8.8

Question 26

"I'm 100% certain Jesus has answered one or more of my prayers—and I can prove it."

Junior Highers *(Grades 7 & 8)*

Strongly Agree	*Somewhat Agree*	*Strongly Disagree*	*Somewhat Disagree*
50%	**33%**	**14%**	**3%**

High School Underclassmen *(Grades 9 & 10)*

Strongly Agree	*Somewhat Agree*	*Strongly Disagree*	*Somewhat Disagree*
62%	**26%**	**7%**	**5%**

High School Upperclassmen *(Grades 11 & 12)*

Strongly Agree	*Somewhat Agree*	*Strongly Disagree*	*Somewhat Disagree*
58%	**26%**	**12%**	**4%**

Christian Teen Girls *(All Grades)*

Strongly Agree	*Somewhat Agree*	*Strongly Disagree*	*Somewhat Disagree*
63%	**26%**	**8%**	**3%**

Christian Teen Guys *(All Grades)*

Strongly Agree	*Somewhat Agree*	*Strongly Disagree*	*Somewhat Disagree*
54%	**27%**	**13%**	**6%**

9

EVANGELISM AND CHRISTIAN TEENS

For I am not ashamed of the gospel.
Romans 1:16 NASB

As you've probably guessed by now, I'm not a person who is easily bedeviled by stage fright. Most often, the opposite is true—I don't know when to keep my mouth shut and so I blather on, winging random and frequent opinions about anything and everything to anyone and everyone who might be nearby. Still, I do recall one particular time when stage fright seized me. I could feel my heart race, my muscles tense, and sweat begin to pool in my armpits while I was speaking to a group of people.

It started out innocently enough. At the time, I was working as an advertising copywriter for a luxury travel company. I found many good people there, but not many religious ones. Obviously (since you know me), it didn't take long for everyone to discover that I was a Christian . . . with opinions. At any rate, my desk was situated right next to the break room. One day, around Easter, a group of about a half dozen folks came in to eat lunch together. They started chatting about the holiday and soon came upon the topic of the Jewish Passover. Since none of them was Jewish, and since they knew I was "religious," they called me over and asked me to tell them what I knew about that Hebrew celebration.

I didn't think much of it. I knew these people and called many of them my friends. So I walked over and started sharing a few basic facts about the Passover. As I was talking, I also included some of my thoughts on how elements of the Passover feast symbolized the promise of Jesus's life, death, and resurrection. It was no big deal, a natural part of the conversation. They asked some questions; I answered as best I could. Then all of a sudden—almost midsentence—it hit me: I wasn't simply chatting with these people. I was actually Sharing The Gospel with them—or "witnessing," or "evangelizing," or whatever the kids are calling it these days.

Honestly, I don't know why that made a difference to me. Although I wouldn't call myself a fervent evangelist, I have spoken about Jesus to lots of people lots of times. But something in that moment choked my thoughts. I was suddenly aware of one woman sitting at the table who, due to unfortunate experiences with family members, was typically hostile to Christianity. And another woman who belonged to a different religion. And a guy who generally seemed to view all Christians as right-wing Republican nutcases. And . . . you get the idea. I started thinking about how I should be careful not to offend anybody, and I worried about my choice of words.

And my heart started pounding.

And I could feel myself beginning to sweat.

And I started stumbling over my thoughts and words.

I'm ashamed to say that I ended the moment a little abruptly, simply because I felt too much pressure from Sharing The Gospel with my coworkers—even though none of them was the least bit unkind to me. Soon their conversation drifted to other topics, and that was that. A few months later I moved on to a different job, and I never had a similar opportunity with those people again.

I regret my cowardice at that moment because, as you must know all too well, it's not easy to be a Christian in today's world. In fact, I often think that Christianity should come with some kind of warning label: "Caution! People don't like Christians—get used to it." When I was a high schooler, I remember other students mocking me as a "Jesus Freak" so much that I finally gave in and bought a T-shirt that proclaimed the same thing. In college a bookstore manager told me that even though I was well-qualified for a job in his store, he wouldn't hire me because my religion opposed pornography, and he didn't want to take a chance that I'd "preach" to his customers and stop them from buying *Playboy* and *Penthouse* magazines. In the years since, I've been singled out for verbal abuse, insult, and discriminatory treatment because of my faith.

I suspect I've gotten off easy—because I know I'm not the only one with these kinds of experiences. After all, we *are* called Christ's witnesses. Interestingly (and perhaps as a sort of heavenly warning label for us), the Greek term for "witness" used in New Testament writings is *martys*. Does that look familiar to you? It should. It's the root from which we get the word *martyr*, "reminding us," says theologian John Drane, "that bearing witness can be a costly business."[1]

Consider the case of a Christian bookstore in Pennsylvania that was banned from buying Christmas advertising in a local media outlet. The company selling the advertising rejected the store's ad on the basis that it was "offensive, questionable or otherwise [not] in good taste." When the owner asked why his ad was offensive, he was told: "The [store's] name. It has the word 'Christian' in it." The store's name is Christian Book and Gift Shop, and it's been in business in that Pennsylvania town for sixty years.[2]

Similarly, a fifth grade girl was banned from performing a dance in her school's talent show because the background song she chose, "We Shine," was labeled "offensive" by school faculty and administrators. Officials at Superior Street Elementary School in Chatsworth, California, insisted that the child "pick a song that does not say 'Jesus' " before they would allow her onstage with her peers—even though there had been no other restrictions on what children could perform in the show.[3]

Or consider bestselling novelist Anne Rice. At the time teens were taking *The Jesus Survey*, she made headlines by declaring that she was so disgusted with Christians she'd decided she was no longer going to be one. As she said on her Facebook page:

> For those who care, and I understand if you don't: Today I quit being a Christian. I'm out. I remain committed to Christ as always but not to being "Christian" or to being part of Christianity. It's simply impossible for me to "belong" to this quarrelsome, hostile, disputatious, and deservedly infamous group.[4]

Or consider John D. Gilland. He says he feels so threatened by Christ and Christians that he actually filed for a judicial restraining order against Jesus Christ. When a judge denied his request, he added NFL quarterback Tim Tebow and President Barack Obama—presumably because they are prominent followers of Jesus—to his petition and resubmitted it. (The judge denied those restraining orders too.)[5]

I hope that last paragraph made you laugh a little, but I also hope you are aware that it's an example—albeit an extreme one—of how our culture makes it difficult for anyone, especially peer-driven teenagers, to speak confidently about Jesus Christ to others.

After three years studying this issue, Barna Group president David Kinnaman reported,

> Christianity has an image problem. . . . Outsiders' most common reaction to the faith: they think Christians no longer represent what Jesus had in mind, that Christianity in our society is not what it was meant to be.[6]

Kinnaman also reports a solidifying, antagonistic viewpoint toward Christians is taking hold among many people outside the church. "A cadre of Mosaics and Busters [teens and young adults] are feeling the brunt of the hostility toward Christianity," he says.[7] For his book on this issue, Kinnaman used the title *unChristian*. He could just as easily called it *unWelcome*, because that's how most Christians feel when it comes time to tell others about Jesus.

Still, regardless of how popular or unpopular it is to talk about Jesus with others, sharing the gospel is both our privilege and obligation as followers of Christ. Jesus himself made this clear when he said, "Go and make disciples of all the nations" (Matt. 28:19), and "You will be my witnesses in Jerusalem, and in all Judea and Samaria, and to the ends of the earth" (Acts 1:8). The apostle Paul further cemented this great calling when he said, "I am not ashamed of the gospel, because it is the power of God that brings salvation to everyone who believes: first to the Jew, then to the Gentile" (Rom. 1:16), and "Preach the Word; be prepared in season and out of season" (2 Tim. 4:2).

So how are the kids in our youth groups faring, in this often hostile climate, with this Great Commission? Do they believe it's important to talk about Jesus with their friends, family, and even strangers? And, regardless of what they believe, are they preaching the Word in season and out of season?

Judging by my "performance" in front of my coworkers, Christian teenagers today are most likely doing a better job at sharing their faith than I am. But with this part of *The Jesus Survey*, I wanted to find out how much better. So I asked them.

Talking the Talk?

In this portion of the content section of *The Jesus Survey*, I wanted to explore Christian teenagers' beliefs and lifestyle as they relate to evangelism. First, I wanted to know if kids felt they were *supposed* to be telling people about Jesus. Next, I wanted to find out if they were *actually* sharing the gospel with someone—anyone—in a typical month.

As for all questions, I listed a one-sentence statement and then asked kids to indicate whether they agreed or disagreed with the statement. In question 27, I asked kids to react to this assertion:

> I believe Christians are expected to tell others about Jesus with the intent of leading them to be Christian too.

Next, for question 28 I asked teenagers to respond to this correlated statement regarding their lifestyle of evangelism:

> I shared about my faith in Jesus with a non-Christian during the past month.

Like the questions on Bible study from chapter 7, these two questions deal with teenagers' values and the real-life expression of those values. Given my own spotty experiences in the ministry of evangelism, both as a teen and as an adult, I felt pretty certain kids' responses would be interesting. I wasn't disappointed.

Question 27: "Christians Are Expected to Tell Others about Jesus."

For starters, continued belief in the Great Commission appears to be widely held among the teenagers in our youth groups. More than 4 out of 5 teenagers (84%) indicated that they at least somewhat supported the assumption that Christians have an obligation to spread the good news of Jesus. Additionally, nearly half of all Christian kids (49%) strongly agreed that this kind of evangelistic effort was to be expected of all Christians—presumably including themselves.

This is significant for this generation of teens for at least one important reason: the statement they agreed to in question 27 clearly included not only an expectation to tell others about Christ, but also an expectation that Christians are to do so "with the intent of leading them to be Christian too." Given previous student opinions about multifaith validity and their general bent toward inclusivity in religious thought, I'd expected larger numbers of these kids to balk at that kind of proselytizing emphasis. After all, attempting to convert someone else to your way of thinking in terms of religion is often frowned upon by our society. Trying to convert others to Christianity specifically is commonly viewed as an intolerant, coercive act and, in fact, is outlawed in many nations of the world. This is particularly true in parts of the globe where doing so would draw people away from the religion of Islam and in places where communist or socialist governments tend to suppress any belief in God as a potentially dangerous social influence.

Figure 9.1

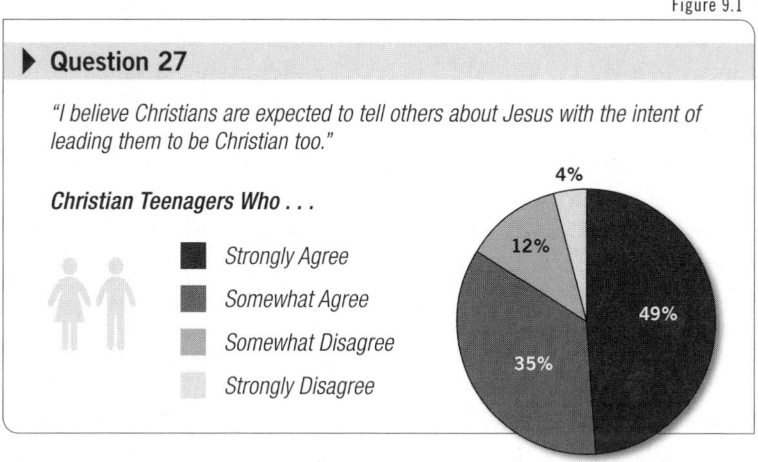

Figure 9.2

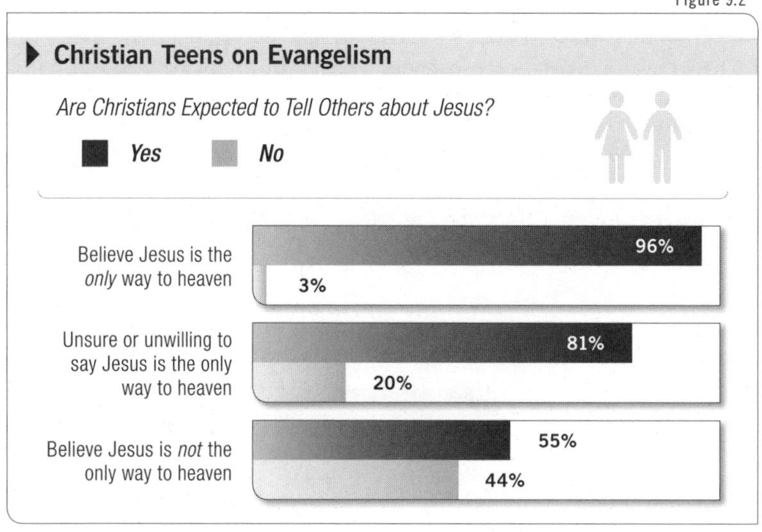

In spite of my expectations, these students showed once again that they are remarkably inconsistent in applying their beliefs across related topics. This time, however, that inconsistency came out in favor of traditional Christianity, with large numbers giving at least nominal backing to the idea that followers of Christ should be talking about Christ and leading others to him.

This support for evangelistic intent showed up in surprising places as well. It's not unexpected that nearly every teen (96%) who believes Jesus is the only way to heaven would also advocate sharing the gospel with others (see fig. 9.2). What is a little bit eye-opening is that, even among those teens who *don't* see Jesus as the sole means of salvation, a clear majority still views evangelism as a Christian obligation. Christian teens who are unsure of Christ's uniqueness in "the saving work" still support evangelistic intent by a 4 to 1 margin (81% to 20%). And even among those Christian kids who deny that Jesus is the only way to heaven, a solid majority (55%) still supports telling other people that he is at least their way to heaven.

There are problems with having evangelists who are likely to spread mistaken belief as part of their efforts (more on this later), but at the same time a Christian who is talking about faith with others is also going to be one who, hopefully, refines and defines his or her experience with God into what is—again, hopefully—a more grounded and defensible faith.

Of course, not all of our students have jumped on the let's-witness-for-Jesus bandwagon. About 1 in 7 Christian kids (16%) sees no real mandate for bringing others into the Christian community. In youth group terms, that's actually a significant minority of believers. By the same token, it may be that these kids are just being honest: they feel no personal compulsion to share about Jesus with others, and thus wouldn't think to impose that expectation on other Christians either.

In another departure from the norm, gender appears to play no role in evangelistic passion. Christian guys and girls were equally likely to indicate that they strongly expect Christians to share the gospel with others. In both cases, nearly half (49%) of our young men and women supported this mandate for leading others to Christ.

Figure 9.3

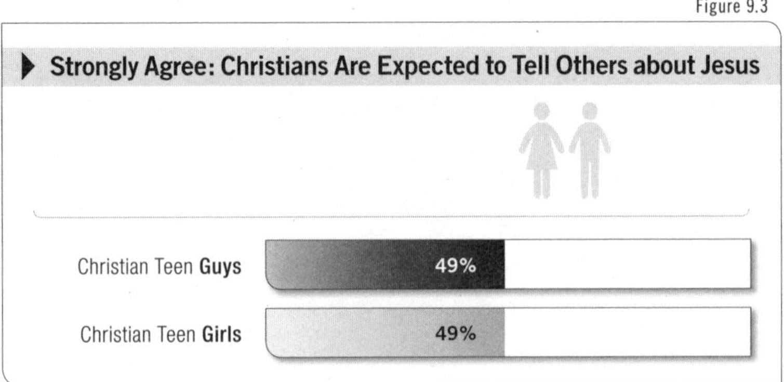

Denominationally, though, a greater variance of belief was evident (see fig. 9.4). By far and away, teens from non-denominational youth groups were the most passionate in their support for Christian evangelism. More than 3 out of 4 of these kids (78%) "strongly agree" that Christians are obligated to spread the word about Jesus. Brethren in Christ students also indicated a significant majority opinion in favor of evangelism, with 64% leaning that direction. At the other end of the spectrum are those students from Episcopalian churches. Only about 1 in 5 (22%) expressed a passionate support for the expectation that Christians lead others to Christ.

Figure 9.4

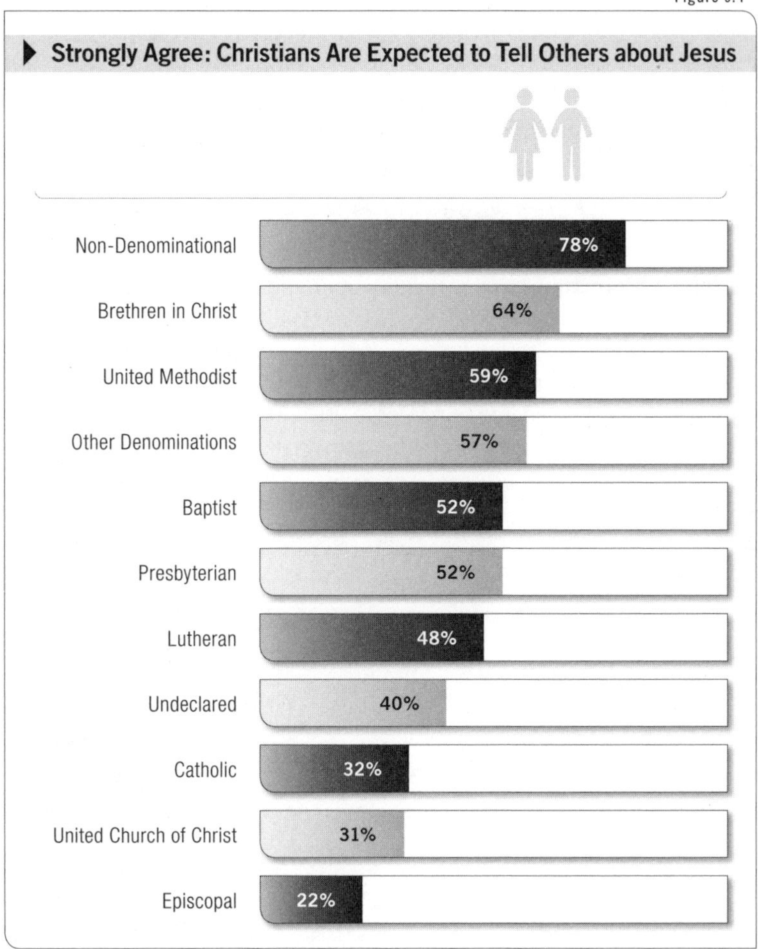

In the case of the Episcopalians, this seems to be a reflection of church leadership (or at least is a known problem to leaders), as youth workers from the Episcopal church predicted those results quite accurately. Among these leaders, 24% predicted passionate support for evangelistic belief from their teens, a number remarkably close to the actual 22% who indicated it.

With the non-denominational group, this strong advocacy for Christian evangelistic expectations is apparently something of a surprise for its youth workers. Less than half of those leaders (44%) predicted that their kids would express strong support for the idea that all Christians should be seeking converts and sharing their faith with others.

Kids from most of the other denominations hovered around the midpoint of passion, with between 40% and 59% expressing strong agreement with the assertion that telling others about Jesus should be the norm for all Christians. Exceptions here were Catholic students (32%) and United Church of Christ kids (31%). In these denominations, Christian teens who feel evangelistic unction are outnumbered 2 to 1 by those who do not see it as a strong priority for believers.

Question 28: "I Shared about My Faith in Jesus."

Still, denominational variances aside, it's clear that the bulk of Christian teenagers see their faith as something to be spoken about and transferred to others—family, friends, coworkers, strangers, whoever. As always, belief begs for action, and so I wanted to see how many of these kids also put a lifestyle of evangelism into practice. For the purposes of *The Jesus Survey*, I decided to use "the past month" as a snapshot of that lifestyle, asking students to report in question 28 how many actually shared about their faith in Jesus with a non-Christian in the last thirty days.

Figure 9.5

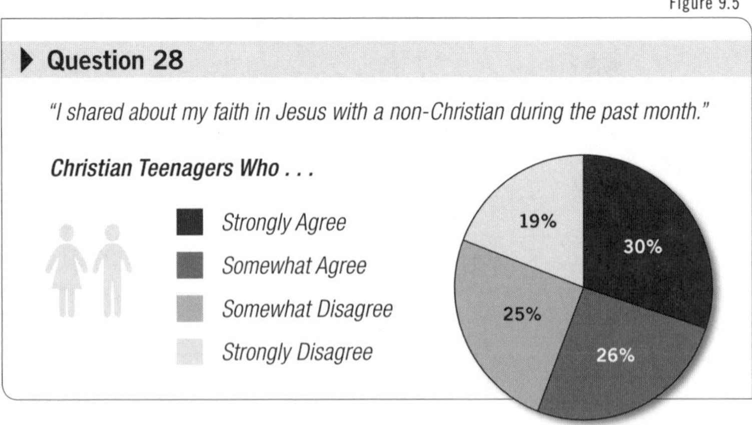

I felt that it was a pretty straightforward question, with concretely measurable criteria for kids. Did you talk to a non-Christian about Jesus in the past month, or not? In spite of that, at least one student objected to that kind of specific indicator of action, saying it wasn't possible to answer the question with either an agree or disagree response. As with the question about personal Bible study back in chapter 7, I understand that reluctance, because answering "disagree" here would hint at hypocrisy for many students and could lead to negative self-esteem. And, for the record, even though I personally strongly agree that Christians have an obligation to share about Christ, I myself would have had to answer "strongly disagree" to question 28. Still, not liking an answer doesn't change the truth of that answer, and gratefully, other students were willing to share their experiences here.

As with the questions on Bible study, there is some subjective interpretation inherent in a "somewhat agree" response. My impression, based on trending from previous, similar questions on *The Jesus Survey*, was this: students who could point clearly to a specific conversation about Jesus in the past month most likely marked "strongly agree." Those who couldn't marked "strongly disagree." Students who may have tried to talk about Jesus but felt unsuccessful or inadequate marked "somewhat agree." And kids who don't generally talk about Jesus to others, but who are open to doing that and can't remember for sure if they did or didn't, marked "somewhat disagree." Yes, these are my own subjective assumptions and you should feel free to replace them with your own subjective impressions instead, but since I'm the one who's writing this book, I get to talk about my own opinions here. (Ah, such power . . .)

Generally speaking, then, more than half of Christian teens (56%) reported at least some kind of faith conversation with a non-Christian in the past thirty days. To my mind, that's actually a high number of kids who are out there spreading the gospel (or some form of it) into their world. It seems that, in this instance, cultural emphasis on tolerance may be working in favor of our youth group kids, making it more acceptable for them to talk about religion among friends than it might be for adults who are more accustomed to avoiding religion as a way of maintaining polite conversation.

These numbers reflect a positive, albeit fluid, trend overall among churchgoing youth. According to recent Barna Group research:

> Among born again Christian teenagers, the proportion who said they had explained their beliefs to someone else with different faith views in the last year had declined from nearly two-thirds of teenagers in 1997 (63%) to less than half of Christian teens in the December 2009 study (45%).[8]

The upward trend evidenced in *The Jesus Survey* may be seasonally influenced, as this study was conducted during summertime, when kids typically have more free time, while the Barna study was done in the middle of the school year. Regardless, even figuring for the margin of error, more than half of the Christian teens in *The Jesus Survey* reported they had shared about Jesus with a non-Christian in the past thirty days. That's encouraging news.

At the same time, a number of Christian teenagers who say they believe in personal evangelism simply aren't acting out that belief as a lifestyle habit—or weren't during the month in question. Recall that fully 84% said they believed that Christians are expected to tell others about Jesus, yet only 56% actually did this in the past month—a difference of 28 percentage points. In other words, more than 1 in 4 kids in our youth groups simply aren't living up to their own expectations in this regard.

Subgroup Comparisons on Evangelistic Belief vs. Practice

This result made me curious enough to run some additional comparison data to see what percentages of the subgroups I identified earlier in this chapter also followed up their belief with action. For this comparison I first tallied the number of kids in each subgroup who indicated a belief in personal evangelism by marking "somewhat agree" or "strongly agree" on question 27 ("Christians are expected to tell others about Jesus"). Next I tallied the number of students who indicated they were living a lifestyle of personal evangelism by marking "somewhat agree" or "strongly agree" on question 28 ("I shared about my faith in Jesus during the past month").

The first subgroups I looked at were those centered on belief in Jesus as the sole Savior of humankind.

Again, it was no surprise to discover that the kids most likely to talk about their faith were those who believe Jesus is the only way to heaven. Nearly 2 out of 3 of these teenagers (65%) reported faith conversations in the past month. Among youth group members who are unsure or unwilling to say Jesus alone saves, more than half (53%) still spoke out on his behalf to a non-Christian in the recent past. Even a significant number of those students who reject the idea that Jesus is the only way to heaven joined in the conversation, with more than 2 out of 5 (43%) saying they'd shared their faith with a non-Christian.

What was surprising here was that those who were most likely to affirm a belief in personal evangelism were also most likely *not* to express that belief in their real lives. Among students who believe the traditional doctrine of salvation (that Jesus is the only way to heaven), the differential between belief in and practice of personal evangelism was 31 percentage points—nearly 1 in 3 students. Conversely, students who deny the traditional doctrine of salvation were most consistent among these three comparison groups, with a belief-to-practice differential of only 12 percentage points.

Next, I checked out how evangelistic belief and practice differed among Christian guys and girls. The number of each gender who affirmed a Christian's responsibility to lead others to Christ is nearly identical (84% and 83%), but the corresponding number of guys and girls who actually practiced what they believed in this regard shows a significant divergence. Among Christian young men, just over half (52%) reported that they'd talked about Jesus with a non-Christian in the last thirty days.

Meanwhile, 3 out of 5 young women (60%) reported that they'd done the same. Apparently Christian girls are either more comfortable with, or have more opportunity for, faith conversations in their regular lives—and a large number of them are capitalizing on those advantages to start discussions about Jesus with others.

Figure 9.6

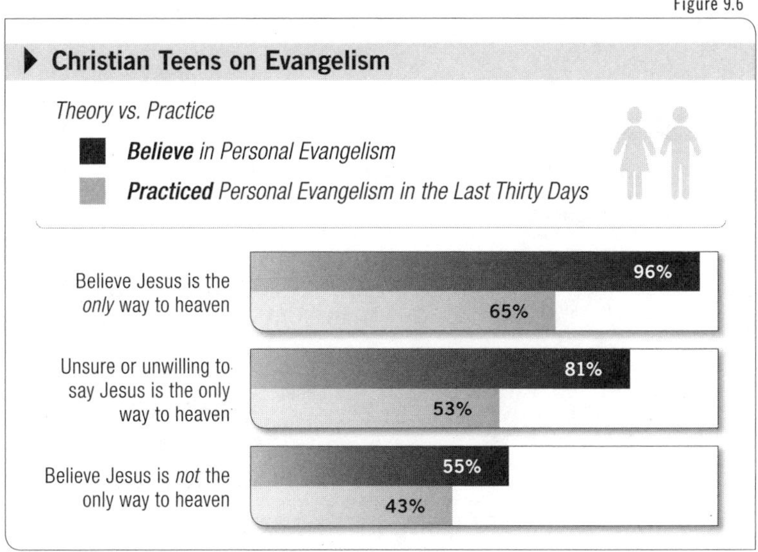

Figure 9.7

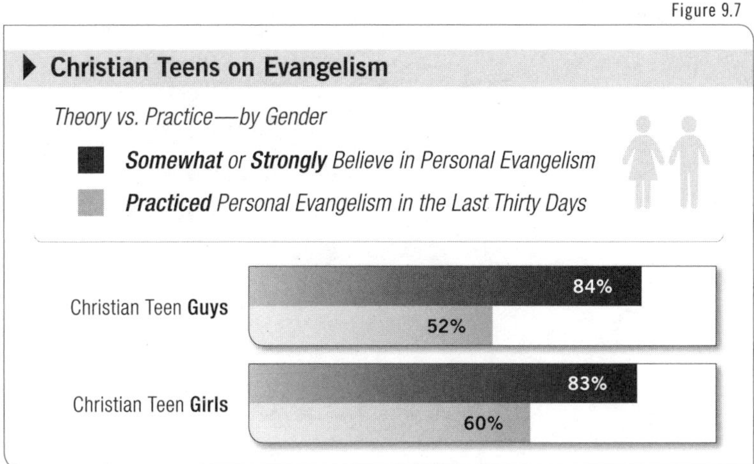

Last but not least, I took a snapshot of how denominational affiliation seemed to influence the expression of evangelistic beliefs in our students' everyday lives. This was interesting. Once again—with one notable exception—those teens who were *most* likely to affirm belief in personal evangelism were also *least* likely to follow through on that belief.

Figure 9.8

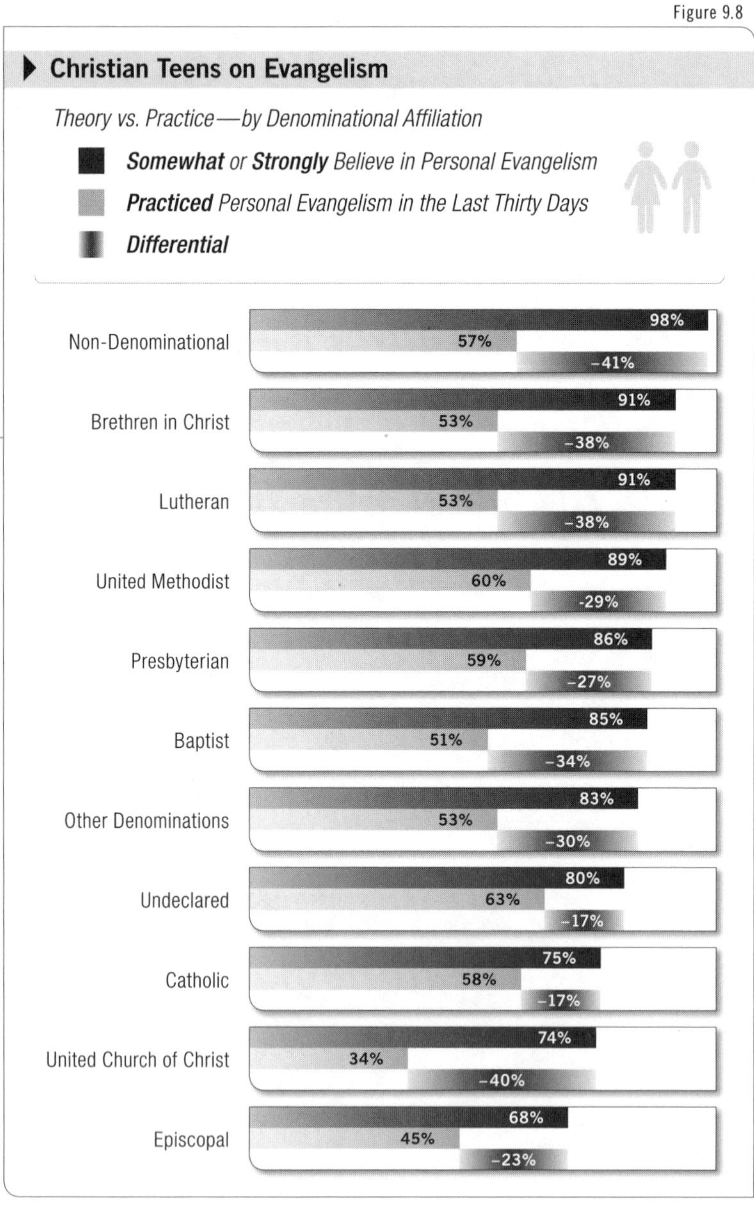

For instance, more than 9 out of 10 non-denominational teens, along with Brethren in Christ and Lutheran kids, indicated a belief in personal evangelism as an obligation for Christian people (98%, 91%, and 91%, respectively). At the same time, all of these groups had a belief-to-life differential of 38 percentage points or more—more than every other denominational affiliation except one. Conversely, two of the bottom four denominations in this category indicated lower levels of belief in personal evangelism (Catholics 75%, and Undeclared 80%), yet had higher levels of actual participation in evangelistic efforts in the past month (Catholics 58%, and Undeclared 63%), than all three denominational groups at the top of the evangelistic belief spectrum.

This seems to present two unique problems. First, there's a clear disconnect between faith and action among all church teens, but particularly among a large number of teenagers in non-denominational, Brethren in Christ, and Lutheran churches. Second, while it's laudatory that Catholic teens are among those who are most often spreading the gospel, data from previous chapters in this book strongly suggests that many of these evangelistic-minded kids are spreading a gospel different from what the Bible teaches. No, I don't believe that means these kids should censor their faith expressions—but I think it does mean we need to do a better job of helping our Christian teenagers (of all denominations) to understand and articulate authentic, biblical Christianity to their world.

The big exception here among the denominations was the United Church of Christ kids. These Christian students were second to last in asserting an obligation to tell others about Jesus (74%), and dead last in actual evangelistic effort in the past month (34%). Those numbers, I think, speak for themselves.

What Kind of Evangelists Are in Our Youth Groups?

Having looked at questions 27 and 28 separately and then by subgroup comparison, I next wanted to see if I could get a clarifying glimpse at what kinds of "evangelist personalities" could be seen in the numbers—and thus in our youth groups. So, as I did with several of the previous question couplets in *The Jesus Survey*, I cross-correlated the data as a whole between the two questions to see what kinds of groupings kids' answers typically fell into. When I was finished, the following four personalities came to the forefront.

Passionate Evangelists. These were the Christian youth who expressed a strong belief in the expectation of Christian evangelism and also claimed (either somewhat or strongly) they'd shared about their faith in Jesus in the past month. These represent about 1 out of 3 (32%) kids in our youth groups.

Irregular Evangelists. These youth group members comprised just over half (51%) of Christian students, and reflected kids who gave somewhat mixed messages about their belief and lifestyle habits. These Christian teens typically expressed—either somewhat or strongly—a belief in evangelistic efforts, but in the last month their actions either exceeded their belief or their belief exceeded their actions. For instance, some only somewhat agreed that Christians have an evangelistic obligation, but also strongly reported that they'd shared their faith in the last thirty days. Others said they strongly supported a belief in sharing their faith, but then couldn't report the same strong confidence—or any confidence at all—about their evangelistic actions in the last month.

Reluctant Evangelists. These Christian kids expressed uniform denial of the idea that followers of Jesus are expected to tell others about the gospel. In spite of that belief, they also reported that in the last thirty days they'd told a non-Christian about their faith in Jesus anyway. This is the smallest grouping of "evangelist personalities" in our youth groups (6%).

Absent Evangelists. Christian students in this category were consistently living out what they believed—which was that Christians are *not* obligated to share the gospel with others. As such, everyone in this group disagreed with question 27 (Christians are expected to tell others about Jesus) and also reported that they had not shared about their faith with anybody over the course of the last month. These kids numbered 12% in *The Jesus Survey*.

Figure 9.9

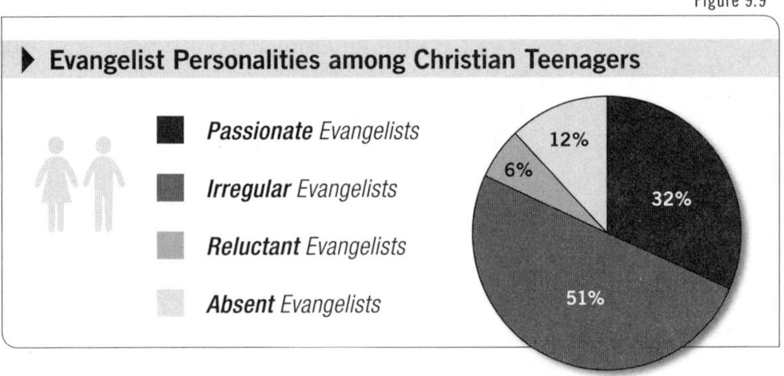

Therefore, I took the four core Christian beliefs about Christ (discussed in the intermission) and applied the appropriate filters to each of the four evangelist personalities to see what that might reveal. I wanted to see what percentage of each evangelist grouping would be likely to share authentic, biblical Christianity when leading others to Christ. The results were a little bit encouraging and also a little disconcerting (see fig. 9.10).

First, the Passionate Evangelists among our teens are—by large margins—also the ones most likely to adhere to traditional Christian doctrine about Christ. For instance, nearly 3 out of 4 (72%) show a strong belief in the physical resurrection of Jesus, whereas no other evangelist personality has more than half who share that belief. Additionally, 50% of the Passionate Evangelists also strongly believe the Bible is trustworthy. Compare that to the other groups and it's nearly double what the Irregular Evangelists believe, twenty-five times more than what the Reluctant Evangelists believe, and seven times more than what the Absent Evangelists believe. So, from that perspective, it appears that those teens who adhere to core Christian orthodoxy are also the ones who are most enthusiastic about sharing their faith with others. As has come to be the norm in this study, right belief has a direct, measurable impact on a Christian student's experience. That's encouraging.

At the same time, the overwhelming majority of our teen evangelists are not strongly rooted in basic Christian belief about Jesus. For instance, while it's great that 50% of our Passionate Evangelists believe the Bible to be trustworthy, that also means that 50% of those evangelists have measurable doubts about God's Word. And while Passionate Evangelists are substantially more likely to be Confident Christians—that is, teens who express confident belief in four core Christian doctrines (see fig. 9.10)—only about 1 in 5 (19%) of these Christian evangelists expresses unshakeable faith in all four of these basic tenets of Christianity. Additionally, combining all groups of evangelists within our youth congregations reveals that barely 1 out of 4 (26%) is likely to share authentic Christian belief when engaged in evangelistic effort.

Figure 9.10

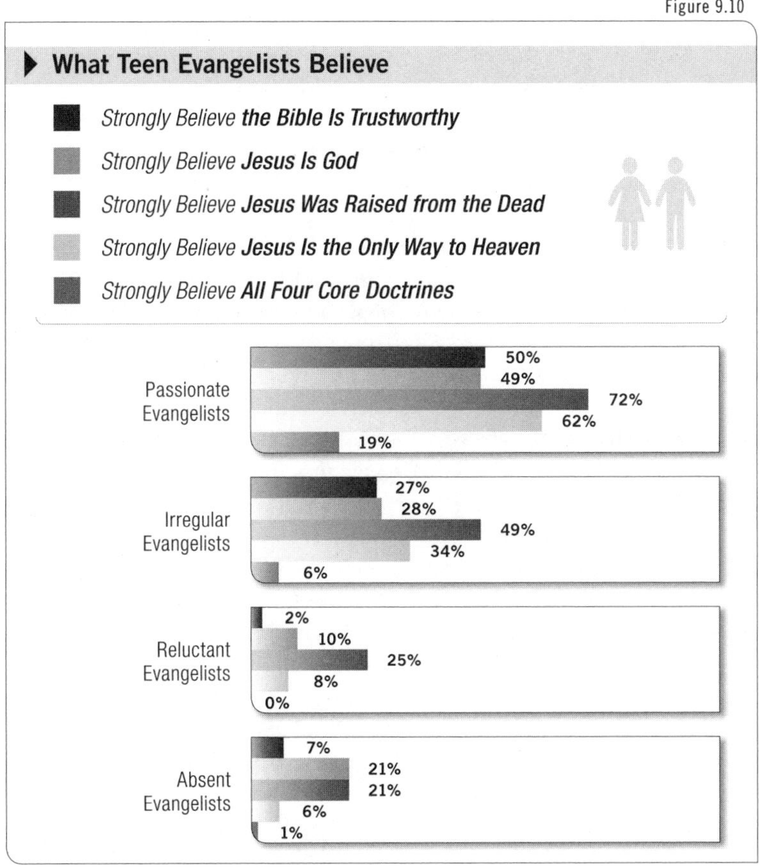

That's a concern—and it's primarily the problem of Christian parents and church leaders who are instructing these kids in the faith. We can be proud of these teens for being willing to stand up and talk about Jesus in often hostile cultural settings, but we must also become better disciplers who are helping our young evangelists experience and discover raw truth about Jesus. If we are successful in doing that, together we might just change the world.

Summary

• Belief in the Great Commission appears to be widely held among the teenagers in our youth groups. More than 4 out of 5 of these teenagers (84%) indicated that they at least somewhat support the assumption that Christians have an obligation to spread the good news of Jesus. This is significant because it indicates that, despite their previous tendencies to assert that all religions are the same, these Christian kids still feel an obligation to convert others to Christianity anyway.

• *Even among Christian teens who believe Jesus is not the only way to heaven, a majority still expresses an obligation to share the Christian faith with others.* More than half of these kids (55%) affirm that every follower of Christ has a responsibility to tell others about Jesus "with the intent of leading them to be Christian too." This is a little surprising, and can likely be attributed at least somewhat to consistent teaching on this topic within Christian churches and families.

• *More than half (56%) of Christian teenagers reported that they had shared about faith in Jesus with a non-Christian during the past thirty days.* This snapshot of teen lifestyle suggests that, even in a culture that's often hostile to their beliefs, Christian youth are generally open and unashamed about their religion.

• *At the same time, a number of Christian teenagers who say they believe in personal evangelism simply aren't acting out that belief as a lifestyle habit.* Fully 84% said they believe that Christians are "expected to tell others about Jesus," yet only 56% actually did that in the past month—a difference of 28 percentage points.

• *Christian girls are more likely to engage in faith conversations than Christian guys.* Just over half of teen guys (52%) reported that they'd talked about Jesus with a non-Christian in the last thirty days. During that same time, 3 out of 5 young women (60%) reported that they'd shared about their faith with a non-Christian.

• *Passionate Evangelists make up about 1 out of 3 (32%) kids in our church youth groups.* These are Christian teens who express a strong belief in personal evangelism and also report that they shared about their faith in Jesus in the past month.

• *Although Christian teens are not shy about telling others of Christ, only 1 out of 4 (26%) is likely to share authentic Christian belief when engaged in evangelistic effort.* The rest share a mix of cultural and religious belief that is similar to Christianity, but often peppered with untrue doctrinal beliefs that are actually anti-Christian in nature. This is cause for concern and a problem that needs to be proactively addressed by Christian parents and church leaders.

Bonus Survey Results

Figure 9.11

Teen Evangelist Personalities (by Grade)

	Passionate Evangelists	*Irregular Evangelists*	*Reluctant Evangelists*	*Absent Evangelists*
7th Grade	**12%**	**61%**	**6%**	**21%**
8th Grade	**43%**	**43%**	**2%**	**13%**
9th Grade	**28%**	**56%**	**4%**	**11%**
10th Grade	**30%**	**55%**	**5%**	**10%**
11th Grade	**29%**	**52%**	**7%**	**12%**
12th Grade	**37%**	**44%**	**8%**	**12%**

Figure 9.12

Teen Evangelist Personalities (by Denomination)

	Passionate Evangelists	*Irregular Evangelists*	*Reluctant Evangelists*	*Absent Evangelists*
Baptist	**31%**	**49%**	**3%**	**17%**
Brethren in Christ	**36%**	**55%**	**0%**	**9%**
Catholic	**22%**	**51%**	**13%**	**15%**
Episcopal	**9%**	**54%**	**10%**	**27%**
Lutheran	**33%**	**57%**	**5%**	**5%**
Non-Denominational	**49%**	**49%**	**1%**	**1%**
Other Denominations	**34%**	**49%**	**3%**	**14%**
Presbyterian	**34%**	**51%**	**6%**	**10%**
Undeclared	**36%**	**42%**	**3%**	**19%**
United Church of Christ	**17%**	**57%**	**6%**	**20%**
United Methodist	**38%**	**51%**	**3%**	**8%**

10

THE SECOND COMING AND CHRISTIAN TEENS

I am coming soon.
Revelation 22:20

When Esther was sixteen, her mother had a dream. In this dream she saw Esther's deceased grandmother. "When is Jesus coming?" asked Esther's mom. "October 28, 1992," replied the grandmother.

When Steven was in fourth grade, a leader in his church prophesied to him, "Jesus is coming when you're seventeen years old." Steven turned seventeen in 1992.

Edward was the pastor at Mission for the Coming Days church in Denver, Colorado. As a result of dreams and visions, Edward and many of his youth group members believed that Jesus would finally return to earth on October 28, 1992, at 8:00 a.m. (Mountain Time). Edward and his youth group weren't alone in their expectation of Christ's return. In Seoul, South Korea, thousands of other sincere Christians, along with many churches, prepared for the second coming of Christ on that date.

On October 26, 1992, two days before the expected time, an interviewer asked Edward what he thought would happen when Christ returned on October 28. Edward described an instantaneous removal of his physical body, leaving his clothes and his lapel microphone to fall to the floor. He finished by saying, "Wednesday morning. That's what we're anticipating."

On October 29, 1992, the headlines in the newspaper read, "Flash: World Didn't End Yesterday. 'We got the message wrong,' frustrated believers say."

Edward, Esther, Steven, and thousands of others were left in disappointment and confusion. As early as 8:15 a.m. on October 28, 1992, Mission for the Coming

Days started receiving calls from concerned Christians all over the world. They were asking, "Are we the only ones left? Are you guys still here?"

"God, why didn't you come?" seventeen-year-old Steven asked.

Likening the situation to that of Jonah and the Ninevites, Edward could offer only one explanation to his youth group and the rest of the world. "It would seem as if the Lord is giving humanity another grace period," he said.[1]

The members of the youth group at Mission for the Coming Days aren't the only ones to get confused about Jesus's imminent return—teens in our Christian homes and churches struggle to understand that future as well. And why not? Few topics of theology have been more hotly debated over the centuries. The fact is, Jesus might very well have come back on October 28, 1992. Or he might delay his return for another ten thousand years.

For many American teenagers, the triumphant return of Christ may seem irrelevant or simply not worth the time spent trying to understand what it really means. But even though we may (correctly) fault Edward and the leaders at Mission for the Coming Days for trying to predict the date and time when Jesus will return, I have to admit that I still admire them a little bit.

They were at least willing to prepare their kids for Jesus's return.

Think of it this way: when our kids are anticipating a big test at school, they want to know all about it. What will be covered? When will it take place? Will it be multiple choice, or essay questions? How thoroughly does one need to know the material? Students want to be ready for an upcoming test; their grade depends on it. In the same way, our Christian students need to anticipate—and prepare—for the upcoming return of Jesus. So much more than a grade in school depends on that heart preparation.

Of course I'm not suggesting that we should begin shouting "Jesus will return on October 28!" or any other specific date. That's both foolish and unkind. But I do believe it's essential to help our Christian teenagers prepare their hearts and lives as if Jesus will return today. After all, there's a reason why theologians often call the second coming of Jesus the "Imminent Return of Christ."[2]

It could happen today, tomorrow, or any day in our lifetimes.

In fact, there is biblical evidence that suggests Jesus's own disciples expected Christ to return in their lifetimes (see 1 Cor. 1:7; Phil. 4:5; 1 Thess. 4:15–18; Rev. 22:20–21; and others). What's more, that "imminent" expectation has persisted throughout the history of Christ's not-yet-returning, inspiring Christians from all ages to persevere, to profess, and to look hopefully toward greater intimacy with Jesus in eternity. Knowing that Jesus's second coming is to be preceded by harsh, antagonistic circumstances for believers (see Mark 13), one also has to wonder how Christian teens will hold up under that coming persecution (promised by Christ!) if they are lackadaisical or halfhearted about anticipating his glorious, redeeming return within their lifetimes.

What if you don't believe Jesus will return before you die? Does that make a difference in the way you live your life? In the way you approach a relationship with Christ? In the way you pursue deeper intimacy with God? In the way you make daily decisions that affect eternity? In the way you relate to your culture and your neighbor? In the way you involve yourself in, or disengage from, the community and support of a local church? In the way you pursue a career and family and outreach and more? I think it does. Actually, I think there's no way it *can't* significantly influence a Christian person's life and lifestyle.

So, with that in mind, in the last content question on *The Jesus Survey* I asked our teenagers what their expectations were regarding the imminent return of Christ. I found a few surprises in their answers.

Jesus's Return: Today, or Someday?

In this portion of the content section of *The Jesus Survey*, I wanted to explore whether or not Christian teenagers viewed the return of Christ as something imminent that would likely happen in their lifetimes or something distant that was not a vital concern for today. I only had room left on the survey for one question at this point, so that was all I asked on this topic. I wish now I'd been able to include a few follow-up questions on this topic, or at least a couplet from which to clarify teen responses, but hindsight is, of course, 20/20. So we will deal here with the data we have. Still, as with previous questions on this survey, I would encourage future researchers to pursue this topic more in-depth with Christian teenagers.

Like all questions on *The Jesus Survey*, I listed a one-sentence statement and then asked kids to indicate whether they agreed or disagreed with the statement. So, in question 29 I asked kids to react to this statement regarding the nearness of Christ's return:

> The anticipated "second coming of Jesus" will occur in my lifetime.

This question, like no other on *The Jesus Survey*, seemed to divide survey respondents—and generated the most "write-in" comments of the whole questionnaire. Additionally, question 29 was, by far, the highest non-response item here, so much so that I need to talk about that phenomenon for a moment.

Typically, in a survey like this one, item non-response (when a student skips a question on his or her survey) happens with regularity, but is also rare enough not to carry much weight in a statistical trend analysis such as this one. For instance, in every case except for question 29, non-response items amounted to anywhere from 0% to just over 2% of all responses. As such, when analyzing trends on individual questions, those item non-responses were excluded from percentage totals for that specific question.

However, when I asked teens about Jesus's imminent return in question 29, the number of non-responses suddenly exploded, accounting for more than 10% of all answers to this question—more even than those who indicated a "strongly agree" response. Given the size of the survey sample, I felt that was a significant number, both in its scope and in its dramatic departure from the norm for all previous questions. So, rather than exclude them from results on this question, I've opted to include them under the category "No Opinion" in the results in this chapter.

Question 29: "Jesus's Second Coming Will Occur in My Lifetime."

So, when asking Christian teenagers whether or not they anticipated Jesus to return in their lifetimes, that meant the final tallies came out like this:

A little more than 1 in 3 (38%) indicated either strongly or somewhat that they expect Jesus to come before they die. Notably, only about 1 in 12 of the kids in our youth groups (8%) strongly believes this—which seems a remarkably low number given the current world circumstances in which these teens have come of age.

Perhaps even more surprising is the number of Christian teenagers who actually *don't* believe Jesus will return in their lifetimes. Nearly half of our youth group members (49%) simply disbelieve that Jesus will indeed "come quickly" as he promised, at least in regard to the next seventy years or so. And another 13% of our teens (about 1 in 7) refuse to even venture an opinion on the topic of Jesus's return.

Figure 10.1

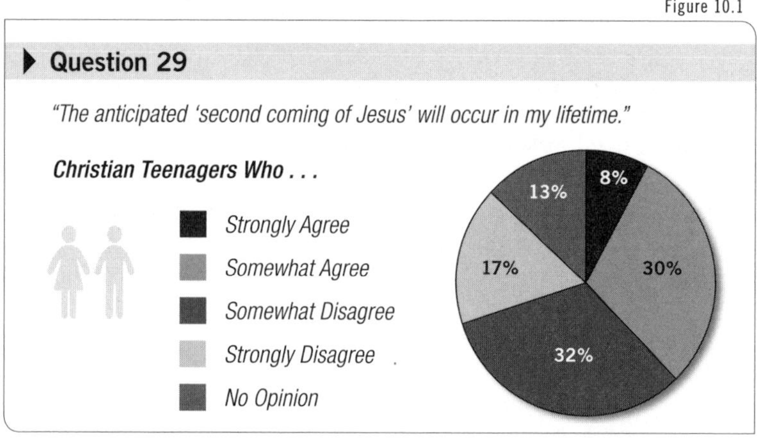

The reason kids gave for refusing to answer this question were generally all the same.

"It will happen when it happens," one 10th grader from Pennsylvania told me. A high school senior from a non-denominational church metaphorically rolled her eyes at the question. "Really?" she said. "If Christ doesn't know, I don't know." Another student, a 10th grade guy from Illinois, lined through the question completely and wrote, "We'll *never* know." A Baptist boy also lined through this one, saying, "There's no way to know, so I'm not gonna act like it." My favorite, though, was a message I got here from a Lutheran teen in Pennsylvania: "I'm not at liberty to say."

For the most part, these kids seem to have taken to heart the latter part of Matthew 24:42: "You do not know on what day your Lord will come" (NIV). However, by refusing to latch onto a tangible hope that Christ will return within their lifetimes, they also appear to be in danger of abdicating their responsibilities outlined in the first part of that same verse: "Therefore keep watch."

For many Christian teenagers, it seems, asking whether or not Christ will come before they die is pretty much the same as asking them to predict that Jesus will return on October 28, or some other specific date and time. That, of course, isn't what responding to this question required, but that's irrelevant. What is relevant is that a number of teenagers thought it did, and like their previously displayed unwillingness to fully commit to other specific matters of faith, this non-response felt like safer ground.

It should also be noted that a few students did answer the question from the opposite extreme. For instance, one Catholic girl from Michigan seems to have mixed up biblical theology with Mayan mythology. She is one of the 8% who strongly believes that Jesus will return in her lifetime—and she made sure I knew when: "2012!" Additionally an Episcopal girl from Texas negated the possibility of any physical return of Christ at all by telling me, "I believe the second coming comes as we die."

Because so many students either rejected the idea that Jesus would return in their lifetimes or avoided answering the issue altogether, I asked a few kids to tell me more about this in their follow-up interviews. Interestingly, the responses were still the same as what many had written on their surveys. "This is a tough question," one United Methodist girl told me. "I honestly have no idea." "I haven't really thought about it," said another student, an 11th grade guy from New York. And a Baptist boy from Alabama was likewise vague about it, saying, "Jesus will return whenever God is ready."

Of course, I agree with these kids in an intellectual way. Clearly we can't know when Christ will return. Still, to use that as a rationale for dismissing any expectation of his return in one's own lifetime seems a dangerous mistake—and it appears to indicate that this issue is being downplayed in our church youth groups as well. To check this hunch, I sent a few follow-up emails to some youth leaders who took the survey and asked them whether or not they felt it was important for Christian teenagers to anticipate the return of Jesus in their lifetimes. Their opinions were split on the issue.

One youth worker from a United Methodist church told me, "[I'm] not sure. . . . I think most of us have become numb to all the hoopla of panic-driven discussions about end times. Honestly, I don't know that it matters." Another Methodist leader felt just the opposite. "Absolutely!" she said. "Teenagers need to [prepare] for the return just as we all do. Why shouldn't they?" A Presbyterian leader from California agreed, saying, "Yes, I think it is clear that we don't know the exact time of Christ's coming and must live as if he will come back at any time and any day. It is the biblically historical approach to how we should be living."

Who's Looking to the Sky?

I tend toward a viewpoint similar to that Californian, but clearly a majority of our teens do not. So who does? Which of our teenagers are actively anticipating the return of Jesus in their lifetimes? I decided to see if I could find out.

First, I sorted the data according to gender. When it comes to guys and girls in our youth groups, the expected stereotypes don't apply. Up to this point, young women most often outnumbered young men in their adoption of Christian belief and practice. However, when it comes to the question of Jesus's impending return, Christian teen guys are slightly more likely to believe he'll show up in this lifetime, with 40% of young men expressing that opinion. Among teen girls, 37% believe the same.

Figure 10.2

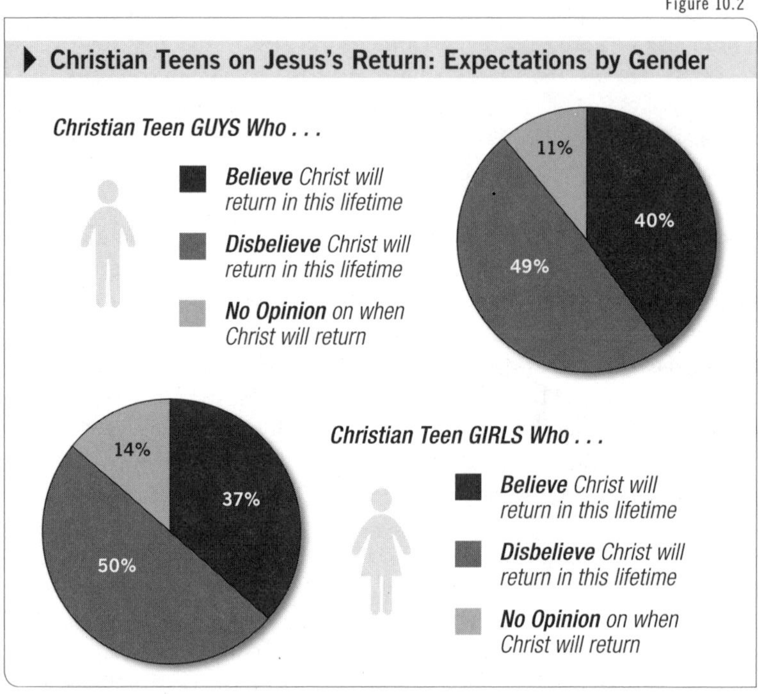

As with the overall population, roughly half of each gender (49% of guys, 50% of girls) disbelieve Jesus will come back anytime soon. Guys, however, are slightly more willing to stake out an opinion on this issue, with only about 1 in 10 (11%) declining to answer while 1 in 7 girls (14%) opted to avoid a decision on this one.

Next, I sorted the data according to denomination. Viewing it this way was informative, if only because it hints at which denominations make Christ's return a priority in youth group ministry. Of all church group affiliations, non-denominational youth were the only ones with a majority anticipating Jesus's second coming within their own lifetimes. More than half of these kids (54%) indicated that expectation, while 1 in 3 (33%) expressed measurable disbelief that Jesus will crack the skies in this lifetime.

Non-denominational youth also had the distinction of being 1 of only 4 affiliations in which teens who believe that Jesus is coming soon outnumber teens who don't believe it. Among Lutheran students, 43% expect his coming, while 38%

don't. For Undeclared students, 38% anticipate being witnesses to Christ's return, while 32% do not. And Baptist boys and girls slightly favor an imminent return by a margin of 37% to 34%.

Figure 10.3

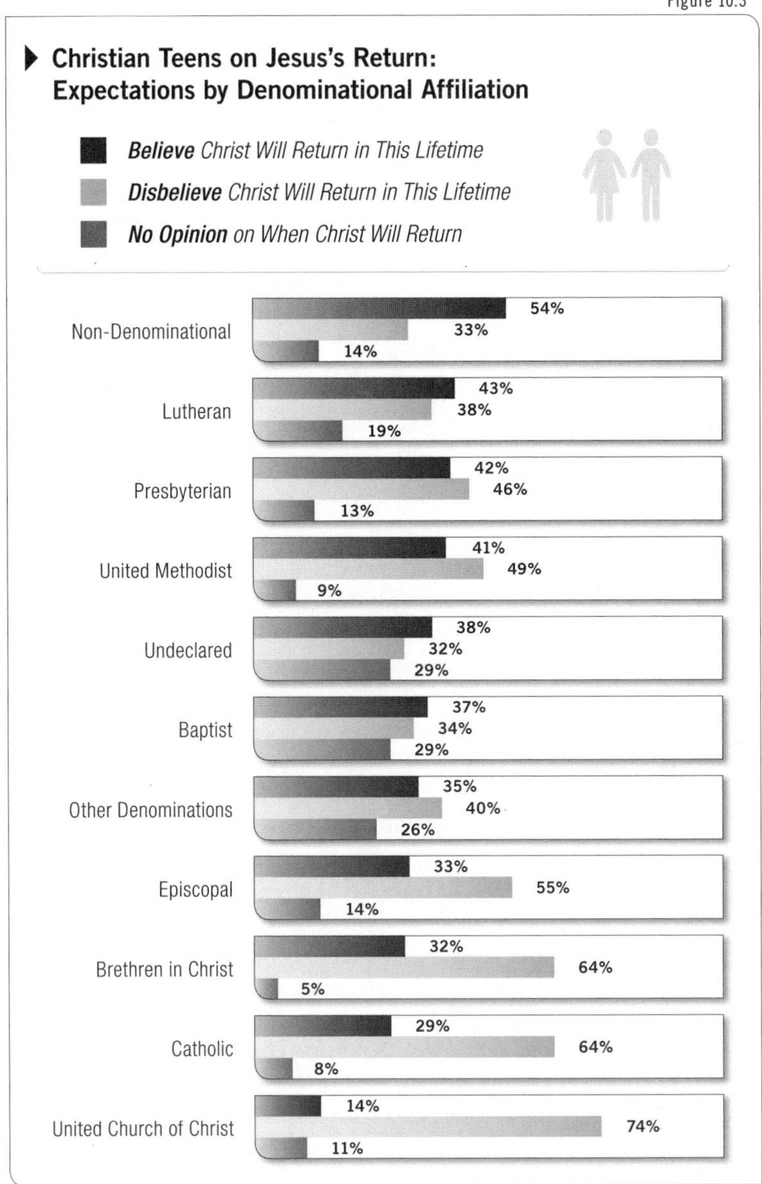

Additionally, Baptist and Undeclared students were the most unwilling to make a commitment on this issue, with 29% of each group opting for a "no opinion" response—more than double the rate of non-response from the general population of the survey. Youth from Catholic and United Church of Christ churches were at the bottom of this list.

Throughout *The Jesus Survey*, there has frequently been a pronounced correlation between the various doctrinal beliefs about Jesus among Christian teens. For instance, those who hold unshakeable belief in the trustworthiness of the Bible are also more likely to strongly affirm that Jesus physically came back to life after his execution. So, for the last breakdown on question 29, I decided to see if a similar correlation showed up in regard to Jesus's return. Using the sixteen doctrinal perspectives I identified back in chapter 8, I sorted survey respondents into those various subgroups of orthodoxy.

Once again, faith in core Christian beliefs appeared to have a significant influence on the issue at hand. In this case, a clear majority (56%) of Confident Christian teenagers (who express strong belief in four key doctrines about Christ) were by far the largest group to express a timely hope in Jesus's second coming. In fact, this subgroup was the only one of all sixteen observed here to include a majority of students who said they anticipated Christ's return within their lifetimes. And within this subgroup, these students outnumbered those who disbelieve Jesus's return is imminent by a 2 to 1 margin (56% to 28%).

Unshakeable teens (who believe the Bible is completely trustworthy), along with teens who believe Jesus is the only way to heaven, were the subgroups with the next highest number of students expecting Jesus's imminent return. Each of these subgroups charted nearly half (48%) with that belief. Interestingly, Unshakeable teens had fewer who disbelieved this, due primarily to the higher percentage of youth group members who chose to avoid taking any opinion at all on the issue (21% to 16%). In fact, Unshakeables were the youth most likely to leave this question blank.

Rounding out the top four subgroups who believe Jesus will return soon were those teens who believe Jesus is God, with 46% saying they expect Christ to come back before they die.

Significantly, no other subgroup of Christian teenagers among these sixteen had a majority express belief in Jesus's soon return. As might be expected, belief in the basics of Christian doctrine also heightens a teenager's expectation in the fulfillment of that belief through Jesus's imminent return.

Student subgroups most likely to disbelieve Jesus's second coming is near are also unsurprising. The overwhelming majority of both Christian teens who don't see the Bible as trustworthy and Christian teens who don't believe Jesus is the only way to heaven simply aren't looking for Jesus to return. More than 3 out of 4 of those who don't trust the Bible (77%) disbelieve Christ will come back in their lifetimes; 4 of 5 who reject the idea that Jesus is the only way to heaven (80%) also disbelieve he will return before they die. And not many have any problem making this commitment: these students were least likely to leave this question blank. Only 6% of each of these subgroups demonstrated item non-response here, or about 3.5 times less than their Unshakeable counterparts. For these kids, it would seem that the return of Jesus is either irrelevant or a myth, and either way is not worth concerning themselves with. That should be sobering news for all of us who are Christian parents or youth leaders in a church.

Figure 10.4 (Part 1 of 2)

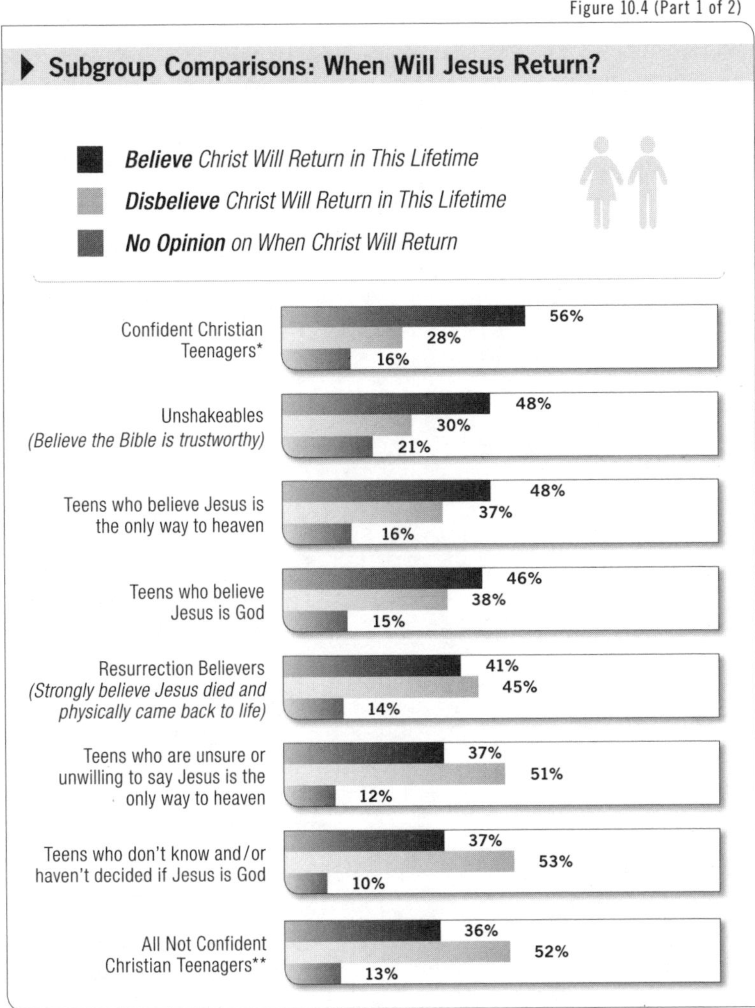

* Express strong confidence in four key Christian doctrines: 1) the Bible is trustworthy, 2) Jesus is God, 3) Jesus died and rose again, 4) Jesus is the only way to heaven.

** Express measurable reservations about one or more of four key doctrines of Christianity.

Figure 10.4 (Part 2 of 2)

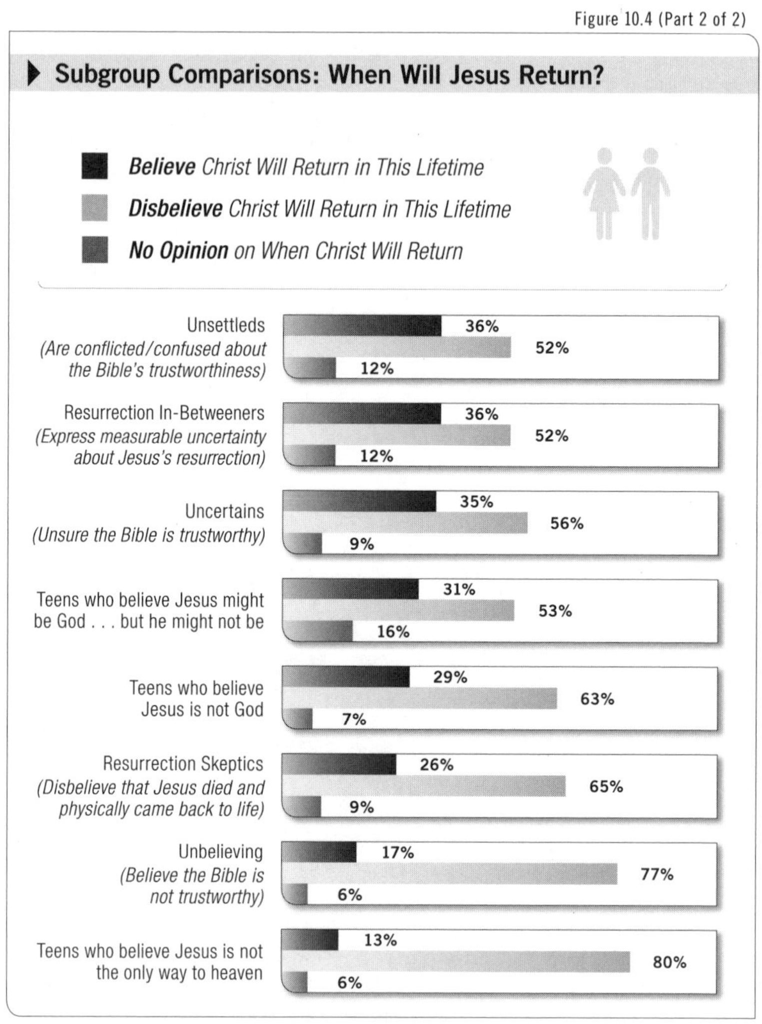

Summary

• About half (49%) of Christian teenagers don't believe Jesus will return within their lifetimes. Additionally, about 1 in 7 (13%) refused to even venture an opinion on the topic.

• *Teen guys are slightly more likely than teen girls to believe Jesus's second coming will happen before they die.* Among Christian guys, 40% of young men say they expect Jesus to return in their lifetime. Among teen girls, 37% believe that.

• *Non-denominational youth are most likely to say they expect Jesus's return in their lifetimes.* More than half of these kids (54%) expressed that opinion—the only denominational affiliation in *The Jesus Survey* to have a majority of students who agreed with this question. Catholic, Brethren in Christ, and United Church of Christ students were the ones most convinced Christ will not return in their lifetime, with 64%, 64%, and 74%, respectively, saying they disbelieve his return is imminent.

• *Belief in the basics of Christian doctrine also heightens a teenager's expectation in the fulfillment of that belief through Jesus's imminent return.* More than half (56%) of Confident Christian teenagers (who express strong confidence in four key Christian doctrines) say they believe Jesus's coming is near, within their lifetimes. Those who are *least* likely to believe Christ will return soon are students who disbelieve that Jesus is God and students who lack faith in the trustworthiness of Scripture. More than 3 out of 4 of those who don't trust the Bible (77%) disbelieve Christ will come back in their lifetimes; 4 out of 5 who reject the idea that Jesus is the only way to heaven (80%) also disbelieve he will return before they die.

Bonus Survey Results

Figure 10.5

Question 29

Adult Leaders Predicted Christian Teenagers Would . . .

	Strongly Agree	*Somewhat Agree*	*Strongly Disagree*	*Somewhat Disagree*	*No Opinion*
"The anticipated 'second coming of Jesus' will occur in my lifetime."	**5%**	**24%**	**35%**	**26%**	**10%**

Figure 10.6

Christian Teens on Jesus's Return: Expectations (by Grade)

	Believe *Christ Will Return in This Lifetime*	***Disbelieve*** *Christ Will Return in This Lifetime*	***No Opinion*** *on When Christ Will Return*
Junior Highers (Grades 7 & 8)	**40%**	**43%**	**18%**
High School Underclassmen (Grades 9 & 10)	**44%**	**44%**	**12%**
High School Upperclassmen (Grades 11 & 12)	**33%**	**55%**	**12%**

AFTERWORD

Every Generation Blames the One Before . . .

Right when I began writing this book, this song came on the radio: "The Living Years" by Mike & The Mechanics.

As you likely know, this melody begins with the lyric, "Every generation blames the one before."[1] I didn't think about it much at the time, but now I kind of think God had a hand in the DJ's timing that day.

During the months that followed, I heard those words in my head at the most unexpected times. When I wrote "the overwhelming majority of our kids (70%) express persistent, measurable doubts—and even outright disbelief in many cases—that what the Bible has to say about Jesus is true" back in chapter 1, Mike & The Mechanics seemed to harmonize in my head. When I tugged out details from teen belief (and disbelief) in Jesus's deity, I heard "The Living Years" playing. When I worked through the nonsense conspiracy theories surrounding Christ's death and resurrection (chapters 3 and 4), the polytheistic viewpoints toward salvation and eternity in chapter 5, and the core belief summary in the intermission of this book, well you guessed it: *every generation blames the one before. . . .*

Then, when subsequent chapters about the Holy Spirit, prayer, and Bible study revealed that right belief translates into real experience, I realized why I kept hearing that song.

Every generation blames the one before.

Look, I know what I blame my parents' generation for—and my list is pretty long. But now I have to ask myself the questions: What will today's teenagers blame me and my generation for? What legacy of faith are we leaving them that'll turn out to be something that makes them grit their teeth in anger and annoyance? That might actually cost them not just a moment but a lifetime in eternity?

Judging from the results of *The Jesus Survey*, there are plenty of things to choose from. So, as I wrap up this long, draining, exhilarating, depressing-and-joyful study on teen beliefs about Jesus, I want to finish with a few private thoughts for you.

First, thank you.

You can't imagine how grateful I am that you took the time to read, and consider, this book. Yes, I know many of you disagreed with my viewpoints and assumptions. And I know that sometimes I can be pretty annoying, especially when I have an opinion about something (and surprise, I have an opinion about everything!). So thanks for sticking it out with me, and for going on this journey with me. I felt your prayers and encouragement—and really tough questions—with every page. And I'm humbled to know that you allowed me to be a part of your perspective on Christian parenting and church leadership of teenagers.

Next (and after spending months digging through absurd details and data from *The Jesus Survey*, I think this is vital) I'd like to suggest one thing to you:

The absolute best thing you can ever do for any Christian teenager, including yours at home and in your church, is to help that teen grow confident in the trustworthiness of Scripture.

Teens who believe the Bible is true also are more likely to embrace authentic Christian beliefs. And these kids, time and time again, are more likely to experience an authentic, noticeable relationship with God. If you hesitate to believe that, then you obviously didn't read this book—or you simply don't want to believe the data.

I don't know how to tell you exactly how to help your kids gain this kind of unshakeable confidence in the Bible—I suspect that every student and every youth group might need something a little bit different. Prayer seems a necessary element. Youth group classes on the history and reliability of Scripture certainly make sense, but there has to be more than simply a once-every-three-years boring Bible course for teens. Frequent challenges to make kids think about what they believe and why also seem like a good idea. And in that spirit, I challenge you, here and now, to wrestle more deeply with this question for both yourself and for the youth in your care:

What can I do today to nurture confidence in Scripture in a teen? What can I do this week? This month? This year? Over the next five years?

I'm enthusiastic about what you'll come up with in answer; I believe Jesus intends to use you in a significant way to spread his gospel through the next generation—and through many, many generations beyond.

If you're interested, you can also visit www.Nappaland.com/TheJesusSurvey to download free pdf "Guides for Extended Study" to go with *The Jesus Survey*. These are designed to prompt deeper exploration of the issues found in this book. Feel free to use them in parent small groups, youth leader volunteer training, teen Bible studies, and for individual devotions. (Did I mention these are free?)

Last but not least, I want you to notice that there's a "permission to reprint" line on *The Jesus Survey* instrument found in appendix A (p. 177) of this book. That's for you, your church, and your community. I encourage you to repeat this survey with the teenagers in your own home, conduct the survey churchwide in your local youth group, or even stage a citywide version of *The Jesus Survey* right where you live. You not only have my permission to do such a thing with my survey, you have my blessing! I would love for you, and your teenagers, to use this tool as a means for discussion and insight in your home and hometown. Thank you for doing that.

Now, as you begin to renew your ministry and parenting to teenagers:

> May the Lord bless you and keep you;
> May he make his face shine on you and be gracious to you;
> May the Lord turn his face toward you
> And give you peace.[2]
> Amen!

Mike Nappa, 2011

ACKNOWLEDGMENTS

Paul C. Richardson and Lori Jones deserve the highest praise for their work on this book. It is no exaggeration to say that without either one of them, *The Jesus Survey* would never have come to pass. Paulie was my database manager for this entire work; he created the data format and tables, and mentored me in how to use them to discover what I needed to know. Lori, bless her heart, volunteered her time for weeks to faithfully handle the mind-numbing chore of inputting every single answer from every single student on every single question. And—get this—she did it cheerfully! (I know, she's weird, huh?) Anyway, my sincere gratitude to both Lori and Paulie for their generosity and support from day one.

Of course, Mike Jones needs to be mentioned here as well. For some reason, he thought it was no big deal to help me pull off this survey—even supporting the project with human resources and picking up the bulk of the expenses associated with conducting it. (Don't tell him what a wonderful, generous thing he did—he still thinks it's no biggie.) His support and enthusiasm were infectious, and much needed. I'm very grateful that he's my friend.

Another friend, Dr. Steven W. Smith, was generous and helpful with his time and encouragement regarding this book. He's on the frontline of ministry to young adults, and I value his heart and his impact in our world. Oh, and it was pretty cool that he was willing to write the foreword to this book as well. Thanks, Steven—tell your dad I said "Hey!"

My wife, Amy, patiently endured more talks on theology and endless questions of faith, life, and ministry than she has had to suffer through since we were both in Bible college—and yet managed to not kick me out of the house. In fact, she often gave me terribly intelligent insights and practical advice that I used repeatedly without giving her a smidgeon of credit. So, you know, thanks, babe. You're the ginchiest.

Once again, Bob Hosack and the entire team at Baker Books deserves to be recognized. Bob is an author's dream—intelligent, encouraging, and visionary. This is the third book Bob and I have collaborated on, and every one has been a good experience—something almost unthinkable in today's publishing world. Thanks, Bob. The rest of the folks at Baker are equally hardworking—so thanks also to Lindsey Spoolstra, Julie Noordhoek, Michael Cook, Ruth Anderson, and everyone else who contributed to this book. It's an honor to be part of your team.

I also owe a debt of gratitude to a number of great thinkers and researchers whose work influenced my own in immeasurable ways: C. S. Lewis, Charles Colson, Charles R. Swindoll, Christian Smith, David Kinnaman, Dinesh D'Souza, Frank I. Luntz, Gabe Lyons, George Barna, George W. Braswell Jr., Gerry Breshears, Hank Hanegraaff, Henry Clarence Thiessen, Jess Rainer, Joani Schultz, Joshua Harris, Kenda Creasy Dean, Lawrence O. Richards, Lee Strobel, Lisa D. Pearce, Louis Berkof, Malcolm Gladwell, Mark Driscoll, Melinda Lundquist Denton, Rick Lawrence, Robert D. Putnam, Thom Rainer, Thom Schultz, Timothy Keller, and Timothy Paul Jones.

Last, but certainly not least, I need to express my gratitude to Jesus Christ, who first put this idea into my head and heart—and then annoyingly kept it there until I finally got off my rear and did something about it. May you always be that persistent with me, leading me daily one step closer toward you.

To the utmost, Jesus saves!

APPENDICES

Appendix A

THE JESUS SURVEY *INSTRUMENT*

NAPPALAND RESEARCH SURVEY: TEEN BELIEFS ABOUT JESUS

Students:

Please answer each question honestly, choosing the response that is closest to your true feelings and opinions. Be assured that your answers are confidential.

Adult Leaders:

Please answer questions 5–30 by choosing the response that you think most teens would choose. Your choices will later be compared to the actual teen responses.

THE JESUS SURVEY INSTRUMENT

TEEN BELIEFS ABOUT JESUS

1. **Which is your gender?**
   ❍ Male ❍ Female

2. **Which is your school grade level? (Adult leaders, please mark "Adult leader" box.)**
   ❍ 7th ❍ 8th ❍ 9th ❍ 10th ❍ 11th ❍ 12th ❍ Adult Leader

3. **What is your home state (for instance, California, Ohio, New York, etc.)?**

   ____

4. **What is your church denomination (Baptist, Catholic, non-denominational, etc.)?**

   ____

Please indicate whether you disagree or agree with the following statements:

5. **I am a Christian.**
   ❍ Strongly Disagree ❍ Somewhat Disagree ❍ Somewhat Agree ❍ Strongly Agree

6. **The Bible is 100% accurate—historically, factually, and theologically—and therefore completely trustworthy in what it says about Jesus.**
   ❍ Strongly Disagree ❍ Somewhat Disagree ❍ Somewhat Agree ❍ Strongly Agree

7. **The Bible, though generally accurate, contains some widely acknowledged errors and can't be completely trusted in everything it says about Jesus.**
   ❍ Strongly Disagree ❍ Somewhat Disagree ❍ Somewhat Agree ❍ Strongly Agree

8. **Other highly regarded religious books, such as the Koran or the Book of Mormon, are just as important as the Bible in teaching people about who Jesus really was.**
   ❍ Strongly Disagree ❍ Somewhat Disagree ❍ Somewhat Agree ❍ Strongly Agree

9. **Jesus, in some mysterious way, is both the Son of God and God himself.**
   ❍ Strongly Disagree ❍ Somewhat Disagree ❍ Somewhat Agree ❍ Strongly Agree

10. **Jesus was a good man, a righteous teacher, and a noble person, but he was not God.**
    ❍ Strongly Disagree ❍ Somewhat Disagree ❍ Somewhat Agree ❍ Strongly Agree

11. **When Jesus walked this earth he never once sinned, not even in a small way.**
    ❍ Strongly Disagree ❍ Somewhat Disagree ❍ Somewhat Agree ❍ Strongly Agree

12. **Jesus was a great, great man, but he was not 100% perfect so he may have sinned.**
    ❍ Strongly Disagree ❍ Somewhat Disagree ❍ Somewhat Agree ❍ Strongly Agree

TEEN BELIEFS ABOUT JESUS

13. It's a fact that Jesus died physically when he was executed by crucifixion.
   ❍ Strongly Disagree ❍ Somewhat Disagree ❍ Somewhat Agree ❍ Strongly Agree

14. It's a fact that Jesus's "death" on a cross was actually some kind of hoax that was later covered up by his followers and the Catholic Church.
   ❍ Strongly Disagree ❍ Somewhat Disagree ❍ Somewhat Agree ❍ Strongly Agree

15. After his execution, Jesus simply could not have physically "come back to life," despite what the legend says.
   ❍ Strongly Disagree ❍ Somewhat Disagree ❍ Somewhat Agree ❍ Strongly Agree

16. Jesus physically came back to life after his execution.
   ❍ Strongly Disagree ❍ Somewhat Disagree ❍ Somewhat Agree ❍ Strongly Agree

17. Jesus actually escaped death on the cross, married Mary Magdalene, and started a political dynasty—but the church hid this information to keep itself in power.
   ❍ Strongly Disagree ❍ Somewhat Disagree ❍ Somewhat Agree ❍ Strongly Agree

18. Jesus was actually a fictional character invented as an extension of pagan mythology.
   ❍ Strongly Disagree ❍ Somewhat Disagree ❍ Somewhat Agree ❍ Strongly Agree

19. Jesus, Mohammed, Buddha, and other great religious leaders all have equal standing in leading people to heaven.
   ❍ Strongly Disagree ❍ Somewhat Disagree ❍ Somewhat Agree ❍ Strongly Agree

20. I'm 100% certain that Jesus is the only way to heaven.
   ❍ Strongly Disagree ❍ Somewhat Disagree ❍ Somewhat Agree ❍ Strongly Agree

21. The Holy Spirit of Jesus resides in every Christian today, leading and empowering that Christian to be more like God.
   ❍ Strongly Disagree ❍ Somewhat Disagree ❍ Somewhat Agree ❍ Strongly Agree

22. I am 100% certain that the Holy Spirit of Jesus is present and active in my life today—and I have proof that this is true.
   ❍ Strongly Disagree ❍ Somewhat Disagree ❍ Somewhat Agree ❍ Strongly Agree

23. Followers of Jesus should study the Bible daily.
   ❍ Strongly Disagree ❍ Somewhat Disagree ❍ Somewhat Agree ❍ Strongly Agree

24. I study the Bible daily.
   ❍ Strongly Disagree ❍ Somewhat Disagree ❍ Somewhat Agree ❍ Strongly Agree

TEEN BELIEFS ABOUT JESUS

25. **Jesus answers prayers.**
   ❍ Strongly Disagree ❍ Somewhat Disagree ❍ Somewhat Agree ❍ Strongly Agree

26. **I'm 100% certain Jesus has answered one or more of my prayers—and I can prove it.**
   ❍ Strongly Disagree ❍ Somewhat Disagree ❍ Somewhat Agree ❍ Strongly Agree

27. **I believe Christians are expected to tell others about Jesus with the intent of leading them to be Christian too.**
   ❍ Strongly Disagree ❍ Somewhat Disagree ❍ Somewhat Agree ❍ Strongly Agree

28. **I shared about my faith in Jesus with a non-Christian during the past month.**
   ❍ Strongly Disagree ❍ Somewhat Disagree ❍ Somewhat Agree ❍ Strongly Agree

29. **The anticipated "second coming of Jesus" will occur in my lifetime.**
   ❍ Strongly Disagree ❍ Somewhat Disagree ❍ Somewhat Agree ❍ Strongly Agree

30. **Some survey respondents will be selected at random to participate in a follow-up email interview. May we contact you via email to participate in that interview?**

   ❍ Yes, my email address is ______________________________

   ❍ No

Thank you for your participation in this survey
from Nappaland Research.

Appendix B

SUMMARY DATA RESULTS FROM **THE JESUS SURVEY**

Figure 1.1

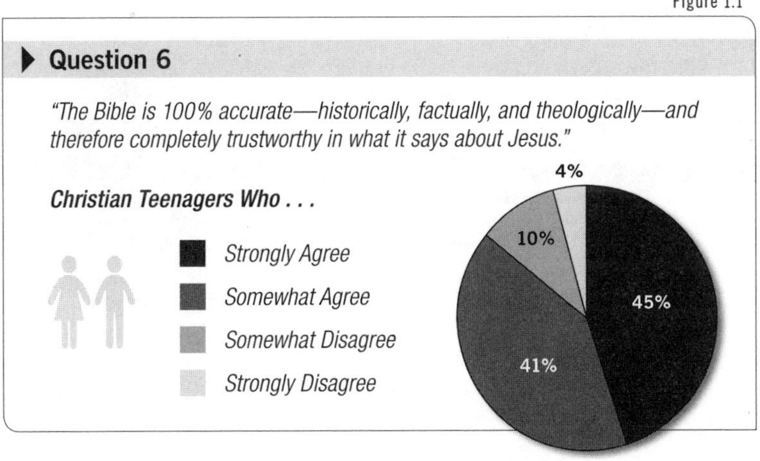

Figure 1.2*

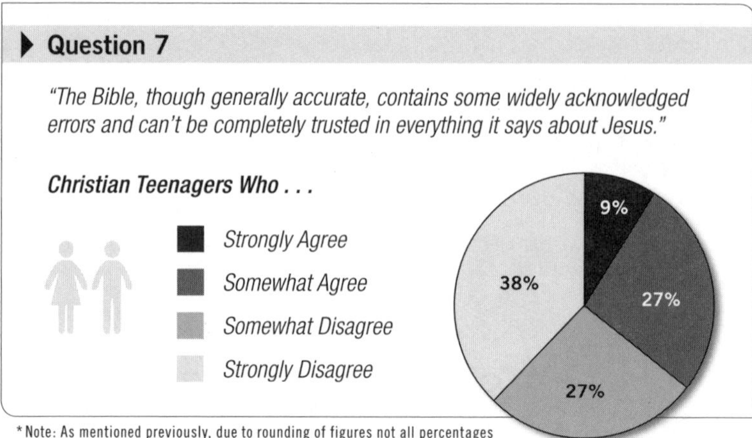

* Note: As mentioned previously, due to rounding of figures not all percentages will always add up to exactly 100%. Just a reminder.

Figure 1.3

Bible Belief Paradigms of Christian Teens

- **Unshakeable Teens**
  (Believe the Bible is ***"completely trustworthy"*** *in what it says about Jesus)*
- **Uncertain Teens**
  *(**Unsure** about the trustworthiness of the Bible, but not willing to dismiss it either)*
- **Unsettled Teens**
  *(Feel **conflicted** and/or **confused** about the issue of the Bible's trustworthiness)*
- **Unbelieving Teens**
  *(**Do not believe** the Bible can be trusted in everything it says about Jesus)*

31%
31%
29%
10%

Figure 1.4

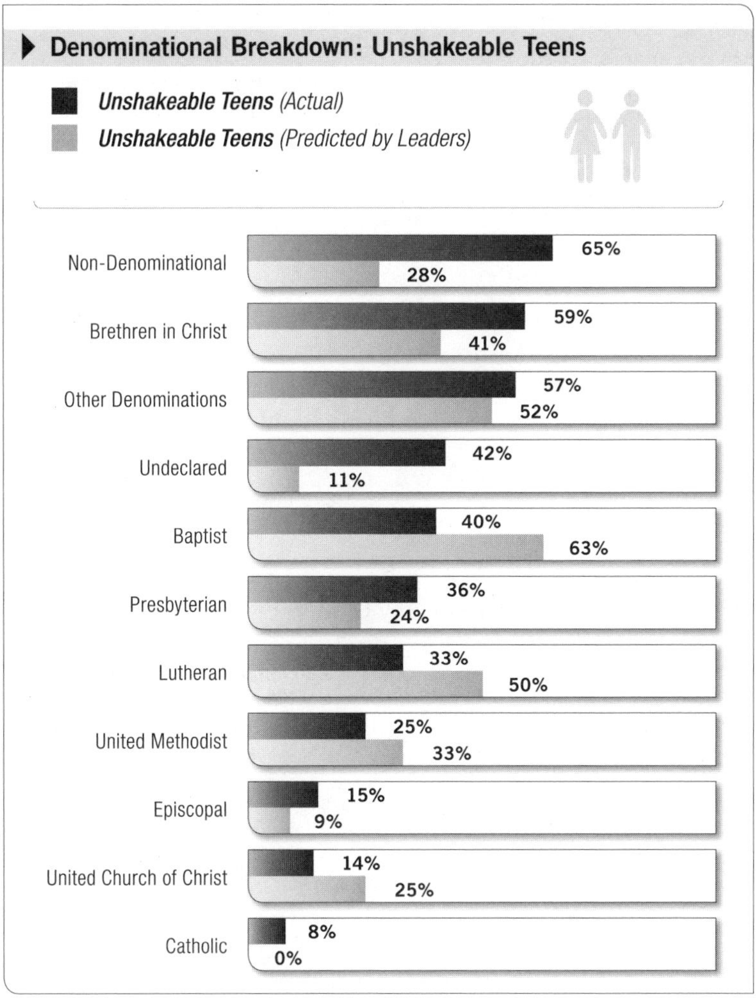

Denominational Breakdown: Unshakeable Teens
Unshakeable Teens (Actual)
Unshakeable Teens (Predicted by Leaders)
Non-Denominational
65%
28%
Brethren in Christ
59%
41%
Other Denominations
57%
52%
Undeclared
42%
11%
Baptist
40%
63%
Presbyterian
36%
24%
Lutheran
33%
50%
United Methodist
25%
33%
Episcopal
15%
9%
United Church of Christ
14%
25%
Catholic
8%
0%

Figure 1.5

Question 8
"Other highly regarded religious books, such as the Koran or the Book of Mormon, are just as important as the Bible in teaching people about who Jesus really was."
Christian Teenagers Who . . .
Strongly Agree
Somewhat Agree
Somewhat Disagree
Strongly Disagree
12%
32%
26%
30%

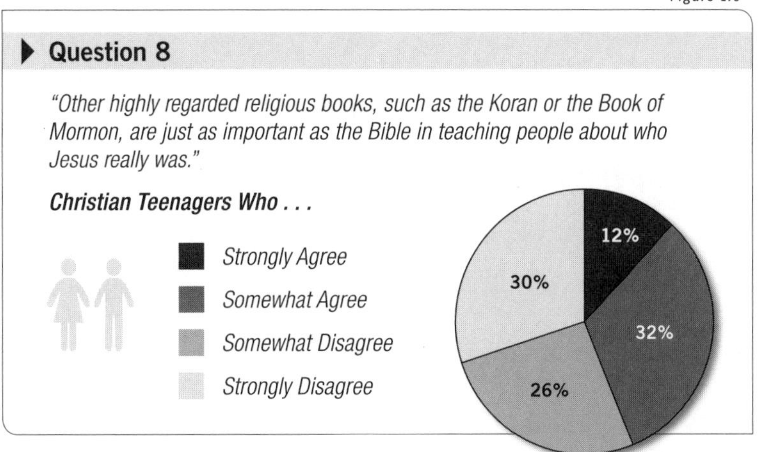

Figure 1.6

Unshakeable Christian Teens (by Grade)

Year in School	***Percentage of Christian Teens Who Are "Unshakeable"*** *(View the Bible as trustworthy when it speaks of Jesus)*
7th Grade	**21%**
8th Grade	**38%**
9th Grade	**33%**
10th Grade	**32%**
11th Grade	**21%**
12th Grade	**34%**

Figure 1.7

Unbelieving Christian Teens (by Grade)

Year in School	***Percentage of Christian Teens Who Are "Unbelieving"*** *(Disbelieve that the Bible is trustworthy when it speaks of Jesus)*
7th Grade	**0%**
8th Grade	**11%**
9th Grade	**6%**
10th Grade	**7%**
11th Grade	**17%**
12th Grade	**12%**

Figure 1.8

▶. **Bible Belief Paradigms of Christian Teens** (by Gender)

	Female	*Male*	*Total*
Unshakeable Teens *(Believe the Bible is "completely trustworthy" in what it says about Jesus)*	17%	14%	31%
Uncertain Teens *(Unsure about the trustworthiness of the Bible, but not willing to dismiss it either)*	17%	14%	31%
Unsettled Teens *(Feel conflicted and/or confused about the issue of the Bible's trustworthiness)*	15%	13%	28%*
Unbelieving Teens *(Do not believe the Bible can be trusted in everything it says about Jesus)*	4%	6%	10%
Total	53%	47%	100%

* Note: This percentage is different from the corresponding one in figure 1.3 due to rounding principles. Combined in figure 1.4, it rounds up to 29%; separated into female and male data sets here, it rounds down to 28%. Go figure.

Figure 2.1

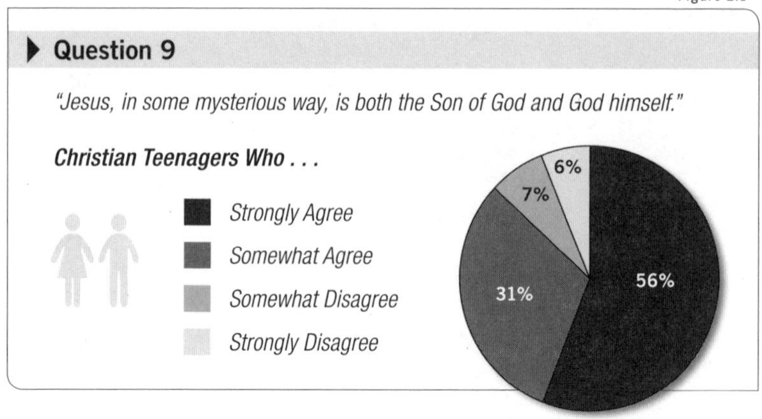

Figure 2.2

Denominational Breakdown: Is Jesus God?

Denomination	Christian Teens Who Believe Jesus Is God	Christian Teens Who **Strongly** Believe Jesus Is God
Other Denominations	94%	60%
Catholic	91%	51%
Undeclared	90%	58%
Brethren in Christ	86%	41%
Non-Denominational	86%	75%
Baptist	86%	54%
United Methodist	85%	52%
Presbyterian	85%	60%
Episcopal	73%	41%
Lutheran	71%	57%
United Church of Christ	71%	40%

Figure 2.3

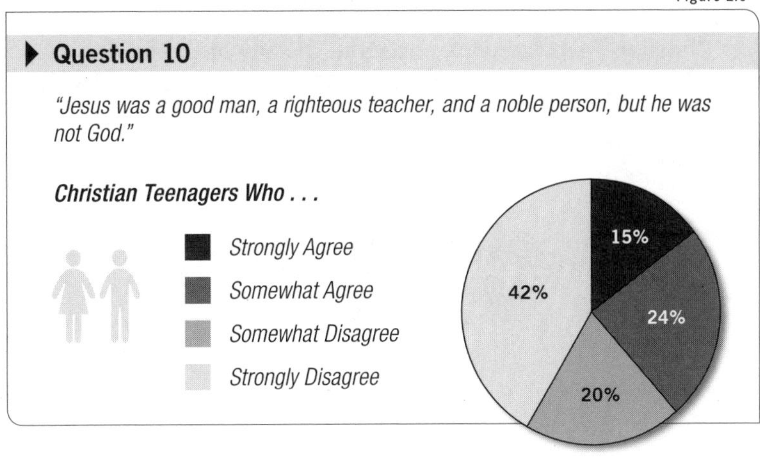

Figure 2.4

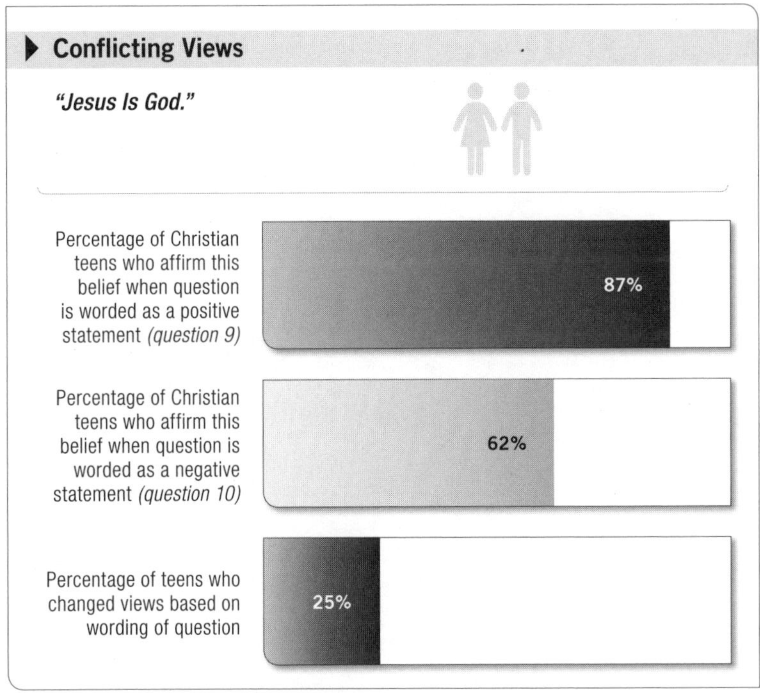

Figure 2.5

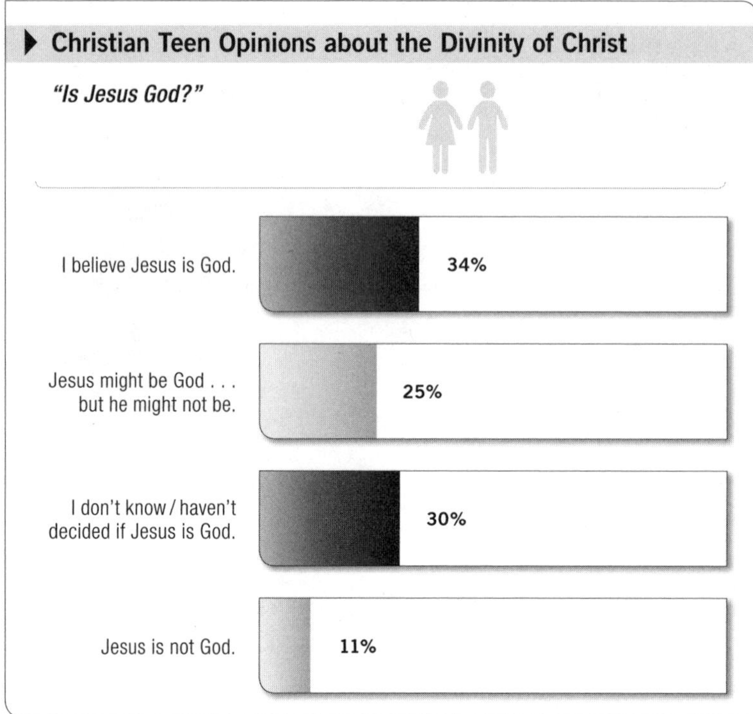

Christian Teen Opinions about the Divinity of Christ
"Is Jesus God?"
I believe Jesus is God.
34%
Jesus might be God . . . but he might not be.
25%
I don't know / haven't decided if Jesus is God.
30%
Jesus is not God.
11%

Figure 2.6

Question 11

"When Jesus walked the earth he never sinned, not even in a small way."

Christian Teenagers Who . . .

Strongly Agree

Somewhat Agree

Somewhat Disagree

Strongly Disagree

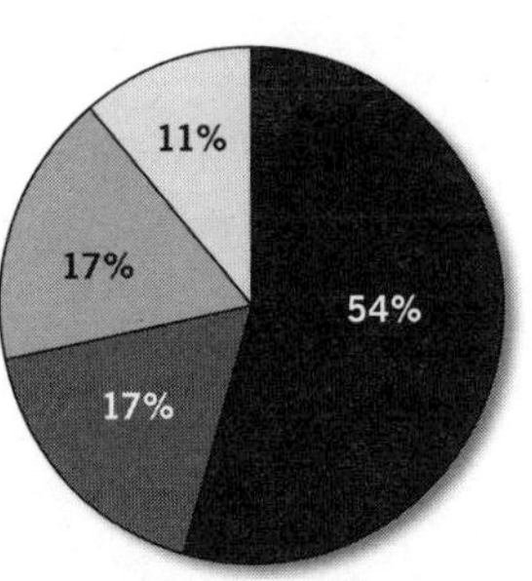

Question 12

"Jesus was a great, great man, but he was not 100% perfect so he may have sinned."

Christian Teenagers Who . . .

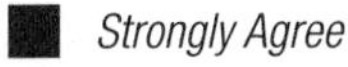

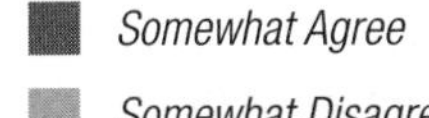

Strongly Agree

Somewhat Agree

Somewhat Disagree

Strongly Disagree

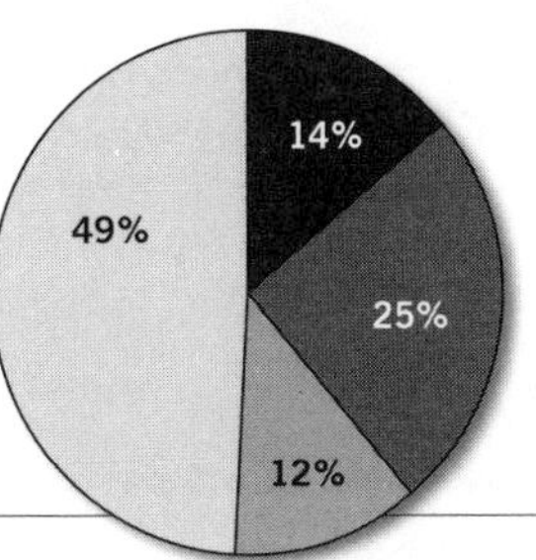

Figure 2.7

Jesus Is God

Total Percentage of Christian Teenagers Who Consistently, Strongly Affirm *(as evidenced by answers to questions 9, 10, 11, and 12)*

Christian Teenagers Who . . .

Strongly Agree

Do Not Strongly Agree

24%
76%

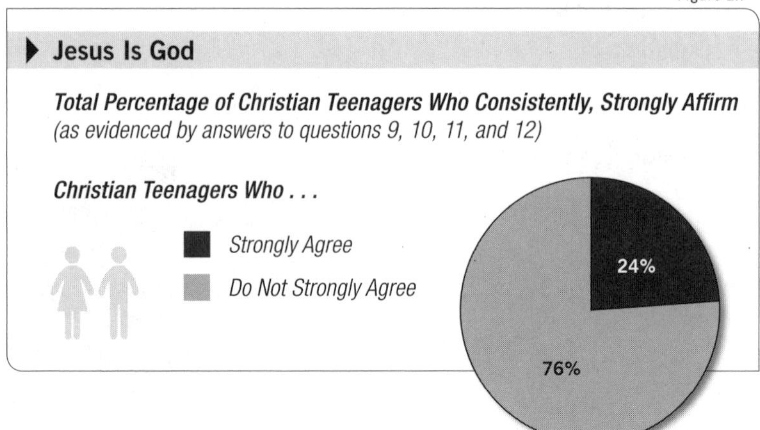

Figure 2.8

Denominational Breakdown: Jesus Is God

Percentage of Denomination Teenagers Who Consistently, Strongly Affirm *(as evidenced by answers to questions 9, 10, 11, and 12)*

Non-Denominational 55%
Other Denominations 34%
Presbyterian 34%
Baptist 31%
Lutheran 29%
Brethren in Christ 23%
United Methodist 21%
Catholic 11%
United Church of Christ 9%
Episcopal 9%
Undeclared 3%

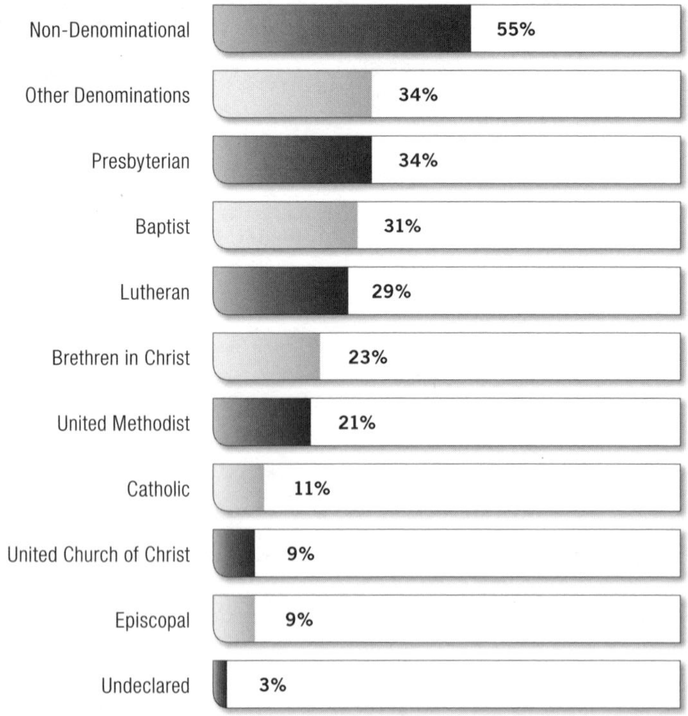

Figure 2.9

Question 9

"Jesus, in some mysterious way, is both the Son of God and God himself."

Adult Leaders Predicted Christian Teenagers Would . . .			
Strongly Agree	*Somewhat Agree*	*Strongly Disagree*	*Somewhat Disagree*
53%	**33%**	**7%**	**7%**

Question 10

"Jesus was a good man, a righteous teacher, and a noble person, but he was not God."

Adult Leaders Predicted Christian Teenagers Would . . .			
Strongly Agree	*Somewhat Agree*	*Strongly Disagree*	*Somewhat Disagree*
12%	**16%**	**18%**	**54%**

Question 11

"When Jesus walked the earth he never sinned, not even in a small way."

Adult Leaders Predicted Christian Teenagers Would . . .			
Strongly Agree	*Somewhat Agree*	*Strongly Disagree*	*Somewhat Disagree*
55%	**20%**	**14%**	**10%**

Question 12

"Jesus was a great, great man, but he was not 100% perfect so he may have sinned."

Adult Leaders Predicted Christian Teenagers Would . . .			
Strongly Agree	*Somewhat Agree*	*Strongly Disagree*	*Somewhat Disagree*
8%	**26%**	**12%**	**54%**

Figure 2.10

Regional Breakdown: Christian Teen Opinions about the Divinity of Christ

Is Jesus God?

	I believe Jesus is God		*Jesus might be God . . . but he might not be*		*I don't know / haven't decided if Jesus is God*		*Jesus is not God*	
	% of Region	*% of Total*	*% of Region*	*% of Total*	*% of Region*	*% of Total*	*% of Region*	*% of Total*
Northeast	**34%**	**17%**	**23%**	**12%**	**33%**	**17%**	**10%**	**5%**
Southeast	**40%**	**7%**	**30%**	**5%**	**19%**	**3%**	**11%**	**2%**
North/Central	**29%**	**6%**	**27%**	**6%**	**32%**	**7%**	**12%**	**3%**
South/Central	**22%**	**2%**	**27%**	**2%**	**33%**	**3%**	**19%**	**1%**
Northwest	**55%**	**1%**	**0%**	**0%**	**36%**	**1%**	**9%**	**<.05%**
Southwest	**79%**	**1%**	**7%**	**<.05%**	**7%**	**<.05%**	**7%**	**<.05%**

Figure 3.1

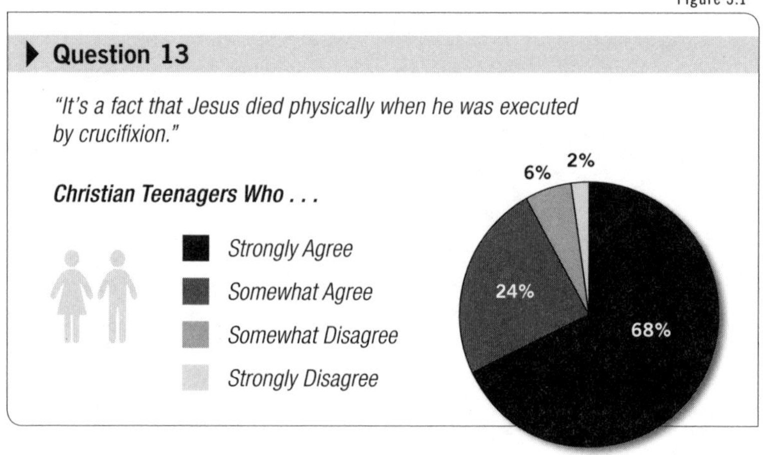

Figure 3.2

By Bible Belief

Percentage Who Strongly Believe Jesus Physically Died on the Cross

Unshakeables (Believe the Bible *is* trustworthy) 84%

Uncertains (Are *unsure* the Bible is trustworthy) 64%

Unsettleds (I don't know / haven't decided if Jesus is God) 58%

Unbelieving (Believe the Bible is *not* trustworthy) 57%

Figure 3.3

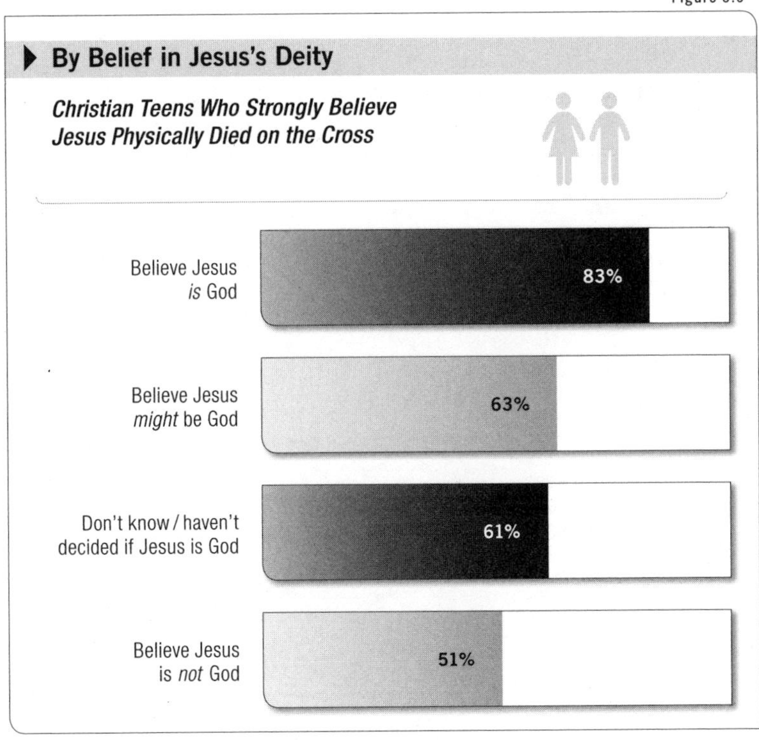

Figure 3.4

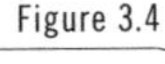

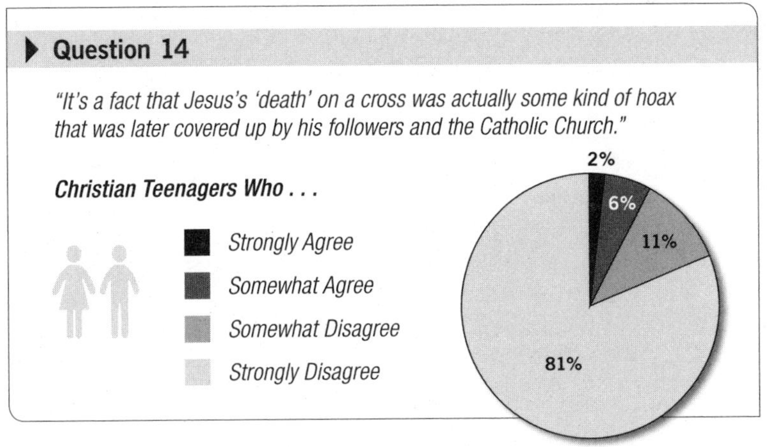

Figure 3.5

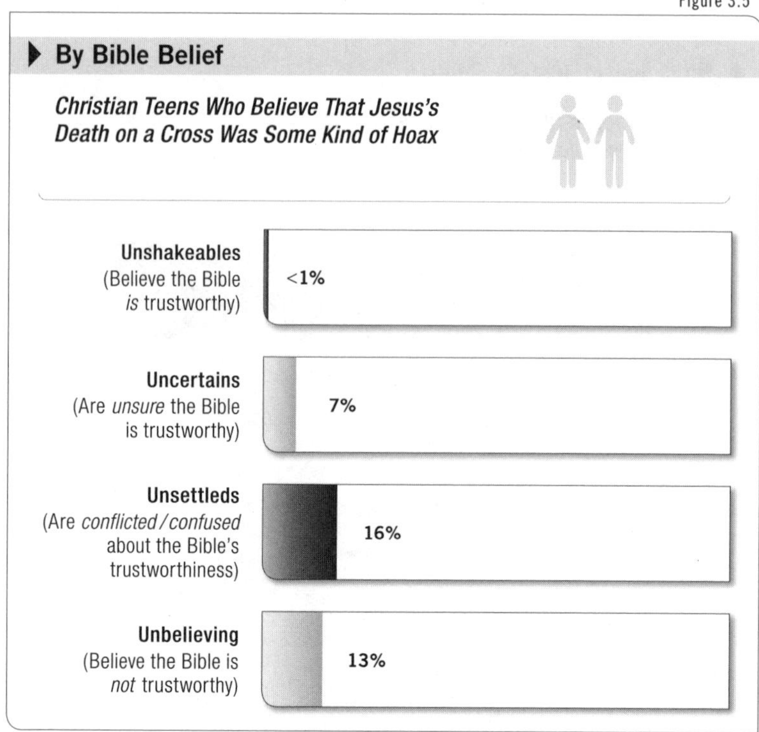

Figure 3.6

By Belief in Jesus's Deity

Christian Teens Who Believe That Jesus's Death on a Cross Was Some Kind of Hoax

Believe Jesus *is* God	2%
Believe Jesus *might* be God	6%
Don't know / haven't decided if Jesus is God	17%
Believe Jesus is *not* God	8%

Figure 3.7

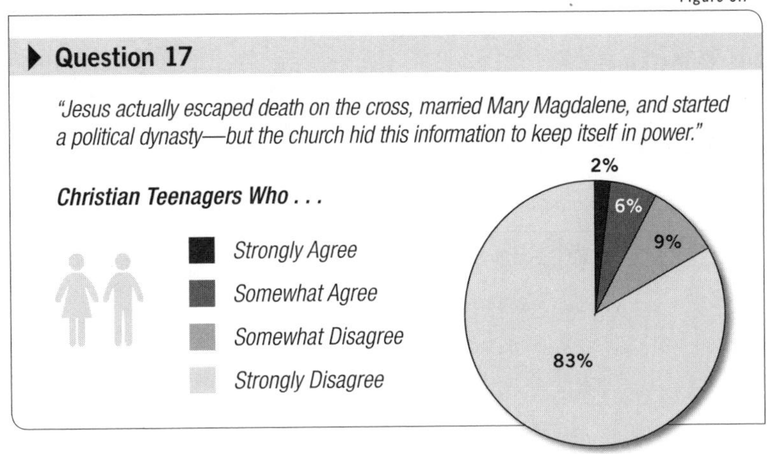

Figure 3.8

By Gender and Grade: Percentage of Christian Teens Who Strongly Believe Jesus Physically Died on the Cross

Girls	65%
Guys	71%
Junior Highers (Grades 7 & 8)	63%
High School Underclassmen (Grades 9 & 10)	67%
High School Upperclassmen (Grades 11 & 12)	69%

Figure 3.9

By Grade: Percentage of Christian Teens Who Believe That Jesus's Death on a Cross Was Some Kind of Hoax

Junior Highers (Grades 7 & 8)	6%
High School Underclassmen (Grades 9 & 10)	10%
High School Upperclassmen (Grades 11 & 12)	8%

Figure 4.1

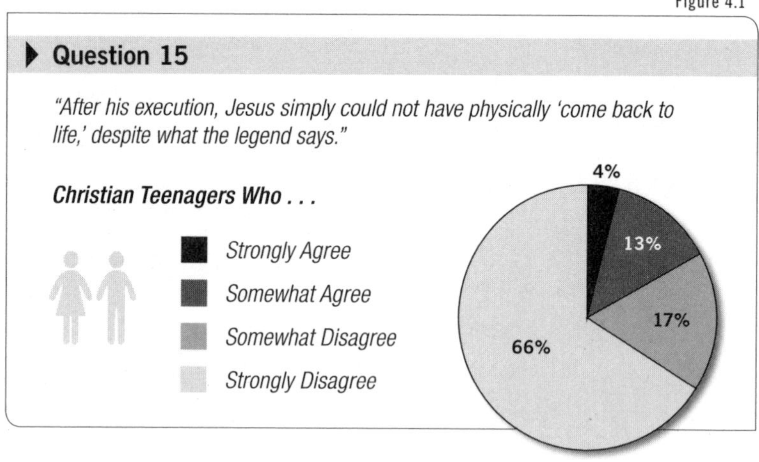

Figure 4.2

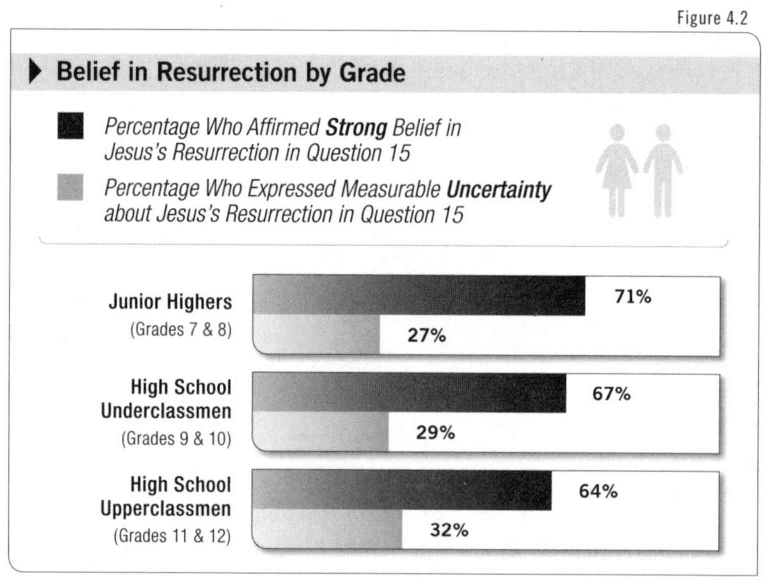

Figure 4.3

Question 16

"Jesus physically came back to life after his execution."

Christian Teenagers Who . . .

Strongly Agree
Somewhat Agree
Somewhat Disagree
Strongly Disagree
60%
25%
10%
6%

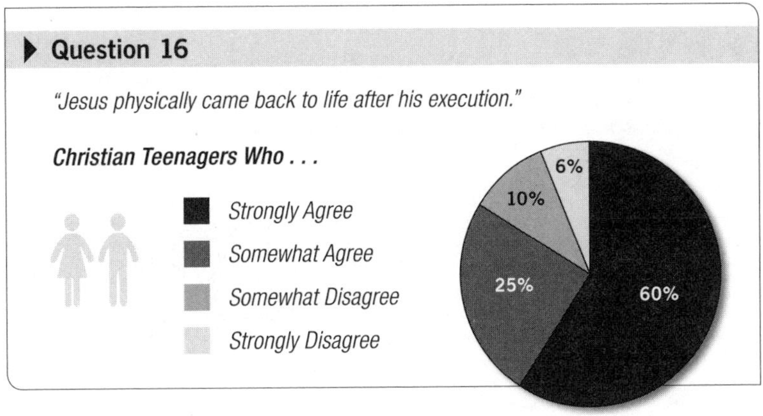

Figure 4.4

Denominational Breakdown: Is Jesus Alive?

Percentage of Teenagers Who Strongly Affirm That Jesus Rose from the Dead *(as evidenced by answers to question 16)*

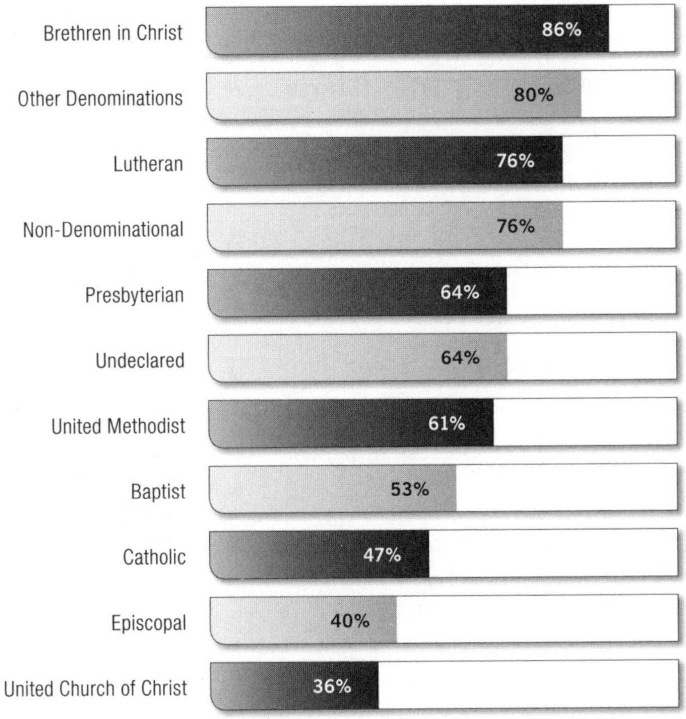

Brethren in Christ
86%
Other Denominations
80%
Lutheran
76%
Non-Denominational
76%
Presbyterian
64%
Undeclared
64%
United Methodist
61%
Baptist
53%
Catholic
47%
Episcopal
40%
United Church of Christ
36%

Figure 4.5

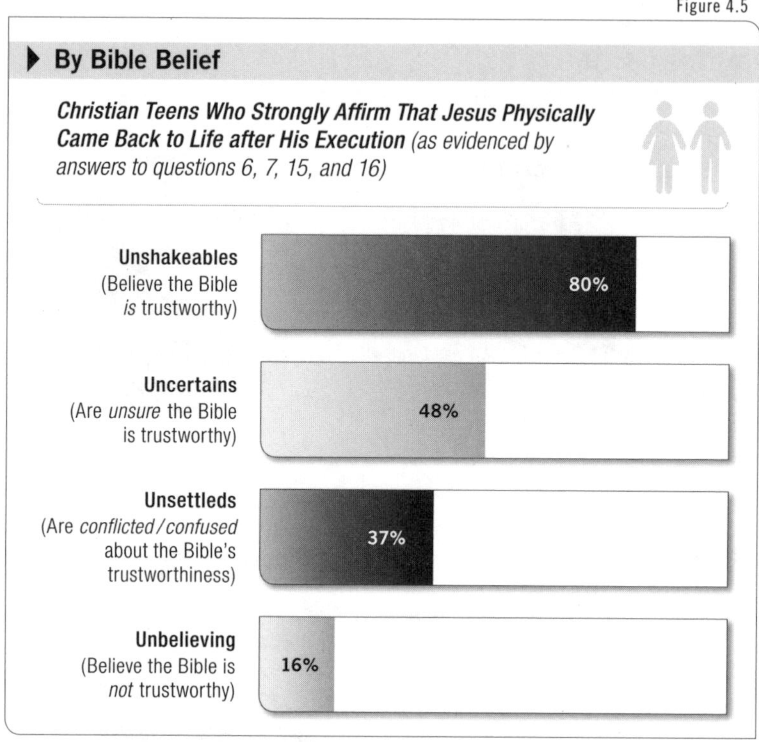

Figure 4.6

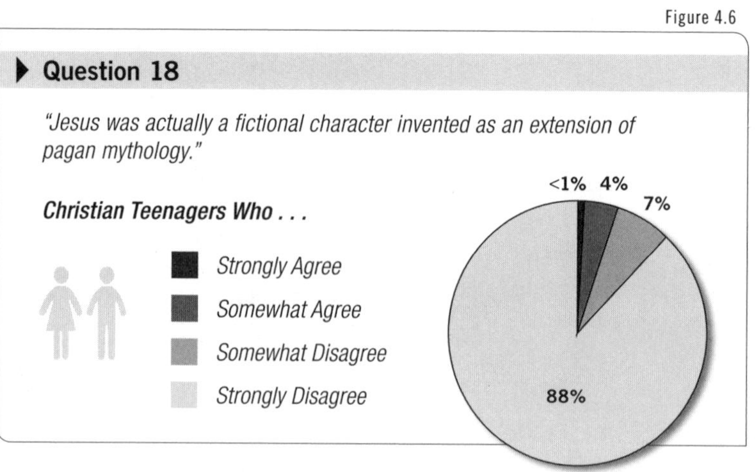

Figure 4.7

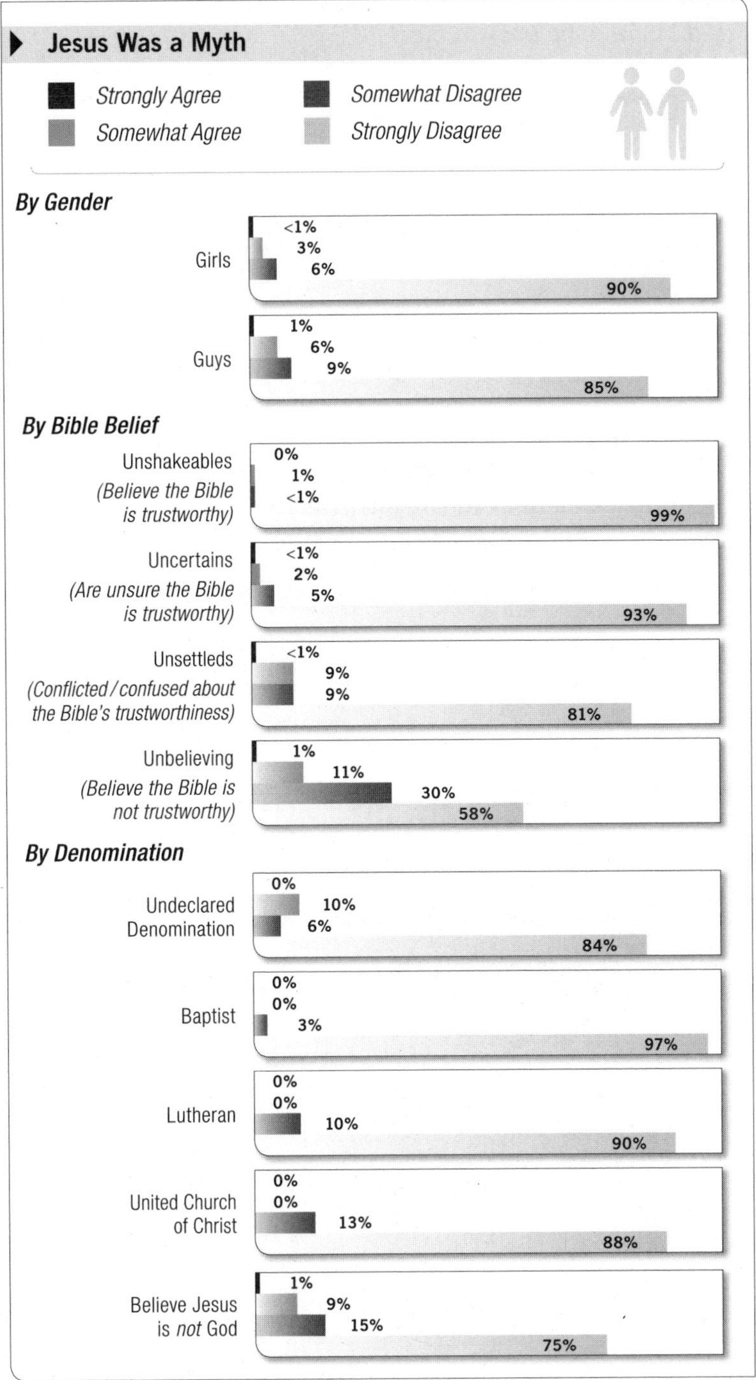

Jesus Was a Myth
Strongly Agree
Somewhat Agree
Somewhat Disagree
Strongly Disagree
By Gender
Girls
<1%
3%
6%
90%
Guys
1%
6%
9%
85%
By Bible Belief
Unshakeables
(Believe the Bible is trustworthy)
0%
1%
<1%
99%
Uncertains
(Are unsure the Bible is trustworthy)
<1%
2%
5%
93%
Unsettleds
(Conflicted/confused about the Bible's trustworthiness)
<1%
9%
9%
81%
Unbelieving
(Believe the Bible is not trustworthy)
1%
11%
30%
58%
By Denomination
Undeclared Denomination
0%
10%
6%
84%
Baptist
0%
0%
3%
97%
Lutheran
0%
0%
10%
90%
United Church of Christ
0%
0%
13%
88%
Believe Jesus is not God
1%
9%
15%
75%

Figure 4.8

Christian Teen Opinions about Jesus's Resurrection
(Did Jesus come back to life?)

Resurrection Believers *(Strongly believe Jesus died and physically came back to life)*	**52%**
Resurrection In-Betweeners *(Express measurable uncertainty about Jesus's resurrection)*	**40%**
Resurrection Skeptics *(Disbelieve that Jesus died and physically came back to life)*	**8%**

Figure 4.9

By Belief in Jesus's Deity: Christian Teens Who Strongly Affirm That Jesus Physically Came Back to Life after His Execution
(as evidenced by answers to questions 9, 10, 15, and 16)

Believe Jesus *is* God	**77%**
Believe Jesus might be God . . . but he might not be	**41%**
Don't know / haven't decided if Jesus is God	**38%**
Believe Jesus is *not* God	**37%**

Figure 4.10

Jesus Physically Came Back to Life

By Region, Christian Teenagers Who . . .

	Strongly Agree	*Somewhat Agree*	*Strongly Disagree*	*Somewhat Disagree*
East Coast / Near East Coast	**61%**	**25%**	**10%**	**5%**
West of the East Coast	**58%**	**25%**	**9%**	**8%**

Figure 5.1

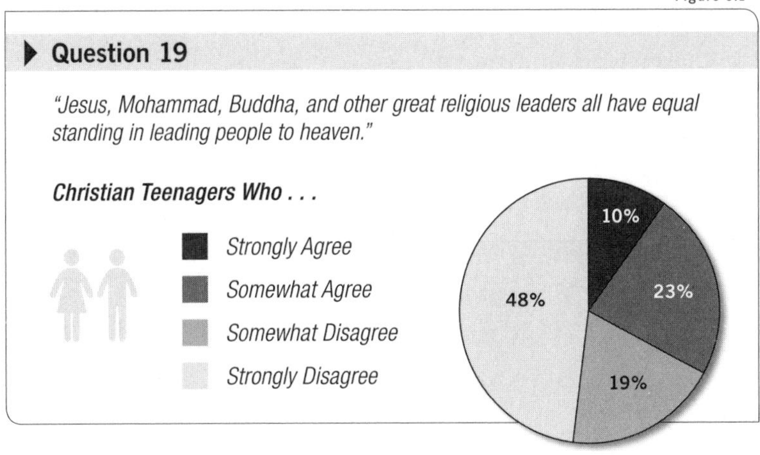

Figure 5.2

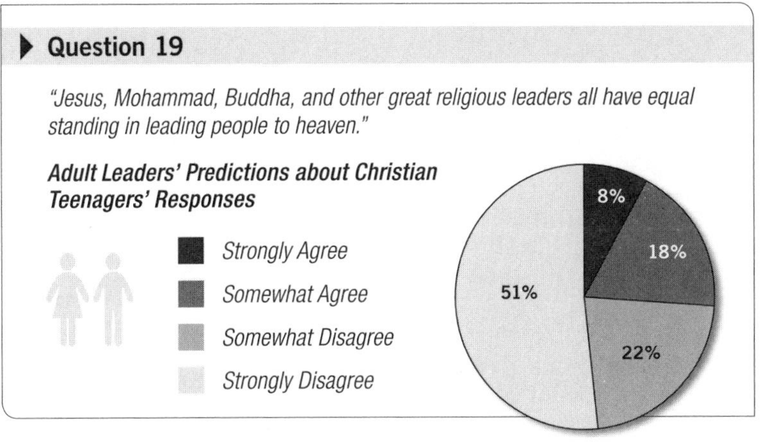

Figure 5.3

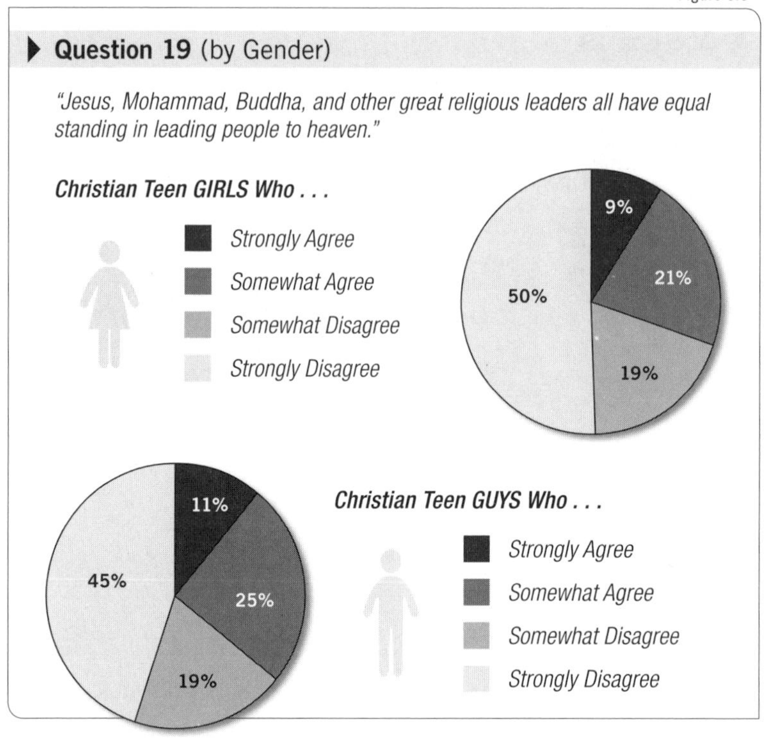
Question 19 (by Gender)
"Jesus, Mohammad, Buddha, and other great religious leaders all have equal standing in leading people to heaven."
Christian Teen GIRLS Who . . .
Strongly Agree
Somewhat Agree
Somewhat Disagree
Strongly Disagree
9%
21%
19%
50%
11%
25%
19%
45%
Christian Teen GUYS Who . . .
Strongly Agree
Somewhat Agree
Somewhat Disagree
Strongly Disagree

Figure 5.4

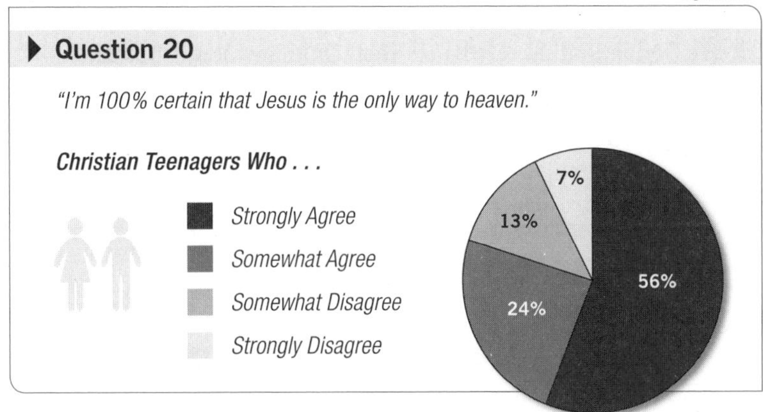

Figure 5.5

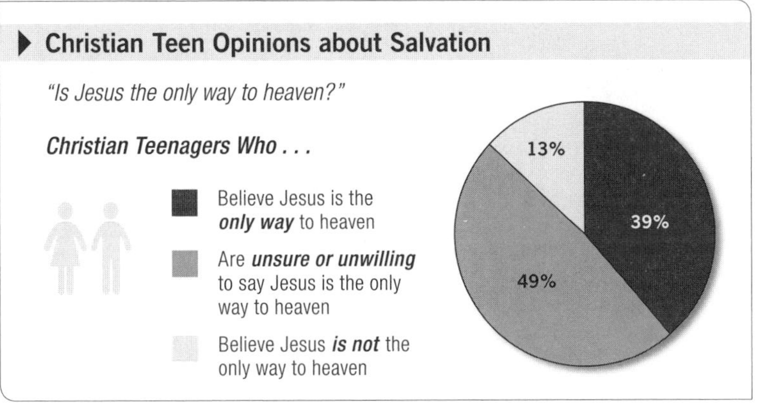

Figure 5.6

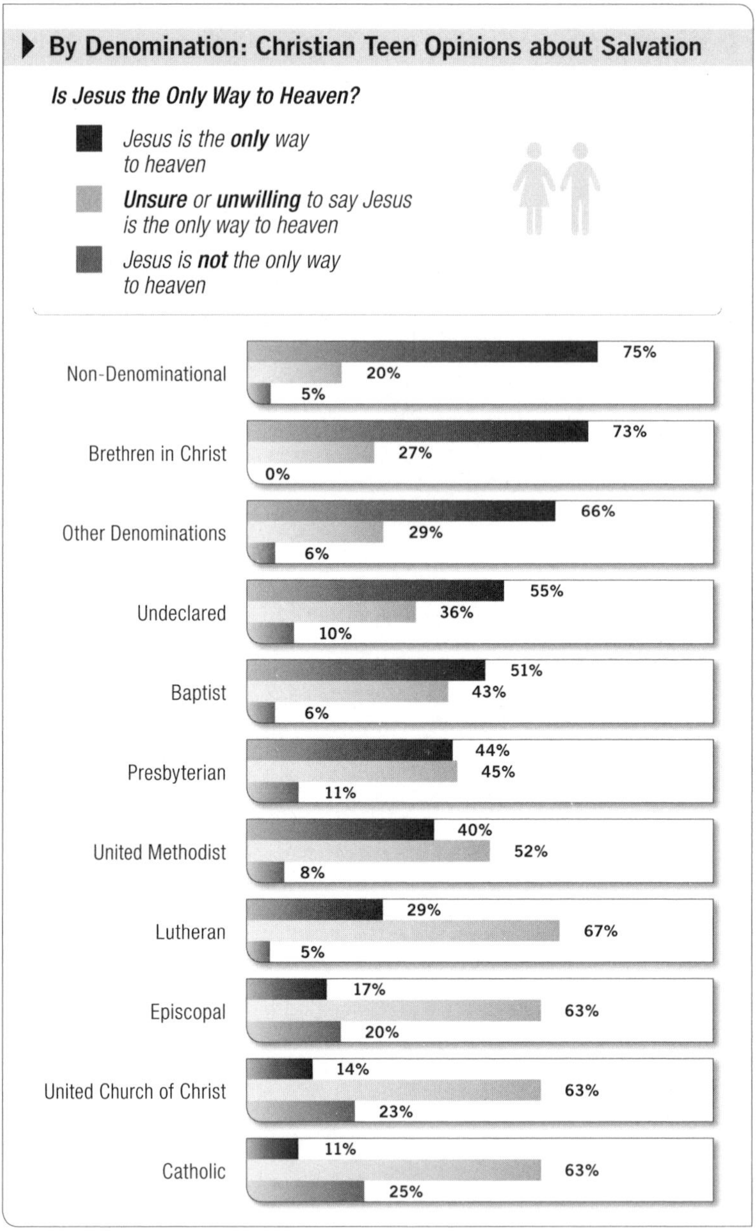

By Denomination: Christian Teen Opinions about Salvation

Is Jesus the Only Way to Heaven?

- *Jesus is the **only** way to heaven*
- ***Unsure** or **unwilling** to say Jesus is the only way to heaven*
- *Jesus is **not** the only way to heaven*

Denomination	Jesus is the only way to heaven	Unsure or unwilling to say Jesus is the only way to heaven	Jesus is not the only way to heaven
Non-Denominational	75%	20%	5%
Brethren in Christ	73%	27%	0%
Other Denominations	66%	29%	6%
Undeclared	55%	36%	10%
Baptist	51%	43%	6%
Presbyterian	44%	45%	11%
United Methodist	40%	52%	8%
Lutheran	29%	67%	5%
Episcopal	17%	63%	20%
United Church of Christ	14%	63%	23%
Catholic	11%	63%	25%

Figure 5.7

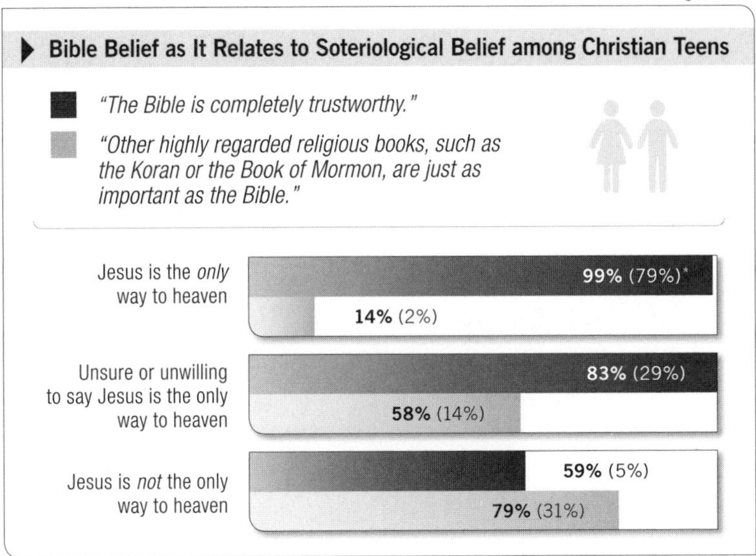

* Percentages in parentheses reflect teenagers who "strongly agree" with the quoted Bible belief statement.

Figure 5.8

Belief in Jesus's Deity as It Relates to Soteriological Belief among Christian Teens

	"Jesus Is Both the Son of God and God Himself"	*"Jesus Never Once Sinned"*
Jesus is the *only* way to heaven	**90%** (72%)*	**89%** (82%)
Unsure or unwilling to say Jesus is the only way to heaven	**86%** (49%)	**66%** (42%)
Jesus is *not* the only way to heaven	**74%** (31%)	**40%** (20%)

* Percentages in parentheses reflect teenagers who "strongly agree" with the quoted Bible belief statement.

Figure 5.9

By Grade: Soteriological Belief among Christian Teens

	7th Graders	*8th Graders*	*9th Graders*	*10th Graders*	*11th Graders*	*12th Graders*
Jesus is the *only* way to heaven	**27%**	**45%**	**40%**	**41%**	**32%**	**40%**
Unsure or unwilling to say Jesus is the only way to heaven	**57%**	**47%**	**50%**	**48%**	**53%**	**45%**
Jesus is *not* the only way to heaven	**15%**	**9%**	**10%**	**11%**	**15%**	**15%**

Figure Int.1

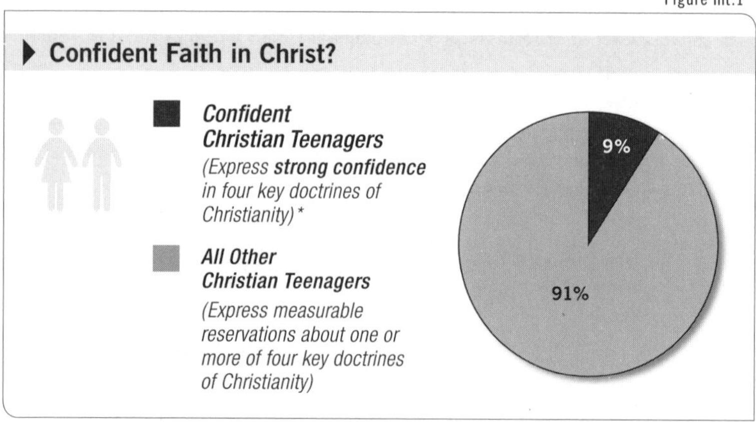

*The four key doctrines are: 1) the Bible is trustworthy, 2) Jesus is God, 3) Jesus died and rose again, 4) Jesus is the only way to heaven.

Figure Int.2

By Denomination: Confident Faith in Christ?

	Confident Christian Teenagers *(Express strong confidence in four key doctrines of Christianity)**	***All Other Christian Teenagers*** *(Express measurable reservations about one or more of four key doctrines of Christianity)*
Non-Denominational	**36%**	**64%**
Other Denominations	**26%**	**74%**
Baptist	**17%**	**83%**
Presbyterian	**12%**	**88%**
Brethren in Christ	**5%**	**95%**
United Methodist	**5%**	**95%**
Undeclared	**3%**	**97%**
Catholic	**1%**	**99%**
Episcopal	**0%**	**100%**
Lutheran	**0%**	**100%**
United Church of Christ	**0%**	**100%**

*Express strong confidence in four key Christian doctrines: 1) the Bible is trustworthy, 2) Jesus is God, 3) Jesus died and rose again, 4) Jesus is the only way to heaven.

Figure 6.1

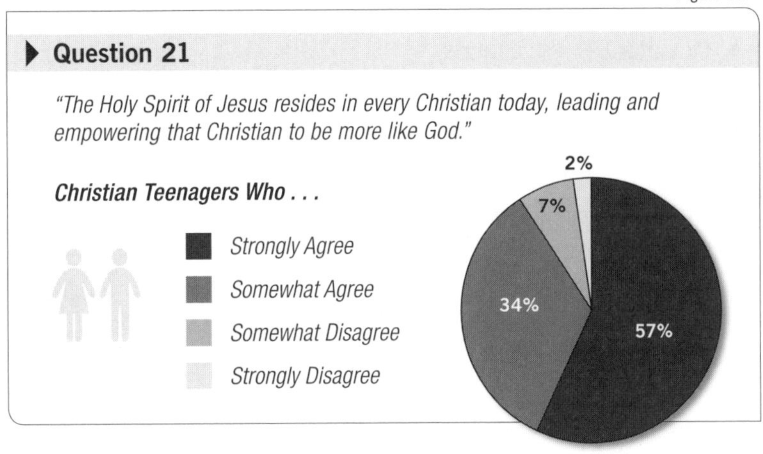

Figure 6.2

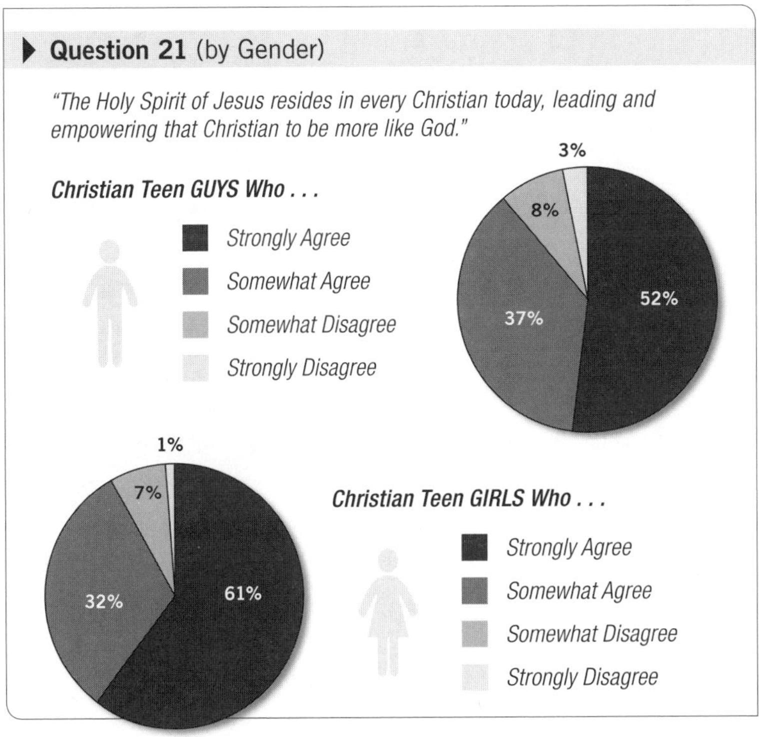

Figure 6.3

▶ **Question 21** (by Grade)

"The Holy Spirit of Jesus resides in every Christian today, leading and empowering that Christian to be more like God."

Christian Teenage JUNIOR HIGHERS
(Grades 7 & 8)

- *Strongly Agree*
- *Somewhat Agree*
- *Somewhat Disagree*
- *Strongly Disagree*

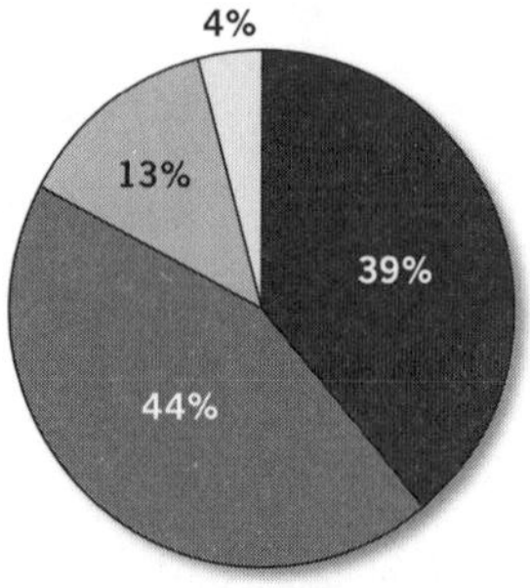

Christian Teenage HIGH SCHOOL UNDERCLASSMEN
(Grades 9 & 10)

- *Strongly Agree*
- *Somewhat Agree*
- *Somewhat Disagree*
- *Strongly Disagree*

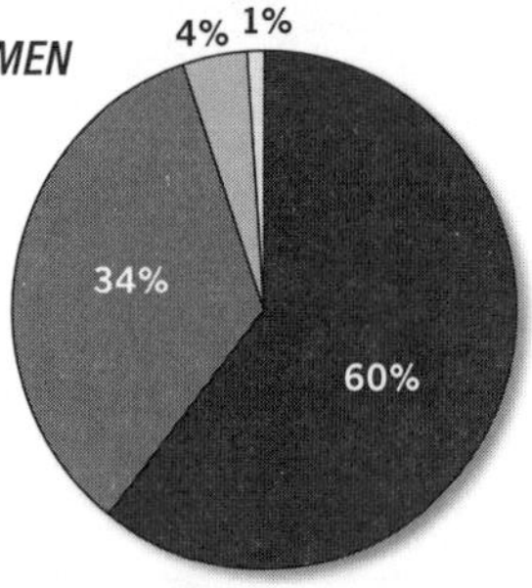

Christian Teenage HIGH SCHOOL UPPERCLASSMEN
(Grades 11 & 12)

- *Strongly Agree*
- *Somewhat Agree*
- *Somewhat Disagree*
- *Strongly Disagree*

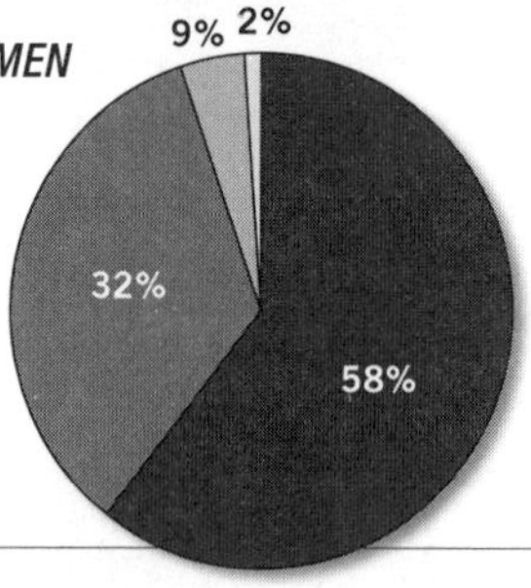

Figure 6.4

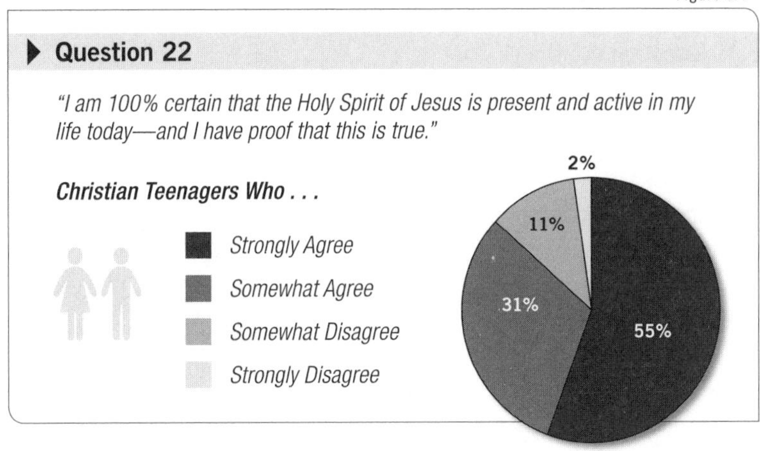

Figure 6.5

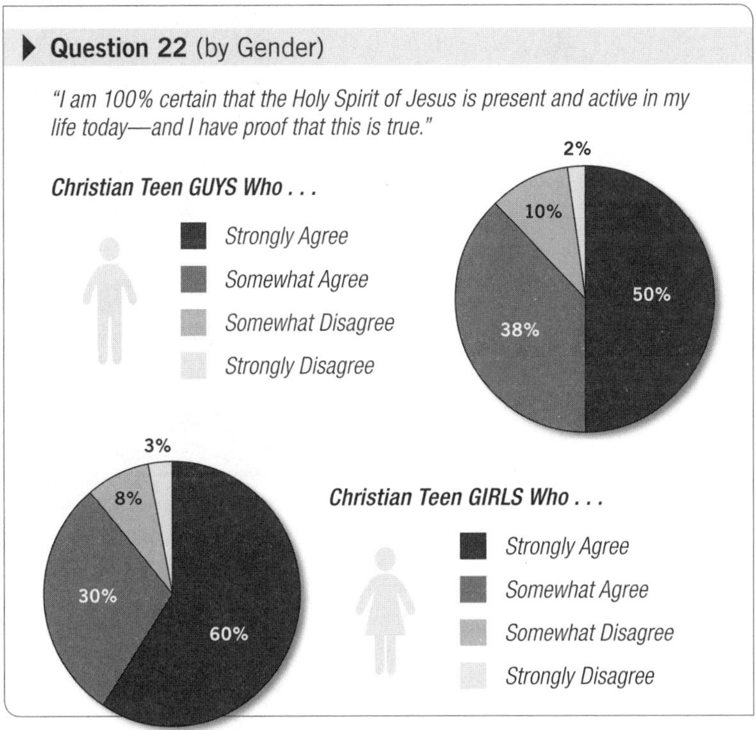

Figure 6.6

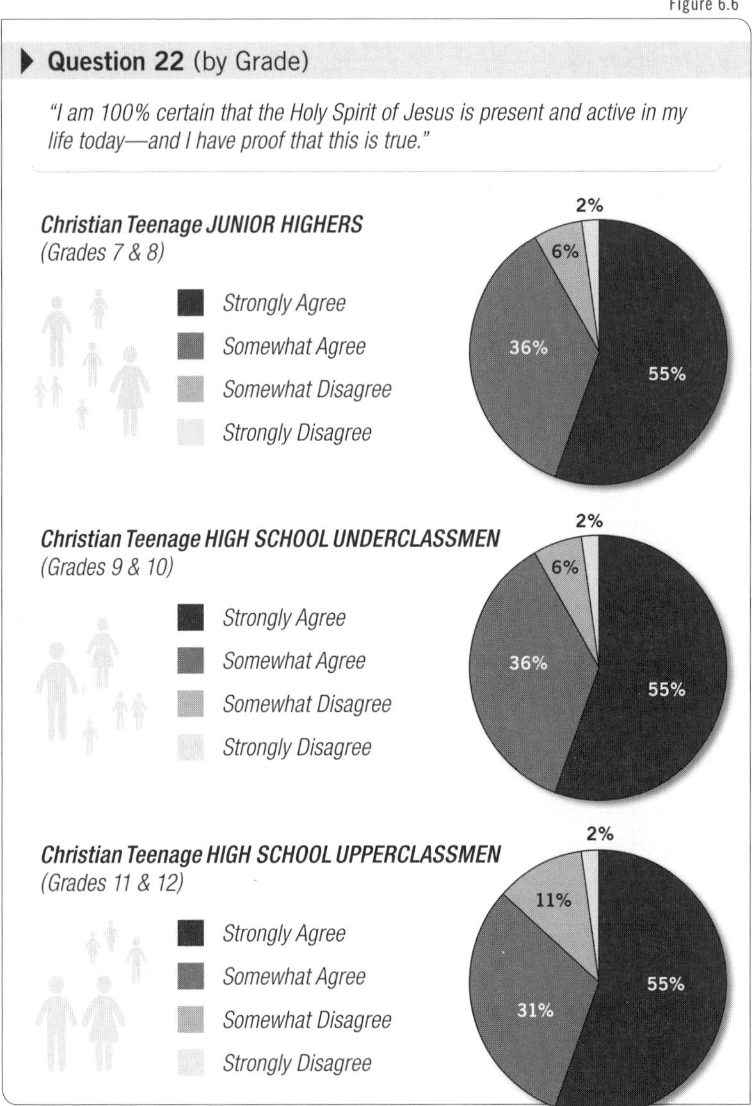

Question 22 (by Grade)
"I am 100% certain that the Holy Spirit of Jesus is present and active in my life today—and I have proof that this is true."
Christian Teenage JUNIOR HIGHERS
(Grades 7 & 8)
Strongly Agree
Somewhat Agree
Somewhat Disagree
Strongly Disagree
2%
6%
36%
55%
Christian Teenage HIGH SCHOOL UNDERCLASSMEN
(Grades 9 & 10)
Strongly Agree
Somewhat Agree
Somewhat Disagree
Strongly Disagree
2%
6%
36%
55%
Christian Teenage HIGH SCHOOL UPPERCLASSMEN
(Grades 11 & 12)
Strongly Agree
Somewhat Agree
Somewhat Disagree
Strongly Disagree
2%
11%
31%
55%

Figure 6.7

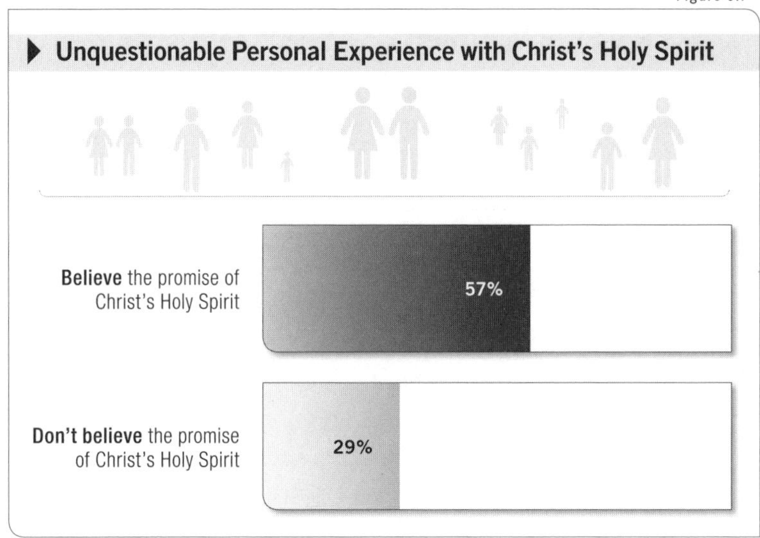

Figure 6.8

Personal Experience with Christ's Holy Spirit (by Doctrinal Belief)

■ ***Strongly*** *Claim Personal Experience with the Holy Spirit*

■ ***Somewhat*** *Claim Personal Experience with the Holy Spirit*

	Strongly	Somewhat
Confident Christian Teenagers *(Express strong confidence in four key doctrines of Christianity)*	86%	14%
All Others *(Express measurable reservations about one or more of four key doctrines of Christianity)*	52%	36%

Figure 6.9

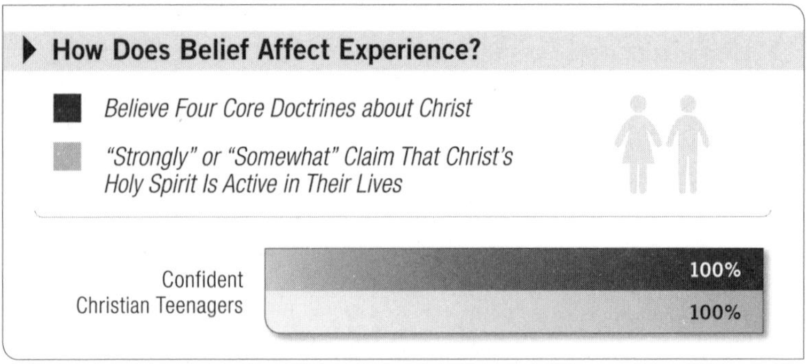

How Does Belief Affect Experience?

Figure 6.10

How Does Belief Affect Experience?

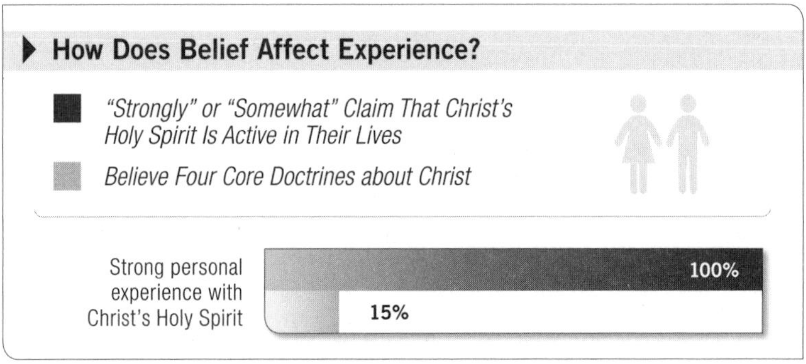

Figure 6.11

By Bible Belief: Christian Teens Who Strongly Claim the Holy Spirit Is Active in Their Lives

Unshakeables *(Believe the Bible is trustworthy)*	**82%**
Uncertains *(Are unsure the Bible is trustworthy)*	**49%**
Unsettleds *(Are conflicted/confused about the Bible's trustworthiness)*	**45%**
Unbelieving *(Believe the Bible is not trustworthy)*	**22%**

Figure 6.12

Comparison: Confident Christian Teens and Denominational Groups

	Believe the Holy Spirit Is Active in All Christians	*Strongly Claim the Holy Spirit Is Active in Their Lives*
Confident Christian Teenagers	**94%**	**86%**
Non-Denominational	**77%**	**70%**
Other Denominations	**71%**	**69%**
Brethren in Christ	**73%**	**68%**
Baptist	**58%**	**66%**
Lutheran	**52%**	**62%**
Undeclared	**39%**	**60%**
Presbyterian	**54%**	**57%**
United Methodist	**59%**	**56%**
Catholic	**51%**	**46%**
Episcopal	**44%**	**44%**
United Church of Christ	**49%**	**34%**

Figure 7.1

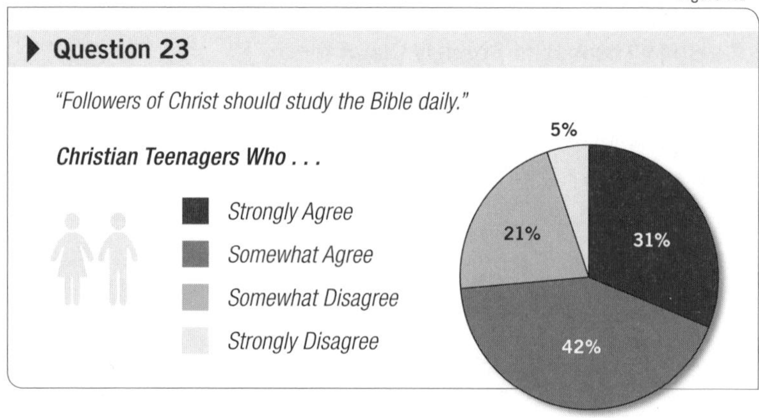

Figure 7.2

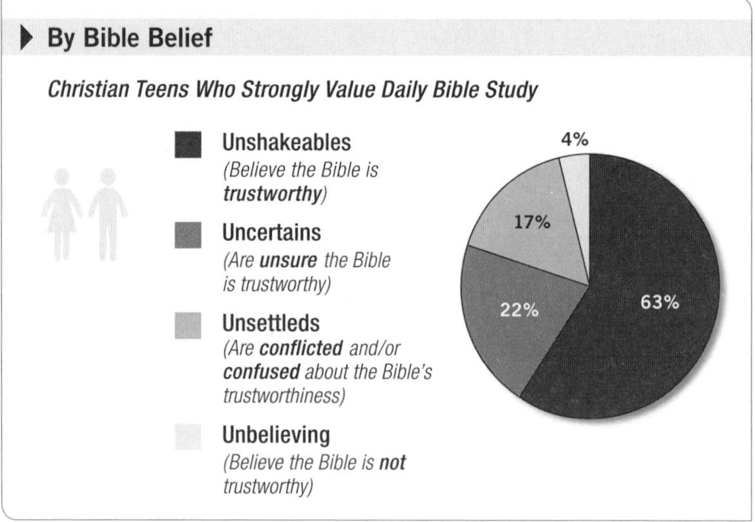

Figure 7.3

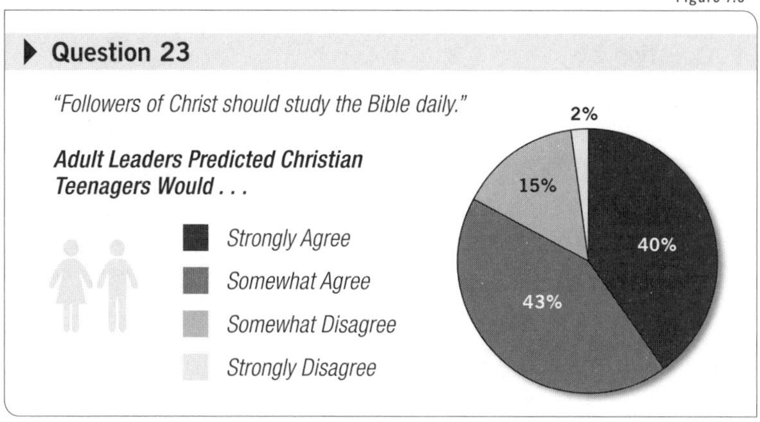

Figure 7.4

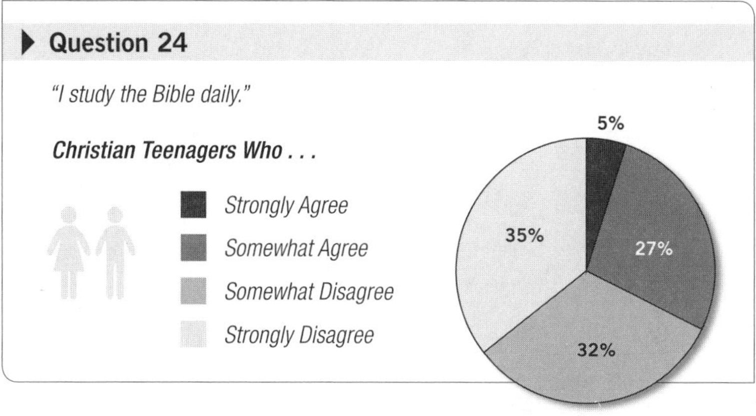

Figure 7.5

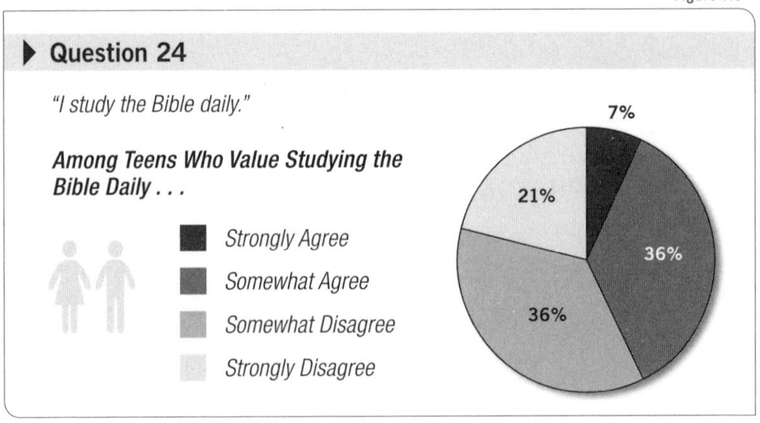

Figure 7.6

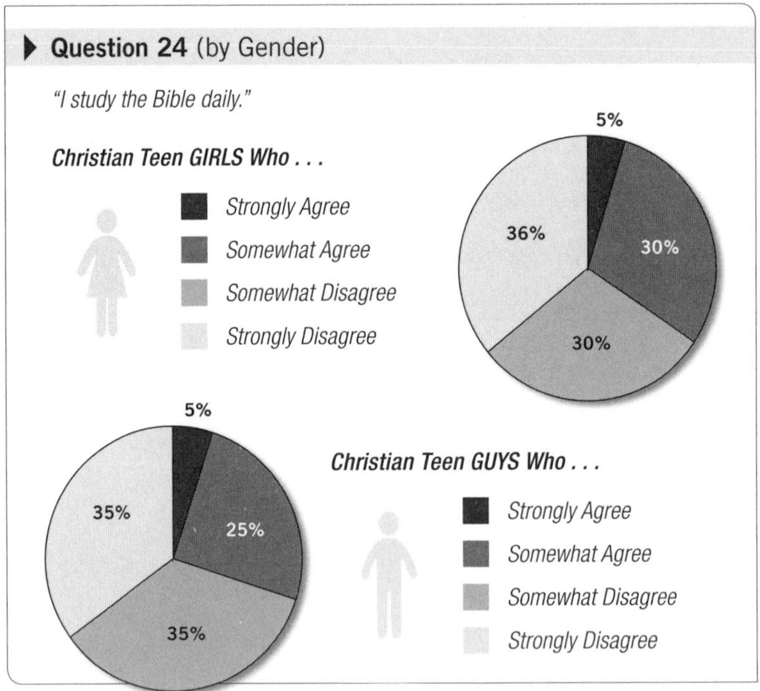

Figure 7.7

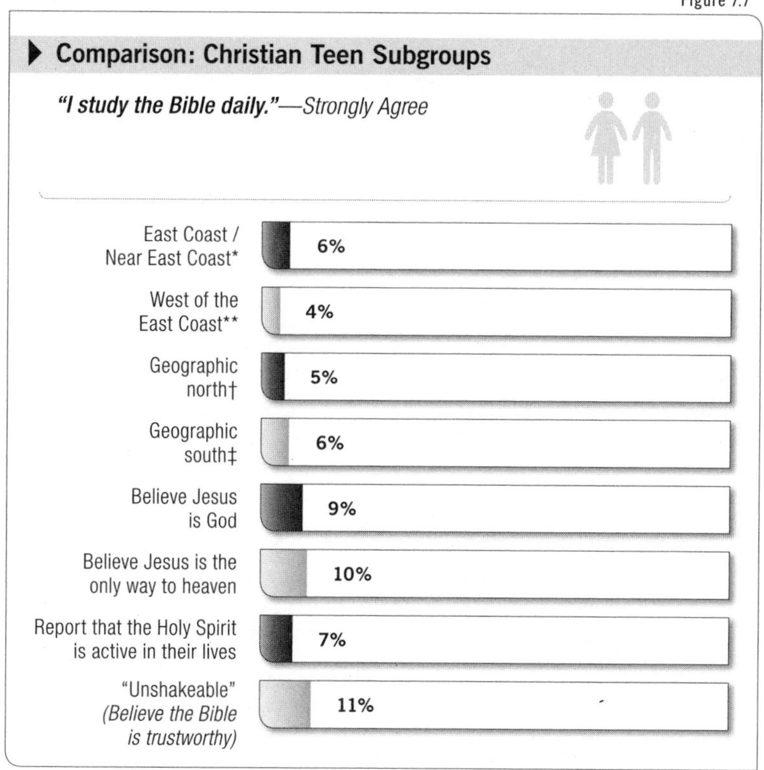

* Roughly from PA east, then down to FL on the map. **Roughly west of PA, then over and across the map. †Roughly from PA and up on the map. ‡Roughly from PA/IL and down the map, including CO and CA.

Figure 7.8

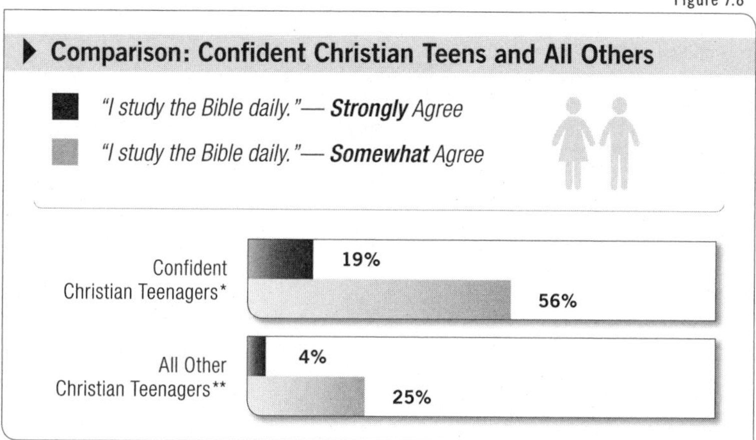

* Express strong confidence in four key Christian doctrines: 1) the Bible is trustworthy, 2) Jesus is God, 3) Jesus died and rose again, 4) Jesus is the only way to heaven.

** Express measurable reservations about one or more of these four key doctrines of Christianity.

Figure 7.9

▶ Comparison: Denominational Groups

	"I Study the Bible Daily." — Strongly Agree	*"I Study the Bible Daily." — Somewhat Agree*
Non-Denominational	**16%**	**35%**
Baptist	**12%**	**30%**
Brethren in Christ	**9%**	**50%**
Other Denominations	**6%**	**31%**
United Methodist	**6%**	**28%**
Presbyterian	**4%**	**34%**
Undeclared	**3%**	**23%**
United Church of Christ	**3%**	**11%**
Catholic	**1%**	**15%**
Episcopal	**0%**	**28%**
Lutheran	**0%**	**25%**

Figure 7.10

▶ Comparison: Age Groups

	"I Study the Bible Daily." — Strongly Agree	*"I Study the Bible Daily." — Somewhat Agree*
Junior Highers (Grades 7 & 8)	**7%**	**37%**
High School Underclassmen (Grades 9 & 10)	**4%**	**27%**
High School Upperclassmen (Grades 11 & 12)	**6%**	**26%**

Figure 8.1

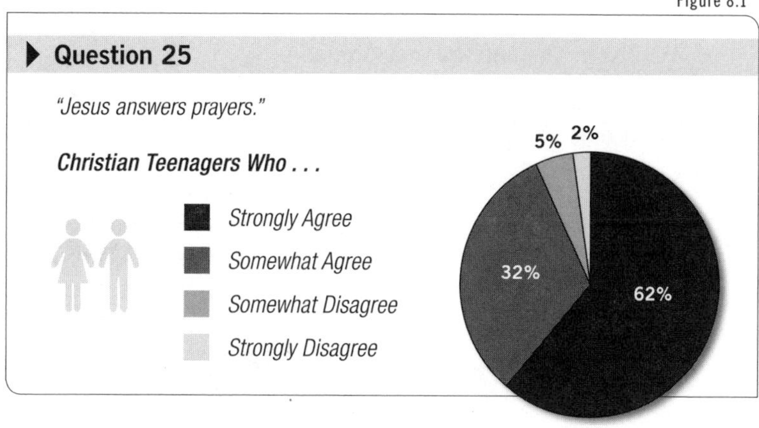

Figure 8.2

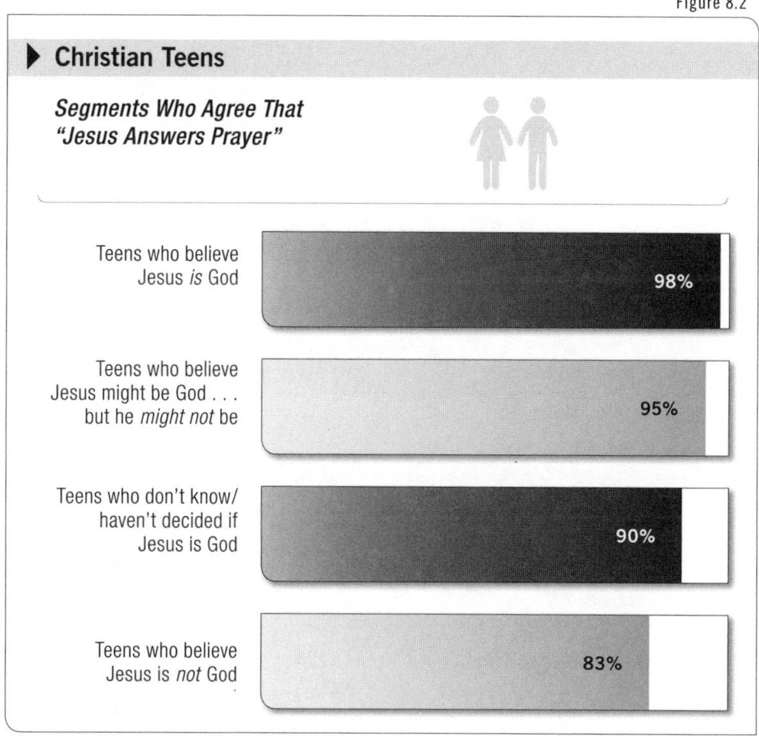

Figure 8.3

Comparison: Denominational Groups

Christian Teens Who Agree That "Jesus Answers Prayer"

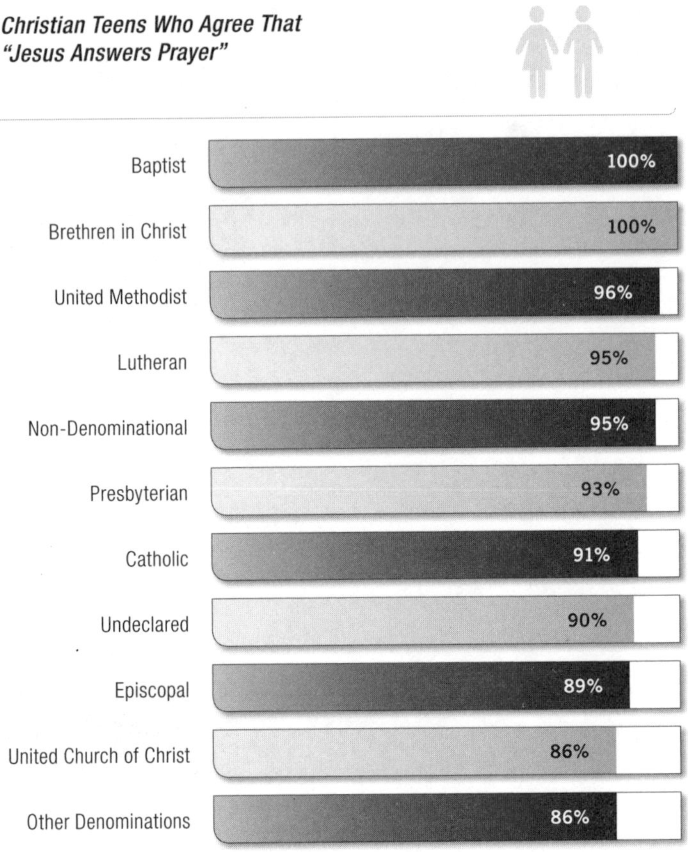

Baptist 100%
Brethren in Christ 100%
United Methodist 96%
Lutheran 95%
Non-Denominational 95%
Presbyterian 93%
Catholic 91%
Undeclared 90%
Episcopal 89%
United Church of Christ 86%
Other Denominations 86%

Figure 8.4

Question 26

"I'm 100% certain Jesus has answered one or more of my prayers—and I can prove it."

Christian Teenagers Who . . .

Strongly Agree
Somewhat Agree
Somewhat Disagree
Strongly Disagree
59%
27%
10%
4%

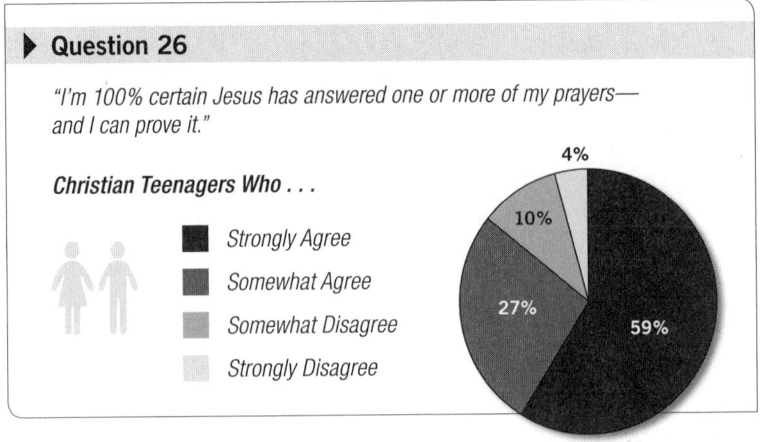

Figure 8.5 (Part 1 of 2)

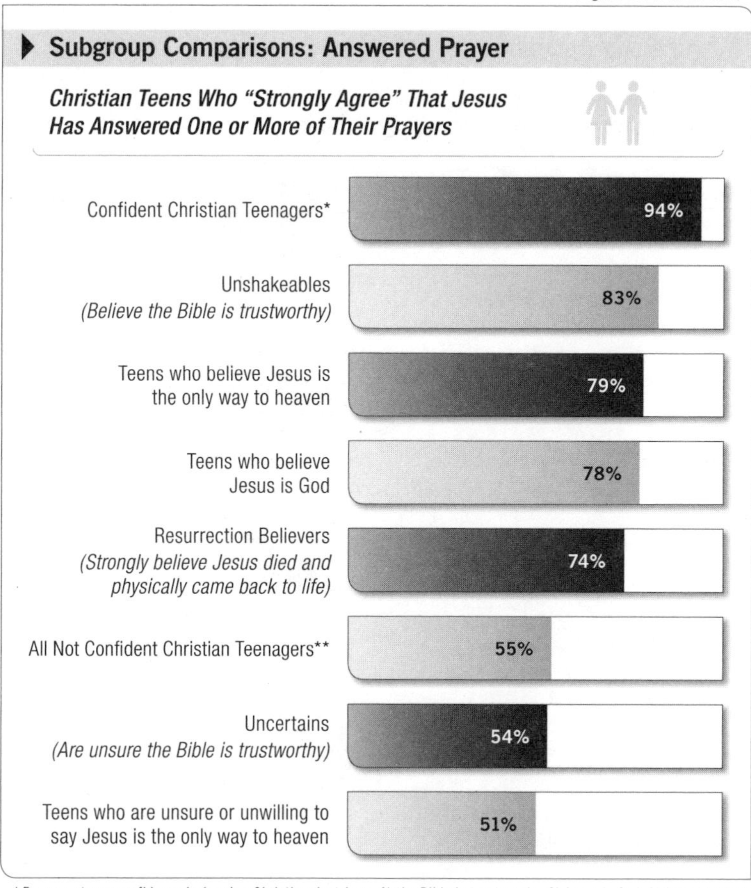

* Express strong confidence in four key Christian doctrines: 1) the Bible is trustworthy, 2) Jesus is God, 3) Jesus died and rose again, 4) Jesus is the only way to heaven.

** Express measurable reservations about one or more of four key doctrines of Christianity.

Subgroup Comparisons: Answered Prayer

Christian Teens Who "Strongly Agree" That Jesus Has Answered One or More of Their Prayers

Subgroup	%
Teens who believe Jesus might be God . . . but he might not be	50%
Unsettleds *(Are conflicted/confused about the Bible's trustworthiness)*	49%
Teens who don't know/haven't decided if Jesus is God	49%
Teens who believe Jesus is not God	48%
Resurrection In-Betweeners *(Express measurable uncertainty about Jesus's resurrection)*	43%
Resurrection Skeptics *(Disbelieve that Jesus died and physically came back to life)*	34%
Unbelieving *(Believe the Bible is not trustworthy)*	30%
Teens who believe Jesus is not the only way to heaven	26%

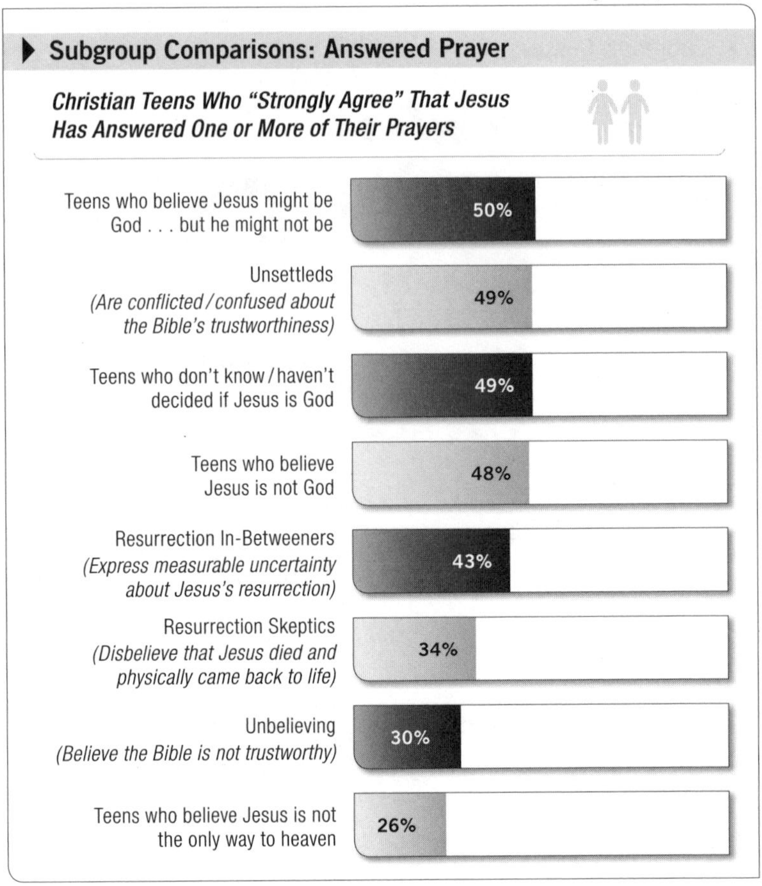

Figure 8.6

▶ Question 25

"Jesus answers prayers."

Adult Leaders Predicted Christian Teenagers Would . . .

Strongly Agree	*Somewhat Agree*	*Strongly Disagree*	*Somewhat Disagree*
54%	**38%**	**7%**	**2%**

Christian Teens' Actual Responses

Strongly Agree	*Somewhat Agree*	*Strongly Disagree*	*Somewhat Disagree*
62%	**32%**	**5%**	**2%**

Figure 8.7

▶ Question 26

"I'm 100% certain Jesus has answered one or more of my prayers—and I can prove it."

Adult Leaders Predicted Christian Teenagers Would . . .

Strongly Agree	*Somewhat Agree*	*Strongly Disagree*	*Somewhat Disagree*
50%	**33%**	**10%**	**7%**

Christian Teens' Actual Responses

Strongly Agree	*Somewhat Agree*	*Strongly Disagree*	*Somewhat Disagree*
59%	**27%**	**10%**	**4%**

Figure 8.8

▶ Question 26

"I'm 100% certain Jesus has answered one or more of my prayers—and I can prove it."

Junior Highers *(Grades 7 & 8)*

Strongly Agree	*Somewhat Agree*	*Strongly Disagree*	*Somewhat Disagree*
50%	**33%**	**14%**	**3%**

High School Underclassmen *(Grades 9 & 10)*

Strongly Agree	*Somewhat Agree*	*Strongly Disagree*	*Somewhat Disagree*
62%	**26%**	**7%**	**5%**

High School Upperclassmen *(Grades 11 & 12)*

Strongly Agree	*Somewhat Agree*	*Strongly Disagree*	*Somewhat Disagree*
58%	**26%**	**12%**	**4%**

Christian Teen Girls *(All Grades)*

Strongly Agree	*Somewhat Agree*	*Strongly Disagree*	*Somewhat Disagree*
63%	**26%**	**8%**	**3%**

Christian Teen Guys *(All Grades)*

Strongly Agree	*Somewhat Agree*	*Strongly Disagree*	*Somewhat Disagree*
54%	**27%**	**13%**	**6%**

Figure 9.1

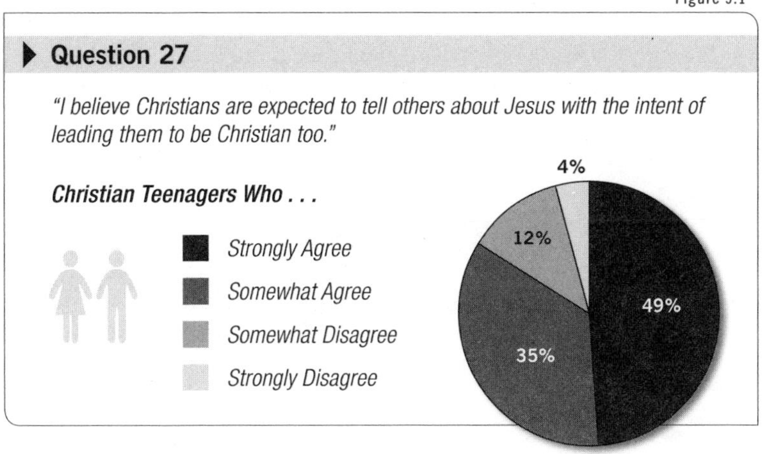

Figure 9.2

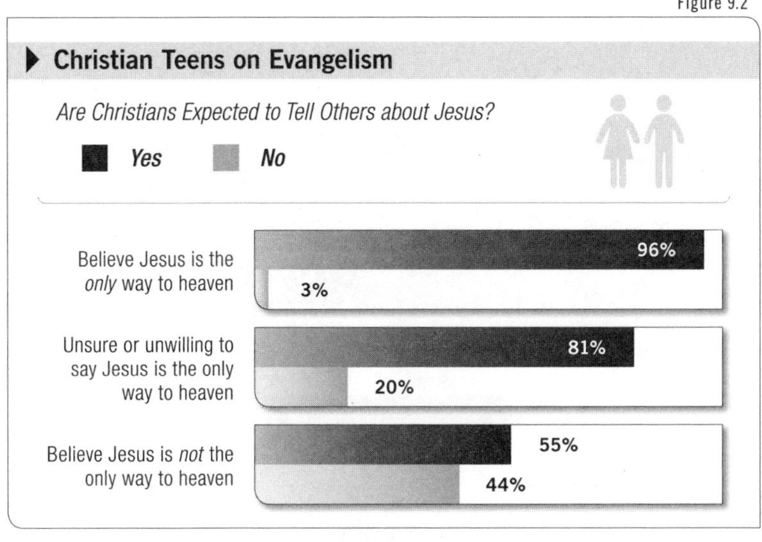

Figure 9.3

Strongly Agree: Christians Are Expected to Tell Others about Jesus
Christian Teen Guys
49%
Christian Teen Girls
49%

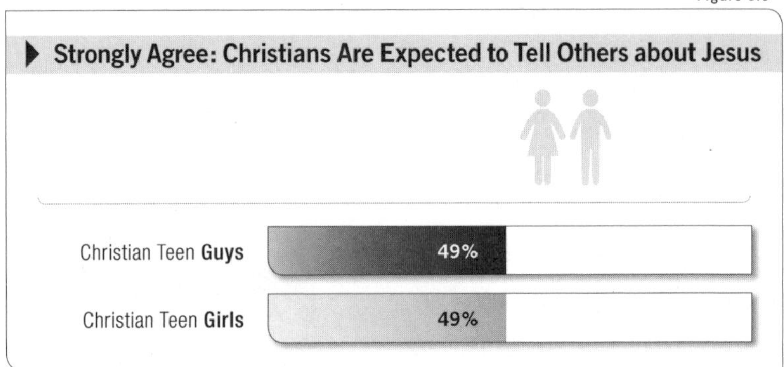

Figure 9.4

Strongly Agree: Christians Are Expected to Tell Others about Jesus
Non-Denominational
78%
Brethren in Christ
64%
United Methodist
59%
Other Denominations
57%
Baptist
52%
Presbyterian
52%
Lutheran
48%
Undeclared
40%
Catholic
32%
United Church of Christ
31%
Episcopal
22%

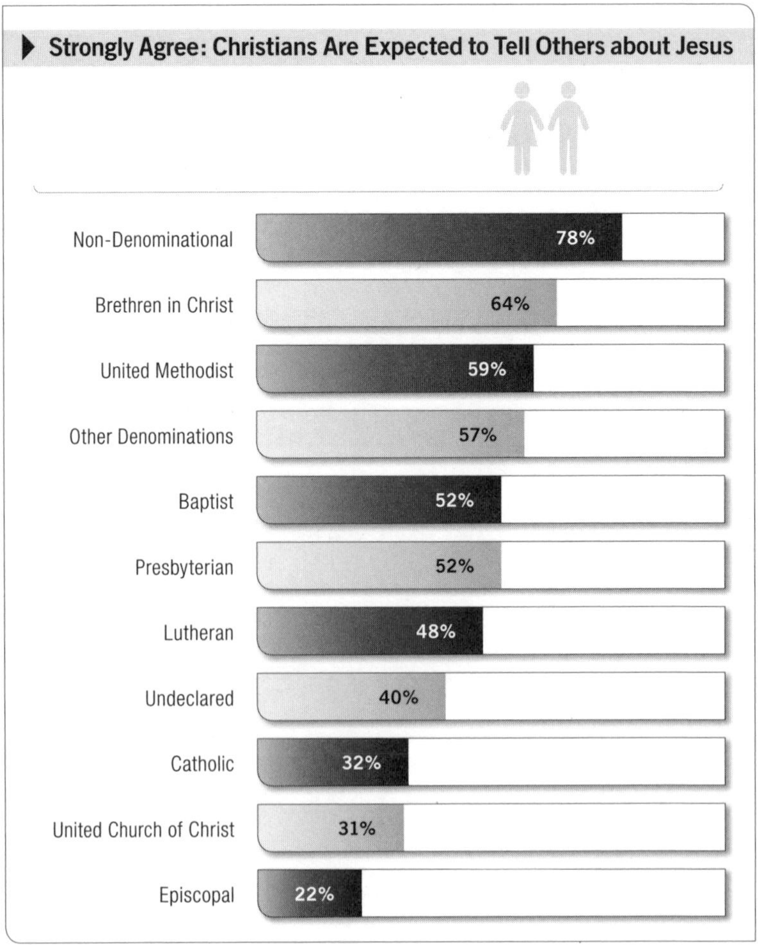

Figure 9.5

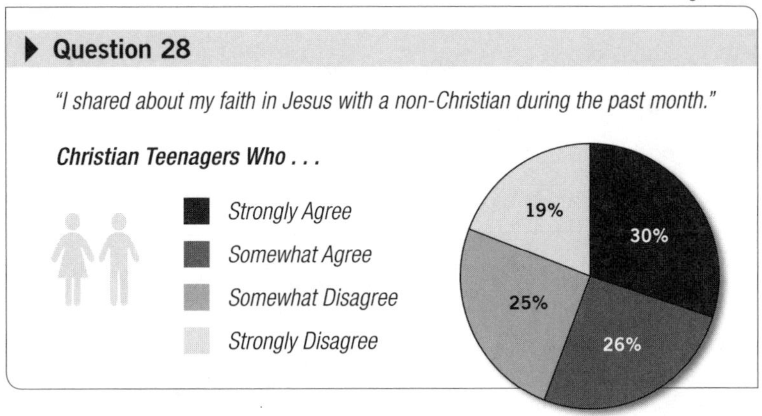

Figure 9.6

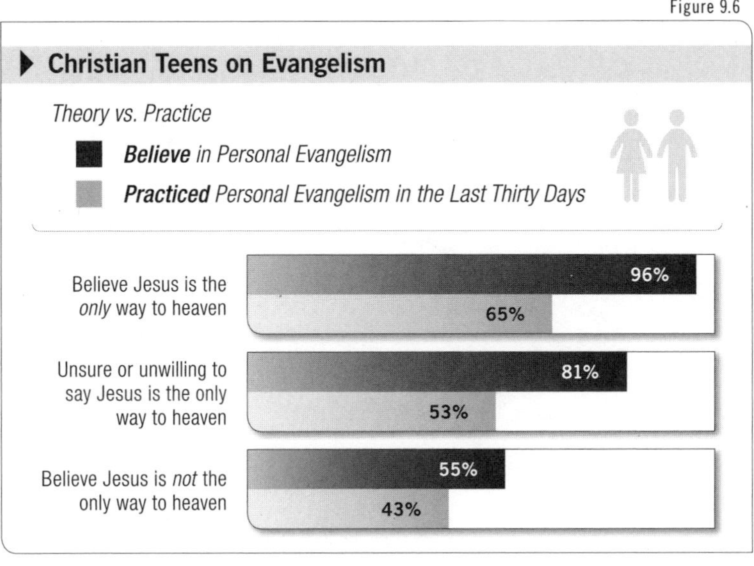

Figure 9.7

Christian Teens on Evangelism

Theory vs. Practice—by Gender

***Somewhat** or **Strongly** Believe in Personal Evangelism*

***Practiced** Personal Evangelism in the Last Thirty Days*

	Somewhat or Strongly Believe in Personal Evangelism	Practiced Personal Evangelism in the Last Thirty Days
Christian Teen **Guys**	84%	52%
Christian Teen **Girls**	83%	60%

Figure 9.8

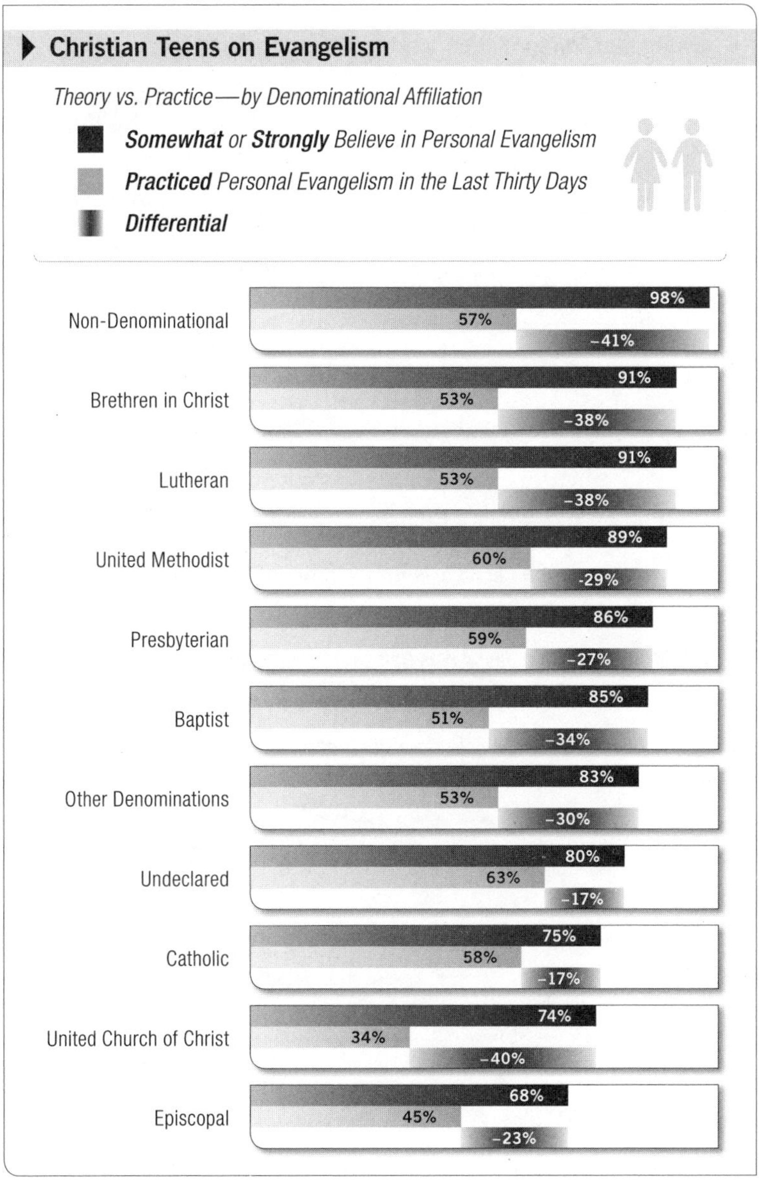

Christian Teens on Evangelism

Theory vs. Practice—by Denominational Affiliation

Somewhat *or* ***Strongly*** *Believe in Personal Evangelism*

Practiced *Personal Evangelism in the Last Thirty Days*

Differential

	Somewhat or Strongly Believe in Personal Evangelism	Practiced Personal Evangelism in the Last Thirty Days	Differential
Non-Denominational	98%	57%	-41%
Brethren in Christ	91%	53%	-38%
Lutheran	91%	53%	-38%
United Methodist	89%	60%	-29%
Presbyterian	86%	59%	-27%
Baptist	85%	51%	-34%
Other Denominations	83%	53%	-30%
Undeclared	80%	63%	-17%
Catholic	75%	58%	-17%
United Church of Christ	74%	34%	-40%
Episcopal	68%	45%	-23%

Figure 9.9

Evangelist Personalities among Christian Teenagers
Passionate Evangelists
Irregular Evangelists
Reluctant Evangelists
Absent Evangelists
12%
6%
32%
51%

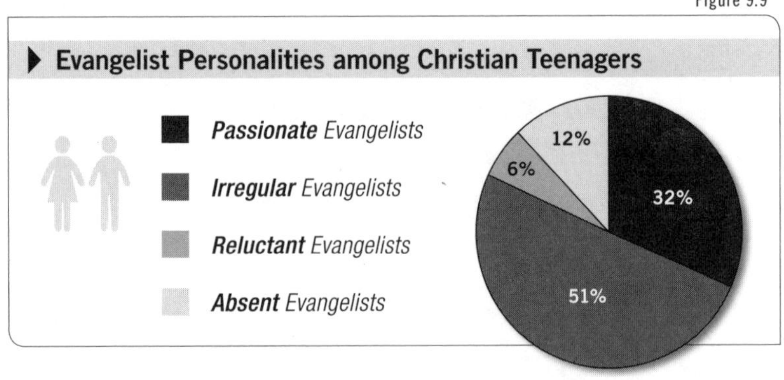

Figure 9.10

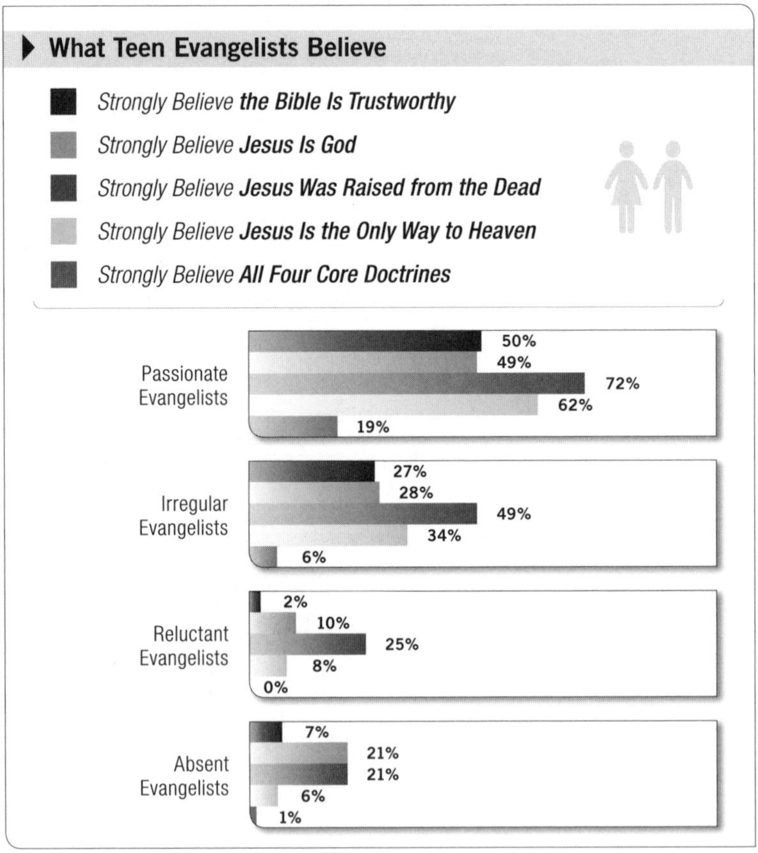

What Teen Evangelists Believe
Strongly Believe the Bible Is Trustworthy
Strongly Believe Jesus Is God
Strongly Believe Jesus Was Raised from the Dead
Strongly Believe Jesus Is the Only Way to Heaven
Strongly Believe All Four Core Doctrines
Passionate Evangelists
50%
49%
72%
62%
19%
Irregular Evangelists
27%
28%
49%
34%
6%
Reluctant Evangelists
2%
10%
25%
8%
0%
Absent Evangelists
7%
21%
21%
6%
1%

Figure 9.11

Teen Evangelist Personalities (by Grade)

	Passionate Evangelists	*Irregular Evangelists*	*Reluctant Evangelists*	*Absent Evangelists*
7th Grade	**12%**	**61%**	**6%**	**21%**
8th Grade	**43%**	**43%**	**2%**	**13%**
9th Grade	**28%**	**56%**	**4%**	**11%**
10th Grade	**30%**	**55%**	**5%**	**10%**
11th Grade	**29%**	**52%**	**7%**	**12%**
12th Grade	**37%**	**44%**	**8%**	**12%**

Figure 9.12

Teen Evangelist Personalities (by Denomination)

	Passionate Evangelists	*Irregular Evangelists*	*Reluctant Evangelists*	*Absent Evangelists*
Baptist	**31%**	**49%**	**3%**	**17%**
Brethren in Christ	**36%**	**55%**	**0%**	**9%**
Catholic	**22%**	**51%**	**13%**	**15%**
Episcopal	**9%**	**54%**	**10%**	**27%**
Lutheran	**33%**	**57%**	**5%**	**5%**
Non-Denominational	**49%**	**49%**	**1%**	**1%**
Other Denominations	**34%**	**49%**	**3%**	**14%**
Presbyterian	**34%**	**51%**	**6%**	**10%**
Undeclared	**36%**	**42%**	**3%**	**19%**
United Church of Christ	**17%**	**57%**	**6%**	**20%**
United Methodist	**38%**	**51%**	**3%**	**8%**

Figure 10.1

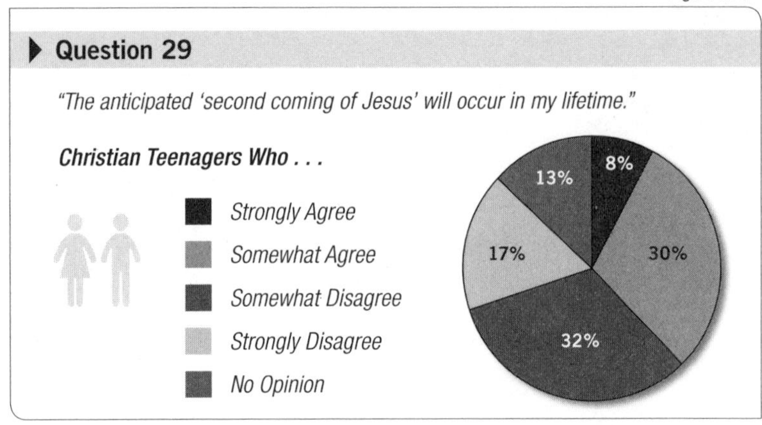

Figure 10.2

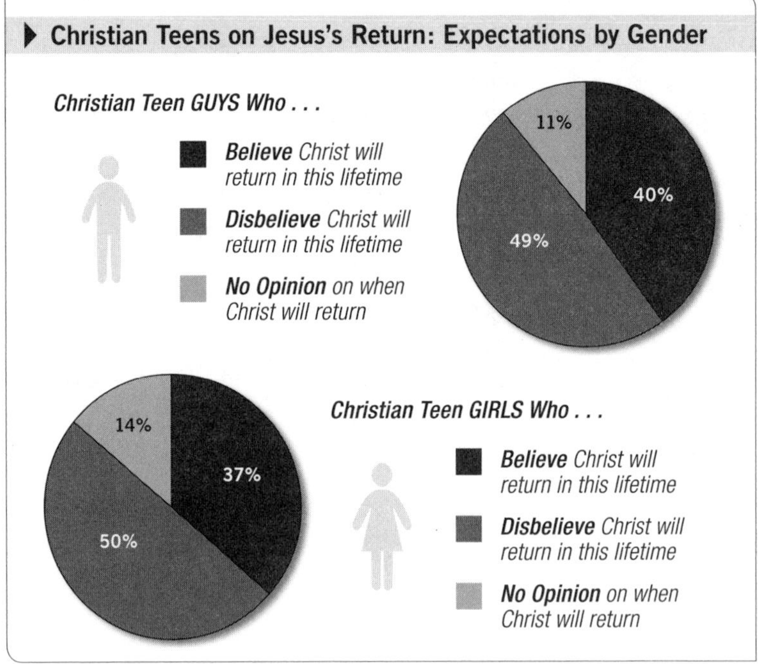

Figure 10.3

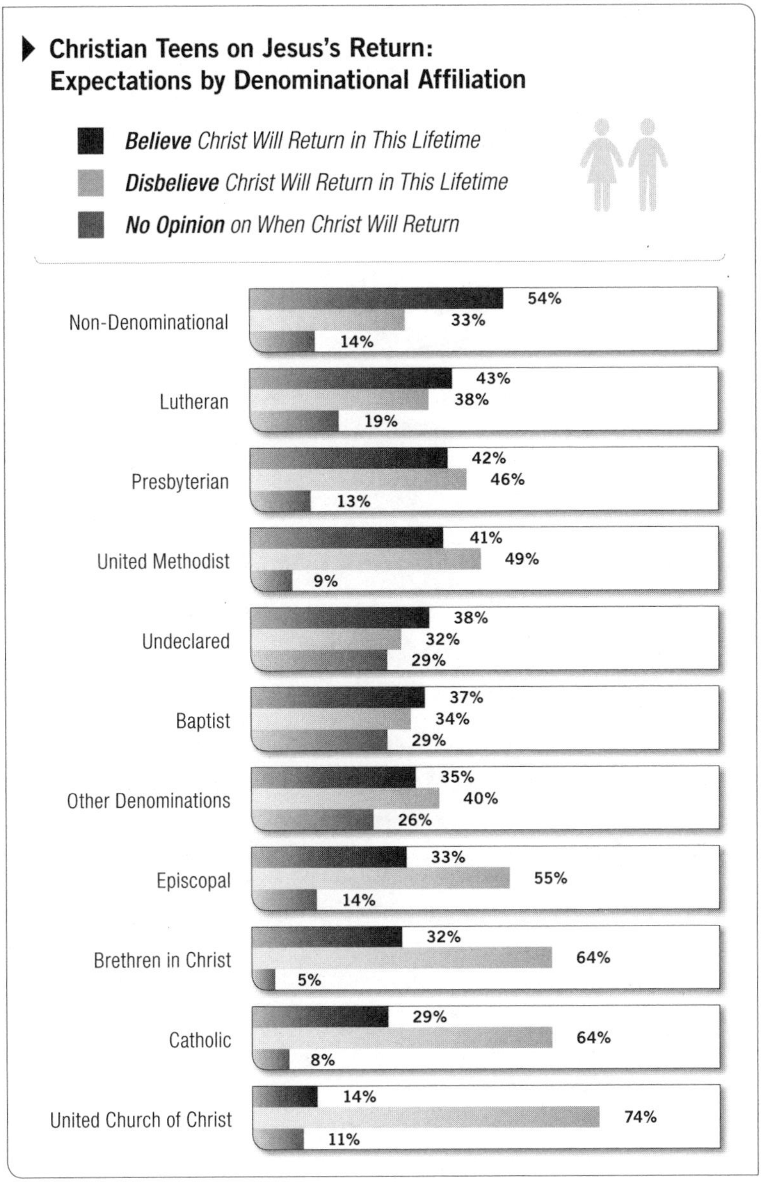

Christian Teens on Jesus's Return: Expectations by Denominational Affiliation

Denomination	**Believe** Christ Will Return in This Lifetime	**Disbelieve** Christ Will Return in This Lifetime	**No Opinion** on When Christ Will Return
Non-Denominational	54%	33%	14%
Lutheran	43%	38%	19%
Presbyterian	42%	46%	13%
United Methodist	41%	49%	9%
Undeclared	38%	32%	29%
Baptist	37%	34%	29%
Other Denominations	35%	40%	26%
Episcopal	33%	55%	14%
Brethren in Christ	32%	64%	5%
Catholic	29%	64%	8%
United Church of Christ	14%	74%	11%

Figure 10.4 (Part 1 of 2)

Subgroup Comparisons: When Will Jesus Return?

	Believe *Christ Will Return in This Lifetime*	***Disbelieve*** *Christ Will Return in This Lifetime*	***No Opinion*** *on When Christ Will Return*
Confident Christian Teenagers*	56%	28%	16%
Unshakeables *(Believe the Bible is trustworthy)*	48%	30%	21%
Teens who believe Jesus is the only way to heaven	48%	37%	16%
Teens who believe Jesus is God	46%	38%	15%
Resurrection Believers *(Strongly believe Jesus died and physically came back to life)*	41%	45%	14%
Teens who are unsure or unwilling to say Jesus is the only way to heaven	37%	51%	12%
Teens who don't know and/or haven't decided if Jesus is God	37%	53%	10%
All Not Confident Christian Teenagers**	36%	52%	13%

* Express strong confidence in four key Christian doctrines:
1) the Bible is trustworthy, 2) Jesus is God, 3) Jesus died and rose again, 4) Jesus is the only way to heaven.

** Express measurable reservations about one or more of four key doctrines of Christianity.

Figure 10.4 (Part 2 of 2)

▶ Subgroup Comparisons: When Will Jesus Return?

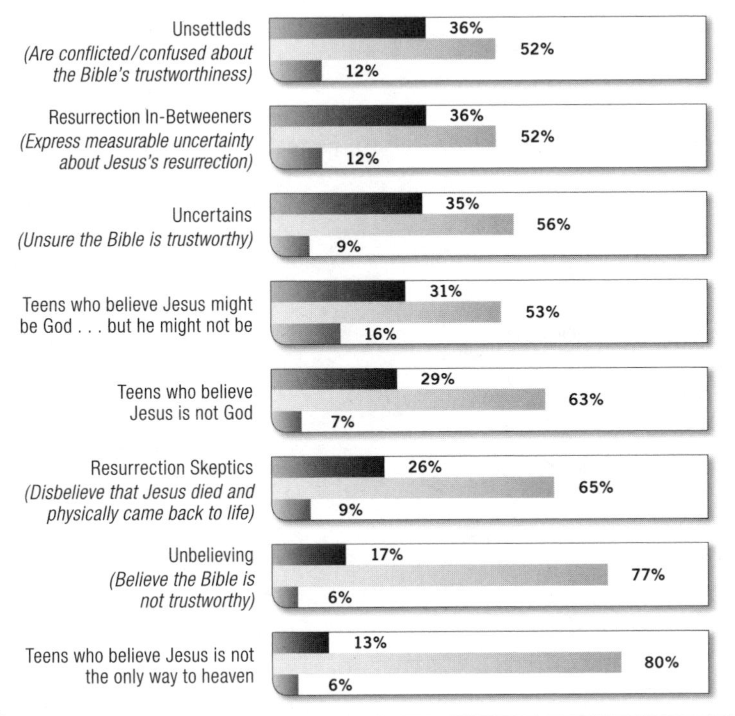

Figure 10.5

Question 29

Adult Leaders Predicted Christian Teenagers Would . . .

	Strongly Agree	*Somewhat Agree*	*Strongly Disagree*	*Somewhat Disagree*	*No Opinion*
"The anticipated 'second coming of Jesus' will occur in my lifetime."	**5%**	**24%**	**35%**	**26%**	**10%**

Figure 10.6

Christian Teens on Jesus's Return: Expectations (by Grade)

	Believe *Christ Will Return in This Lifetime*	***Disbelieve*** *Christ Will Return in This Lifetime*	***No Opinion*** *on When Christ Will Return*
Junior Highers (Grades 7 & 8)	**40%**	**43%**	**18%**
High School Underclassmen (Grades 9 & 10)	**44%**	**44%**	**12%**
High School Upperclassmen (Grades 11 & 12)	**33%**	**55%**	**12%**

Appendix C

RECOMMENDED RESOURCES

Books

- Berkof, Louis. *Systematic Theology*. Grand Rapids: Eerdmans, 1941.
- Colson, Charles, and Harold Fickett. *The Faith*. Grand Rapids: Zondervan, 2008.
- D'Souza, Dinesh. *What's So Great About Christianity*. Washington, DC: Regnery, 2007.
- Dean, Kenda Creasy. *Almost Christian*. New York: Oxford University Press, 2010.
- Driscoll, Mark, and Gerry Breshears. *Vintage Jesus*. Wheaton, IL: Crossway, 2007.
- Hanegraaff, Hank. *Resurrection*. Nashville: Thomas Nelson, 2000.
- Harris, Joshua. *Dug Down Deep*. Colorado Springs: Multnomah, 2010.
- Jones, Timothy Paul. *Christian History Made Easy*. Torrance, CA: Rose, 2005.
- ———. *Conspiracies and the Cross*. Lake Mary, FL: Frontline, 2008.
- ———. *Misquoting Truth*. Downers Grove, IL: InterVarsity, 2007.
- Keller, Timothy. *The Reason for God*. New York: Riverhead, 2008.
- Kinnaman, David, and Gabe Lyons. *unChristian*. Grand Rapids: Baker, 2007.
- Nappa, Mike. *The Courage to Be Christian*. West Monroe, LA: Howard, 2001.
- Smith, Christian, and Melinda Lundquist Denton. *Soul Searching*. New York: Oxford University Press, 2005.
- Smith, Christian, and Patricia Snell. *Souls in Transition*. New York: Oxford University Press, 2009.
- Strobel, Lee. *The Case for the Real Jesus*. Grand Rapids: Zondervan, 2007.
- Thiessen, Henry Clarence. *Introductory Lectures in Systematic Theology*. Grand Rapids: Eerdmans, 1956.

Bibles

- *ESV Study Bible* (Crossway).
- *Quest Study Bible* (Zondervan).

Websites

- *Christianity Today* (www.ChristianityToday.com).
- Lifetree Café (www.LifetreeCafe.com).
- Reach Workcamps (www.ReachWC.org).

NOTES

Introduction

1. "Light Pollution," *World English Dictionary*, as quoted on Dictionary.com, http://dictionary.reference.com/browse/light+pollution. Accessed November 17, 2010.

2. See Matthew 4:16.

About *The Jesus Survey*

1. Note: These six denominations, taken together, were represented by less than 5% of the total number of students who participated in *The Jesus Survey*.

2. US Census Bureau, "United States: ACS Demographic and Housing Estimates: 2006–2008," http://factfinder.census.gov/servlet/ADPTable?_bm=y&-geo_id=01000US&-qr_name=ACS_2008_3YR_G00_DP3YR5&-ds_name=ACS_2008_3YR_G00_&-_lang=en&-_sse=on. Accessed August 26, 2010.

3. "What Teenagers Look for in a Church," Barna Group online, October 8, 2007, http://www.barna.org/barna-update/article/16-teensnext-gen/93-what-teenagers-look-for-in-a-church?q=teenagers+teens. Accessed August 26, 2010.

4. Special thanks to Creative Research Systems for providing a "Sample Size Calculator" to accurately figure the confidence level and margin of error for this survey. http://www.surveysystem.com.

Part One Who Is Jesus?

1. See Mark 8:29.

Chapter 1 Can I Trust What the Bible Says about Jesus?

1. Yes, yes, I know that Christianity is not a "religion" in the personal, intimate sense—that in truth it's a relationship between God and his children. But for the sake of discussion in this book, that distinction is mostly semantics. Christianity in general is considered a religion by most definitions, so I'm comfortable referring to it as such here.

2. Charles Colson and Harold Fickett, *The Faith* (Grand Rapids: Zondervan, 2008), 45.

3. OK, for the record, *The Big Bang Theory* and *How I Met Your Mother* are two of my favorite TV shows—consistently funny and entertaining. At the same time, I'm often dismayed at how people as funny as the writers of those shows feel the need to use their humor as a tool for mockery and insults aimed at people of faith.

4. Richard Dawkins, *The God Delusion* (New York: Houghton Mifflin, 2006), 92–93.

5. Ibid., 94.

6. From email correspondence between the author and Dr. Timothy Paul Jones, September 13, 2010.
7. Christian Smith and Melinda Lundquist Denton, *Soul Searching* (New York: Oxford University Press, 2005), 42.
8. David Kinnaman and Gabe Lyons, *unChristian* (Grand Rapids: Baker, 2007), 23.
9. Ibid.
10. Lisa D. Pearce and Melinda Lundquist Denton, *A Faith of Their Own* (New York: Oxford University Press, 2011), 51–52.
11. Ibid., 112.
12. Christian Smith and Patricia Snell, *Souls in Transition* (New York: Oxford University Press, 2009), 48–49.

Chapter 2 Jesus—Merely Great, or Simply Divine?

1. "Blasphemy," Dictionary.com, http://dictionary.reference.com/browse/blasphemy. Accessed November 17, 2010.
2. See John 10:32.
3. See John 10:33.
4. See Matthew 26:63–67.
5. Kenda Creasy Dean, *Almost Christian* (New York: Oxford University Press, 2010), 11.
6. Ibid., 12.
7. Louis Berkof, *Systematic Theology* (Grand Rapids: Eerdmans, 1941), 318.
8. Joshua Harris, *Dug Down Deep* (Colorado Springs: Multnomah, 2010), 84.
9. Thom Rainer and Jess Rainer, *The Millennials* (Nashville: B & H Publishing, 2011), 242.
10. George Barna, *Real Teens* (Ventura, CA: Regal, 2001), 128–29.

Chapter 3 What about the Christ Conspiracies? (Part One: The Cross)

1. Colson and Fickett, *The Faith*, 127.
2. 1 Corinthians 1:23–24.
3. Dr. Robert Schoen, *What I Wish My Christian Friends Knew about Judaism* (Chicago: Loyola, 2004), 11.
4. George W. Braswell Jr., *Islam* (Nashville: Broadman & Holman, 1996), 283.
5. Charles R. Swindoll, *Insights on John* (Grand Rapids: Zondervan, 2010), 334–35.
6. Ibid., 335.
7. Lee Strobel, *The Case for the Real Jesus* (Grand Rapids: Zondervan, 2007), 102–3.
8. Mark Driscoll and Gerry Breshears, *Vintage Jesus* (Wheaton, IL: Crossway, 2007), 118–19.
9. Timothy Keller, *The Reason for God* (New York: Riverhead, 2008), 194.
10. Ibid., 200.
11. Neil Leifer and Thomas Hauser, *Muhammad Ali Memories* (New York: Rizzoli International, 1992), 37.
12. Timothy Paul Jones, *Conspiracies and the Cross* (Lake Mary, FL: Frontline, 2008), 153.
13. Hank Hanegraaff, *Resurrection* (Nashville: Thomas Nelson, 2000), 34.

Chapter 4 What about the Christ Conspiracies? (Part Two: The Empty Tomb)

1. Strobel, *Case for the Real Jesus*, 105.
2. See 1 Corinthians 15:17–20.
3. Strobel, *Case for the Real Jesus*, 105.
4. Hanegraaff, *Resurrection*, 7.
5. Ibid., 4–5.
6. Keller, *Reason for God*, 216.
7. Hanegraaff, *Resurrection*, 28.
8. Jones, *Conspiracies and the Cross*, 154.
9. Hanegraaff, *Resurrection*, 28–29.

10. Jones, *Conspiracies and the Cross*, 155–58.
11. Hanegraaff, *Resurrection*, 9–10.
12. Driscoll and Breshears, *Vintage Jesus*, 141.
13. Richard Abanes, *Cults, New Religious Movements, and Your Family* (Wheaton, IL: Crossway, 1998), 79, 86.
14. Jones, *Conspiracies and the Cross*, 101–3.
15. Ibid., 100.

Chapter 5 Jesus—*The* Way or *One* Way to Heaven?

1. I. Howard Marshall, *The Acts of the Apostles* (Grand Rapids: Eerdmans, 1980), 100–101.
2. Rainer and Rainer, *Millennials*, 23.
3. Henry Clarence Thiessen, *Introductory Lectures in Systematic Theology* (Grand Rapids: Eerdmans, 1956), 274.
4. Smith and Denton, *Soul Searching*, 160.
5. Barna Research Group, "Six Megathemes Emerge from Barna Research Group in 2010," *Barna Update* e-newsletter, December 13, 2010.
6. Ibid.
7. Colson and Fickett, *Faith*, 26.
8. Robert D. Putnam and David E. Campbell, *American Grace* (New York: Simon and Schuster, 2010), 536.
9. Pearce and Denton, *Faith of Their Own*, 92–93.
10. Colson and Fickett, *Faith*, 26.
11. Smith and Denton, *Soul Searching*, 160.

Intermission Where We've Been, Where We're Going

1. Harris, *Dug Down Deep*, 1.
2. Barna Research Group, "Six Megathemes Emerge from Barna Research Group in 2010," *Barna Update* e-newsletter, December 13, 2010.
3. Rainer and Rainer, *Millennials*, 232.

Part 2 What Difference Does Jesus Make?

1. See 2 Corinthians 5:17.

Chapter 6 The Holy Spirit and Christian Teens

1. Ted Van Cleave, *Totally Absurd Inventions* (Kansas City, MO: Andrews McMeel Publishers, 2001), 3, 17, 21, 77, 122.
2. Lawrence O. Richards, ed., *The Revell Bible Dictionary* (Grand Rapids: Revell, 1990), 491. Italics mine.
3. Jeanne Phillips (Dear Abby), "Tween Wants to Make Changes," *Reporter-Herald*, October 30, 2010, B3.
4. Pearce and Denton, *Faith of Their Own*, 60.
5. Dean, *Almost Christian*, 162.
6. Barna Research Group, "Six Megathemes Emerge from Barna Research Group in 2010," *Barna Update* e-newsletter, December 13, 2010. Italics mine.

Chapter 7 Bible Study and Christian Teens

1. Charles R. Swindoll, *The Tale of the Tardy Oxcart* (Nashville: Word, 1998), 48–49.
2. "U.S. Religious Knowledge Survey—Full Report," Pew Forum on Religion and Public Life (Washington, D.C., Pew Research Center, 2010), 4, 7.
3. Thiessen, *Introductory Lectures in Systematic Theology*, 86–87.
4. St. Augustine, *Confessions*, trans. Hal M. Helms (Orleans, MA: Paraclete, 1986), 160–61.

5. The Gideons International, "God's Word Changes Lives," Gideons.org, http://www.gideons.org/ChangedLives/ChangedLivesText.aspx. Accessed November 17, 2010.
6. Ibid.
7. Ibid.
8. See Hebrews 4:12.
9. Smith and Denton, *Soul Searching*, 269.
10. Dean, *Almost Christian*, 128–29.
11. "Take Time to Learn," *The Youth Bible* (Dallas: Word, 1991), 1266.
12. Ibid.
13. Barna, *Real Teens*, 132–33.

Chapter 8 Prayer and Christian Teens

1. All these stories are documented in Mike Nappa, *True Stories of Answered Prayer* (Wheaton, IL: Tyndale, 1999).
2. Steve Brown, *Approaching God* (Nashville: Moorings, 1996), ix–x.
3. Mike Nappa, *The Courage to Be Christian* (West Monroe, LA: Howard, 2001), 8.

Chapter 9 Evangelism and Christian Teens

1. John Drane, "Witness," *The Complete Book of Everyday Christianity*, ed. Robert Banks and R. Paul Stevens (Downers Grove, IL: InterVarsity, 1997), 1121, 1123.
2. "Store Rejected Over 'Offensive' Christian Name," *Christian Retailing* online, September 30, 2010, http://www.christianretailing.com/index.php/newsletter/latest-etailing/22074-store-rejected-over-offensive-christian-name-. Accessed September 30, 2010.
3. Jennifer LeClaire, "Cali School Bans Christian Student's Talent," *Charisma Magazine* online, February 1, 2011, http://charismamag.com/index.php/news/30117-cali-school-bans-christian-students-talent. Accessed February 5, 2011.
4. NPR Staff, "Writer Anne Rice: 'Today I Quit Being a Christian,'" *NPR* online, August 2, 2010, http://www.npr.org/templates/story/story.php?storyId=128930526. Accessed August 9, 2010.
5. Fanhouse Staff, "Tim Tebow, Obama, and Jesus Target of Florida Man's Restraining Order," *NFL.Fanhouse.com*, November 10, 2010, http://nfl.fanhouse.com/2010/11/10/tim-tebow-obama-and-jesus-target-of-florida-mans-restraining-o/. Accessed November 10, 2010.
6. Kinnaman and Lyons, *unChristian*, 11, 15.
7. Ibid., 34.
8. "How Teenagers' Faith Practices Are Changing," Barna Group online, July 12, 2010, http://www.barna.org/teens-next-gen-articles/403-how-teenagers-faith-practices-are-changing?q=teenagers+teens. Accessed August 26, 2010.

Chapter 10 The Second Coming and Christian Teens

1. "The Rapture of 1992," parts 1 and 2, on *Hot Talk-Starters Video, Series 3* (Loveland, CO: Group, 1993).
2. And, yes, I understand that the phrase "imminent return of Christ" comes with some scholarly baggage and disagreements over pretribulation rapture and posttribulation doctrines, but for the purposes here I'm using the term to simply refer in general to Christ's return—not as an exercise in theological hairsplitting.

Afterword

1. Mike & The Mechanics, "The Living Years," song lyrics as quoted on elyrics.net, http://www.elyrics.net/read/m/mike-&-the-mechanics-lyrics/the-living-years-lyrics.html. Accessed August 9, 2010.
2. See Numbers 6:24–26.

ABOUT **THE AUTHOR**

Mike Nappa is a bestselling and award-winning author of many books for families and church leaders. A former youth pastor, he holds a master's degree in English and a bachelor's degree in Christian Education with a minor in Bible theology. Learn more about Mike at www.MikeNappa.com.

ABOUT **REACH WORKCAMPS**

Ministering since 1992, Reach Workcamps is a weeklong mission of service to low-income communities.

Working with local agencies and/or local churches, the camps seek to make an impact on residents, communities, students, and adult sponsors who attend. It is a life-changing experience as campers participate in activities that build community and self-esteem, encourage spiritual growth, and enable them to understand their role in combating poverty.

Reach held its first workcamp during the summer of 1992 in Madisonville, Kentucky. Since then, over 25,000 junior and senior high school students and their adult sponsors have attended a Reach workcamp in thirteen different states and Mexico. To date, there have been 117 Reach workcamps since its birth. Over the years, Reach Workcamps has experienced a 70% youth group return rate.

Reach Workcamps is a nonprofit organization based in Colorado and maintains a 501(c)(3) tax-exempt status from the Internal Revenue Service. Additionally, Reach is an interdenominational ministry. It is not affiliated with any one church but serves all Christian churches.

To request a free workcamp information packet for your church youth group, visit Reach Workcamps online at www.ReachWC.org, or call toll free: (888) 732-2492.